Early childhood services
Theory, policy and practice

Edited by
Helen Penn

Open University Press
Buckingham · Philadelphia

This book is dedicated to my grandson
Mothibi 'Tiger' Kekana

Open University Press
Celtic Court
22 Ballmoor
Buckingham
MK18 1XW

email: enquiries@openup.co.uk
world wide web: www.openup.co.uk

and

325 Chestnut Street
Philadelphia, PA 19106, USA

First Published 2000
Reprinted 2001

A catalogue record of this book is available from the British Library

ISBN   0 335 20330 2 (hb)   0 335 20329 9 (pb)

Library of Congress Cataloging-in-Publication Data
Early childhood services: theory, policy, and practice/Helen Penn
   (ed.).
      p.   cm.
   Includes bibliographical references and index.
      ISBN 0-335-20330-2 (hard). – ISBN 0-335-20329-9 (pbk.)
      1. Early childhood education – Europe.   2. Early childhood education –
Great Britain.   3. Child care services – Europe.   4. Child care services – Great
Britain.   I. Penn, Helen.
LB1139.3.E85E35   1999
371.21'094–dc21   99-13284
                                                                            CIP

Typeset by Type Study, Scarborough

Printed and bound in Great Britain by
Marston Lindsay Ross International Ltd,
Oxfordshire

Contents

Contributors

Priscilla Alderson is Reader in Sociology and Children's Rights at the Social Science Research Unit, Institute of Education, London University.

Jessica Ball is coordinator of the Canadian First Nations Programme in the School of Youth and Childcare at the University of Victoria, Canada.

Roland Burgard is Director of Architecture in the City of Frankfurt.

Margaret Carr is Associate Professor of Early Childhood at the University of Waikito, New Zealand.

Anne Edwards is Professor of Education at the University of Birmingham.

Gunilla Dahlberg is Associate Professor at the Stockholm Institute of Education.

Chris Holligan is Senior Lecturer at the Faculty of Education, University of Paisley, Scotland.

Marta Mata y Garriga was an MP, and then a Senator in the Spanish Upper House, and chairwoman of the Education and Culture Committee in Barcelona.

Helen May is Professor of Early Childhood at the University of Wellington.

Peter Moss is Professor of Early Childhood Services at Thomas Coram Research Unit, Institute of Education, London University.

Alan Pence is Professor of Child and Youth Care at the University of Victoria.

Helen Penn is Professor of Early Childhood at the University of East London, and Visiting Fellow at the Social Science Research Unit, Institute of Education, London University. She is also Early Years Consultant to Save the Children UK.

Harriet Strandell is Professor in the Department of Sociology, Abo Akademi University, Finland.

Martin Woodhead is Senior Lecturer in the School of Education, The Open University.

Introduction

This book is based on a series of international seminars, originally given at the Institute of Education, 1995–6, exploring ground breaking aspects of theory and practice in early childhood. The seminars, which were funded by the Baring Foundation, were intended to explore the strengths and limitations of present practices in early childhood and to suggest ways in which new initiatives might be developed. Contributors to the seminars were academics and practitioners from Denmark, Canada, Germany, Spain, Sweden and the UK and they presented their views and conclusions for discussion with a mixed audience of academics and practitioners. The seminars attracted much interest and there were lively debates about the issues raised. Childcare and education policy and practices in the UK rely on a particular rhetoric about children and what they need, and these seminars provided an opportunity to look at traditional ideas and practices with new eyes.

In this book the authors develop the ideas about theory, policy and practice raised in the seminar series, and their complex interrelationships. The book brings together papers; some have already been published as journal articles; some have been especially commissioned; and some were originally presented at the seminars. They give new angles on early childhood services from a variety of perspectives. They do not always agree in their approach, and they are not intended to present an alternative blueprint for how such services should be run. Instead, hopefully, they give us some fresh insights and new understandings about the services we currently have and may choose to develop.

The current debate in the UK about care and education in the early years relies on implicit and explicit theories about children's development and the roles that adults adopt in relation to young children, and is sited in a particular policy context. The very language we use to describe what is provided for young children expresses our confusion and ambivalence, both about theory and about policy: nursery education, nursery school-ing, nursery units, reception classes, preschools, kindergartens, nurseries, day nurseries, family centres, workplace nurseries, private nurseries, child-care, crèches, mother and toddler groups, playgroups, community groups, community nurseries, childminding, nannies, *au pairs*, out of school cen-tres, play centres. In general in this book 'early childhood services' is used as an umbrella term to cover all these different kinds of arrangements, but some contributors may use different words, or may use one word in a more inclusive way to describe the arrangements in their own country.

At a policy level, then, the system in the UK is characterized by frag-mentation of services for younger children into these many kinds of pro-vision, then very early entry to school and pursuance of formal learning at age 4 (5 in Scotland) rather than at age 6 or 7, which is the policy in most countries. Although the system of part-time nursery education and early entry to school appear to be non-negotiable, there have been new Governmental attempts to integrate the education and welfare or care tra-ditions, and to reconcile them with a burgeoning private market in child-care as more women are drawn back into the workforce. At the same time as there is a move to integrate education and welfare approaches, the frag-mentation is being increased, with competitive bidding for resources, and a mixture of private and public initiatives to develop services in particular areas. In this fragmented system, the competencies for staff, and the per-formance outcomes and indicators for children, become still more import-ant in order to give a veneer of comparability over very diverse situations. The kinds of approaches developed in the UK represent a very particular way, and a very particular history, of promoting and developing services for young children.

It is often assumed that practice is somehow separate from policy and belongs to the domain of professionals. Enlightened policy makers may heed the words of researchers and practitioners, but essentially policy has its own rationale and imperatives. However the work of many recent theorists suggest that practice is inseparable from context, and that what people do in their daily lives, with children or anyone else, inescapably has a powerful contextual meaning and inevitably reflects what is hap-pening around them. The relationship between practice and theory is also subject to various interpretations. Practice in working with young chil-dren is assumed, implicitly or explicitly, to draw on theory, but doing and knowing are also inextricably linked. Daily tasks are continually modified, and practitioner judgements of what works, or seems to work, is both a commentary on and an addition to the knowledge base – in other words people learn from their own experiences.

Much of the new material becoming available is not from the UK, but concerns experiences of working in and documenting practice in other countries, including the developing or majority world countries, where 75 per cent of the world's children live. In Europe and North America, the minority world, we are mostly in ignorance of majority world traditions and understandings about childhood, although the reverse is not true; minority world ideas have percolated everywhere, first through colonialism, and now through the global market. It is in the majority world that some of the greatest theoretical and practical challenges lie, since ways of understanding childhood and providing for young children are sometimes so radically different that they necessarily throw into question the validity of what is commonly taken for granted in everyday practice in the UK and elsewhere in the minority world.

The first two chapters in this book raise the questions of how children learn in very different sociocultural contexts, and what assumptions and values inform such learning. Martin Woodhead offers a critique of child development as the underpinning discipline for work in early years. He argues that its theorists neglect to take into account evidence from the majority world, and cannot claim to make universalistic assumptions about how children learn and what conditions best suit their learning until they adopt a broader perspective. Alan Pence and Jessica Ball recount their experiences in working with aboriginal or First Nation peoples in Canada, and also conclude that universalist assumptions about the patterns of children's learning and the ways to assist it are deeply problematic and have to be reassessed. Margaret Carr and Helen May have also struggled to reconcile very different cultural stances, and in Chapter 3 document the process in New Zealand to develop a bicultural early years curriculum. They too raise fundamental questions about theory and practice in early childhood services, working in a situation with Maori peoples and Pacific islanders where traditional Euro–American or minority world assumptions about childhood could no longer be taken for granted. Margaret Carr and Helen May also illustrate how necessary it was to position themselves very carefully within a wider education policy debate, in order to make their case for curricular change.

The need to be alert to, or even try to influence the policy climate is referred to in a number of contributions. Although the relationship between theory, policy and practice is usually tenuous and indirect, in some countries, practice has arisen, or been fostered, as a direct result of informed political initiatives. Marta Mata y Garriga is a respected Spanish stateswoman, and was previously a member of the Spanish senate. Her views on the importance of providing an educational environment for very young children were influential in shaping the Spanish Education Reform Act, *La Ley Orgánica de Ordenación General del Sistema Educativo* (known as the LOGSE), which locates provision for children aged 0–6 firmly within the Spanish Ministry of Education, and emphasizes the need to regard even very young children primarily as active learners. In Chapter 4 she illustrates the complexities of policy making and the many levels at which policy is developed. In a recent paper for the Organization for Economic Co-operation and Development (OECD), Chapter 6, Peter Moss provides an overview of the policy issues concerned with training. In Chapter 7 the editor draws on her research on childcare training undertaken for the Department for Education and Employment (DfEE) to discuss the disadvantaged status and career opportunities for those working with young children, and how they too arise out of a particular policy environment.

The rapidly expanding field of sociology of childhood raises another set of perspectives; how children feel and think about the services they experience, and how adults are finding ways to listen to and understand what children say and do. In Chapter 10 Priscilla Alderson gives an account of children's rights and their implications for early childhood services. In Chapter 8 Chris Holligan attempts to apply the ideas about control and surveillance of the French sociologist Foucault to understanding everyday life in a nursery from the point of view of the child. His research into the behaviour of staff at two nursery schools offers a challenging critique and a re-interpretation of the effectiveness of methods of observation and assessment that have been regarded as a bedrock for nursery education practice. Harriet Strandell uses her ethnomethodological research to deconstruct conventional thinking about children's play in Chapter 9, and argues that it is both more subversive and more unknowable than is commonly supposed. In the same vein, but as an architect, rather than as a sociologist, Roland Burgard describes attempts in the Frankfurt kindergarten programme to envision space and surroundings as children might see and experience them in Chapter 5.

The question of how practice changes and develops, in response to new theoretical thinking, in philosophy and psychology, is addressed in the last part of the book. In Chapter 11 Gunilla Dahlberg pays homage to the psychologist Loris Malaguzzi, who, in the supportive political climate of Reggio Emilia in northern Italy, was able to develop a collective and collaborative group of nurseries whose social constructivist policies have since become world famous. Anne Edwards discusses the work of sociocognitive theorists and their ideas about a 'community of practice', and 'situated learning' in her description of working with practitioners in Chapter 12. Both writers hold that learning is not an individual internalized process by which a child or adult absorbs relevant knowledge, but is created out of social interactions.

The contributions from these different perspectives have been grouped into six interlinked and overlapping themes. Each theme has a brief introduction, setting the issues raised in the current context. These themes are as follows.

- *How* do young children learn? What assumptions are made about children as learners?
- *What* should young children be learning? What is an appropriate approach to curriculum for young children?
- *Where* should young children learn? What arrangements are made for them? What kinds of spaces do children inhabit?
- *Who* should help them learn? What role do adults take in supporting children learning?

- *Children* are participants and knowledgeable persons. What contribution can children themselves make to the plans that are made for them?
- *How* does practice, particularly embedded practice, change or develop?

Part one
How do children learn?
Early childhood services in
a global context

Early childhood services exist in almost every country in every continent. Even in countries where there is considerable poverty or repression, in urban areas if not in rural ones, there are nurseries and attempts to provide out of home care for young children, in cities as different as Dar es Salaam in Tanzania, Manila in the Philippines, Rangoon in Burma (Myanmar), Medellín in Colombia or Ulaanbaatar in Outer Mongolia. The pattern and availability of nursery education and childcare services for young children differ across countries, and in every country they have changed over the century in response to shifts in family and work patterns, as well as reflecting changes in educational thought. A number of cross-cultural European (European Commission Network on Childcare 1996) and global studies (Lamb *et al.* 1992; Cochran 1993) have tried to chart the ways in which provision has developed in each country, and the reasons and rationales for the policy twists and turns that have occurred in them. Most recently the OECD has commissioned another review of early childhood education across member states (Moss 1998). Everywhere there has been continuous change and modification of services and any comparative snapshots need continual updating.

Although the levels of provision, and the access to them, may differ, there has been less work on divergences in day-to-day practice with children and how theories about early childhood and learning, implicit or explicit, inform such practices. The extent, distribution, types and costs of provision are matters of policy and resources – or policy by default – but what takes place between adults and young children in education and care settings is commonly regarded as building on a solid base of internationally acceptable theory that applies, with minor variations, equally in New York or Cape Town or Beijing. It is often argued that daily practice in early childhood is, or should be, based on understandings about the intellectual, emotional, social and physical needs of children, which are essentially the same everywhere. These categories of need, and the practices that have emerged to meet them, so the argument runs, have been empirically derived from within the discipline of child development; what is sometimes called 'developmentally appropriate practice' (Bredekamp 1987).

The notion of 'ages and stages', that children learn and behave in certain ways at certain ages, and those concerned with young children should know what these patterns and norms are, is widespread. For example a recent project by Save the Children in Scotland claimed to have found that: 'parents often thought they had a problem with their child, whereas the real problem lay with the fact that they were under-informed about child development and how each stage affected behaviour and ability' (*Guardian* 1998). Proponents of this approach argue that research in child development can give clear indications of what constitutes best practice for different age groups and different target groups.

In fact, it is increasingly argued that many of the 'scientific' or 'empirical' findings about young children reflect a particular, Euro–North American worldview or way of looking at children and ignore the situation of the majority of the world's children, who live and learn in more diverse and often more vulnerable circumstances (Jahoda and Lewis 1988; Elder *et al.* 1993; Burman 1994; Penn 1997a, 1997b). Most research in the field of early childhood development originates from the minority world, and reflects minority world norms of childhood. The African writer Chinweizu (1975) neatly captures the imbalance and one-way flow of information between the majority and minority worlds in the title of his book, *The West and the Rest of Us*.

This Euro–North American research is in turn translated into a series of tests, programmes and guidelines to inform practice in working with young children. As Woodhead (1998: 8) has commented elsewhere:

> Programme approaches, curriculum models, and evaluation strategies are strongly informed by the child development literature, which in turn becomes part of an export/import trade through books, international conferences, training programmes and commercial packages. With few exceptions 'textbook' child development originates mainly in Europe and North America, and mainly within a fairly narrow socio-economic band within these Continents. Theories, programmes and evaluation strategies don't just convey well-researched knowledge about development. They also transmit hidden messages through rhetorical devices, notably about children's 'nature', their 'needs' what aspects of the 'environment' are 'harmful' or 'beneficial' for healthy development. The problem is that much of this rhetoric has as much to do with particular socio-cultural contexts (of the research community as well as of the children they have studied) as with shared features of early human development.

Those working in the field of early years, as researchers or practitioners, frequently cite Bronfenbrenner's (1979) model of the child as evidence that they recognize the importance of sociocultural factors. In Bronfen-brenner's model the universal child, essentially the same everywhere, is at the centre of concentric circles of influences – the family, the immediate context, the wider cultural context and so on – that impinge on him. This model of 'the child at the centre' is used by many international agencies who promote child development projects in the majority world, including United States Aid (USAID) programmes and the United Nations Children's Fund (UNICEF). Thorpe (1994), a native American, is one of many who argue that Bronfenbrenner's model is culturally insensitive, in treating 'culture' as one more set of variables that have to be taken into account in their impact on the child. Instead, Thorpe claims, the circumstances pro-duce the child; children are socially constructed, the child is 'a cultural invention' (Kessen 1979). Thorpe proposes an 'inverted cone' model, whereby the broad cultural framework is gradually narrowed down by par-ticular communities and families to create an individual child.

Similarly, cross-cultural studies, of which there are an increasing number, are not necessarily illuminative if they assume there are common criteria or dimensions against which each country's variation can be measured; since each country, and subgroup within it, may represent a radically different viewpoint or set of expectations, towards what children are, what they can or cannot, should or should not do, and such 'world-view' accounts of childhood and culture cannot be simply normatively compared (Penn 1998b). Indeed, as the authors of many of the chapters in this book suggest, in lieu of a universalistic approach towards young chil-dren and early childhood services, the only way to arrive at common understandings and common ways of proceeding, at a theoretical and a practical level, is through open dialogue and negotiation about implicit and explicit values.

The notion that it is possible to extrapolate from research findings that implicitly rely on Euro–North American or minority world cultural norms is increasingly seen as problematic because the norms they describe and refer to are not universal but a reflection of particular kinds of cultures and worldviews. These cultural frameworks are closely linked to economic frameworks; the cultural roles we assign to children both determine and reflect their economic status within societies. De Vylder (1996) has pointed out some of the negative effects on children and childhood of an economic framework in which there is a heavy reliance on market solu-tions, a reluctance to introduce regulatory measures and a free market approach that leads to an economically polarized society.

The solid base of theory on which early years practitioners rely is per-haps not so solid after all. Even the basic categories of 'physical', 'intellec-tual', 'emotional' and 'social' (sometimes known as PIES) can be viewed as arbitrary constructs that may have outlived their usefulness. For instance, in societies as different as the Japanese and the Chewa (Zambian) the notion of intelligence is inextricable from that of helpfulness; an unhelp-ful child may have a superficial cleverness but is essentially a stupid child

(Tobin *et al.* 1989; Serpell 1993). Young child herders in pastoralist or nomadic communities may routinely and unproblematically undertake physical feats of endurance that would be regarded as dangerous and even barbaric in sedentary Euro–North American societies (Penn 1998a). Gardner (1984) has elaborated some of these ideas in his notion of seven different kinds of intelligence, but as Shweder (1990: 33) has argued, the position is richer and more complex by far: 'Some cultures of the world are virtuosos of grief and mourning, others of gender identity, and still others of intimacy, eroticism and ego striving . . . selections from the arc of human possibility'.

Globalism means not only that Western ideas and influence spread throughout the world, but that vice versa, what was once strange and exotic and faraway, is now part of our everyday lives and likely to become more so. The response to globalism, and the gradual understanding that human diversity is both precious and in danger of disappearing has been an impetus to rethinking child development. The global context of which we in the minority world are slowly becoming aware, and the limitations of current theoretical thinking, have led to an approach, sometimes called 'cultural psychology' (Goldberger and Veroff 1995; Cole 1996), which takes as its starting point the importance of particularity and locality.

In a lucid article, Rogoff and Chavajay (1995) have traced some of the recent developments in ideas about the effect of society and culture on thinking and learning, concluding that 'inherent to sociocultural approaches is a premise that individual, social and cultural levels are inseparable' (1995: 873). This ties in with research on the idea of a 'community of practice' and a view that psychologists can profitably investigate the way in which individuals and groups enter, negotiate and become skilled within and are shaped by particular communities of practice (Lave and Wenger 1991). In other words, people become skilled practitioners or children become good learners, only in relation to a very specific domain or context. To quote Shweder (1990: 23) again, 'Indeed what seems to differentiate an expert from a novice is not some greater amount of content free pure logical or psychological power. What experts possess that neophytes lack is a greater quantity and quality of domain-specific knowledge of stimulus properties, as well as didactic mastery of the specialized or parochial tools of a trade.'

To give an everyday example, young children in the UK are expected to achieve certain measurable performance outcomes as a result of their attendance at preschool. One of these outcomes is the ability to recognize basic colours: red, green, blue, yellow and so on. Mongolian herder children of the same age will have learnt to distinguish horses by their colour. Horses come in varying shades of black, white and grey and a Mongolian child would be expected to distinguish about 320 of these combinations by name. The expectations of the level of visual discrimination the children can achieve, and the uses to which it is put, are very different in each community. Another very obvious example is language. Most of the world's children, in order to survive, are routinely bilingual or even trilingual, a feat we would consider exceptional in secondary age children in the UK.

One frequently cited example of this local and particular approach to understanding learning is that of the anthropologist Shirley Brice Heath (1983), who was a participant observer over many years in two small midwest American communities in 'Trackton'. One community was black, and the other working-class white. She noted how children were socialized by their local community, and how they developed particular ways of communicating and behaving that reflected the values and social position of those communities. In subsequent research (Heath 1990) she followed up the children she had observed who were now parents themselves. The poor black community had been rehoused and dispersed. Brice Heath chillingly documents how, isolated from their peers, friends and relatives, the children of Trackton's children showed none of the communal learning that their parents had experienced. And as the parents had become more isolated, and lost their communal supports, they lost their own skills and effectiveness and their ability to transmit the values with which they grew up. Conolly (1998) also shows, in Northern Ireland, how community values shape children's learning.

There are other longitudinal anthropological studies that also illustrate the powerfulness and particularity of time and place: Serpell (1993) in Zambia, LeVine *et al.* (1994) in Kenya, Scheper-Hughes (1987) in Brazil, Rabain (1979) in Senegal and Riesman (1992) in Burkina Faso all provide dramatic examples of childhoods where the everyday assumptions made about young children differ widely from the norms presented in the standard textbooks on child development. However, as Palacios and Moreno (1996) have pointed out, one does not need to travel to exotic locations to find examples of diversity. Most nations are not homogenous but accommodate within their boundaries many different types of communities and cultural assumptions.

But we should also exercise caution about using the word 'culture'. Ngugi Wa Thiong'o (1993), the Kenyan-Gikuyu writer, has provided a brilliant definition of culture, created by economic conditions and in turn creating them; culture as a process that is always being adjusted, and that may shrivel when held in contempt by others who are more powerful.

> Culture develops within the process of a people wrestling with their natural and social environment. They struggle with nature. They struggle with one another. They evolve a way of life embodied in their institutions and certain practices. Culture becomes the carrier of their moral, aesthetic and ethical values. At the psychological level, these values become the embodiment of the people's consciousness as a specific community . . . Within a given community any change in the major aspect of their lives, how they manage their wealth for

instance, or their power, may well bring about changes at all the other levels and these in turn will bring about mutual action and reaction on all the other aspects. Here there is no stillness but constant movement and the problem about study of cultures . . . is how to study them in their movement and linkages to other processes in that society or community. It is like studying a river in its very movement.

(1993: 29)

Child development, it would be fair to argue, no longer presents a coherent point of view or a unified subject matter, but encompasses a variety of competing approaches and overlapping or even unreconcilable topics at different levels of detail and generality. Yet it is regarded as not merely useful but as a *necessary* underpinning for practice in work with young children. Part of the intention of this book is to illustrate that there are many different theories, practices and policies concerning early childhood, even within a minority Euro–North American context, let alone within the majority world. Understanding the range of this diversity, and the challenges it poses for understanding and dialogue, is a critical task for students of early childhood.

In the first of the chapters in this part, Martin Woodhead tellingly points out that most of the world's children, are expected from a very early age to contribute to family resources and well-being through some kind of work, paid or unpaid: helping to grow vegetables; caring for animals; looking after younger siblings; doing household tasks; selling; scavenging; doing outwork; and so on. Lancy (1996) has also commented on the need to recast definitions of work and play. His research in West Africa shows how children as young as four contribute to household tasks and take responsibility for marketing produce. 'Make-believe play can provide opportunities for children to acquire adult work habits and to rehearse social scenes. In many cases the transition from play work to real work is nearly seamless' (Lancy 1996: 89).

Woodhead's interviews with majority world children suggest that work tasks are not regarded as an imposition, but are mostly done willingly because that is what is normal, expected and respected, in the situations in which children live their daily lives. Whatever one's views about child labour, the effect of such everyday assumptions and practices on children's lives cannot be ignored. Yet as he points out, most textbooks on child development, although including many generalizations about 'play', with one exception simply do not consider or mention 'work' or discuss whether children might have a useful contribution to make to household and domestic life.

Alan Pence and Jessica Ball develop the theme of contradictory cultural interpretations of childhood and childrearing in their work with aborigine or First Nation peoples in Canada. Because of the hegemony and dominance of Western or minority world ideas in most fields, local or indigenous knowledge systems are in danger of being dismissed as superstition, and undermined, or even obliterated (Hobart 1993). The oppressiveness of Western knowledge systems is particularly acute where the people concerned are themselves a minority group within an industrialized country and, as with Aboriginal peoples in Australia, separate development and separate education systems may be an important way to preserve indigenous cultures and childrearing practices (Thomas 1994). Ball and Pence confront these difficulties and explore how they can be addressed.

References

Bredekamp, S. (ed.) (1987) *Developmentally Appropriate Practice in Early Childhood Programmes Serving Children from Birth through Age 8*. Washington: National Association for the Education of Young Children.

Bronfenbrenner, U. (1979) *The Ecology of Human Development. Experiments by Nature and Design*. Cambridge, MA: Harvard University Press.

Burman, E. (1994) *Deconstructing Developmental Psychology*. London: Routledge.

Chinweizu (1975) *The West and the Rest of Us*. New York: Random House.

Cochran, M. (ed.) (1993) *International Handbook of Child Care Policies and Programs*. Westport, CT: Greenwood Press.

Cole, M. (1996) *Cultural Psychology: A Once and Future Discipline*. Cambridge, MA: Belknap Press.

Conolly, P. (1998) *Racism, Gender Identities and Young Children*. London: Routledge.

De Vylder, S. (1996) *Development Strategies, Macro-economic Policies and the Rights of the Child*, discussion paper for Radda Barnen, Stockholm.

Elder, G.H., Model, J. and Parke, R.D. (eds) (1993) *Children in Time and Place: Developmental and Historical Insights*. Cambridge: Cambridge University Press.

European Commission Network on Childcare (1996) *A Review of Services for Young Children in the European Union. 1990–1995*. Brussels: European Commission Directorate General V.

Gardner, H. (1984) *Culture Theory: Essays on Mind, Self and Emotion*. Cambridge: Cambridge University Press.

Goldberger, N.R. and Veroff, J.B. (1995) *The Culture and Psychology Reader*. New York: New York University Press.

Guardian (1998) Society, *Guardian*, 9 September.

Heath, S. Brice (1983) *Ways with Words: Language, Life and Work in Communities and Classrooms*. Cambridge, MA: Cambridge University Press.

Heath, S. Brice (1990) *The Children of Trackton's* Children, in J.W. Stigler, R.A. Shweder and G. Herdt (eds) *Essays on Comparative Human Development*. Chicago, IL: Chicago University Press.

Hobart, M. (ed.) (1993) *An Anthropological Critique of Development: The Growth of Ignorance*. London: Routledge.

Jahoda, G. and Lewis, I.M. (eds) (1988) *Acquiring Culture: Cross Cultural Studies in Child Development*. London: Croom Helm.

Kessen, W. (1979) The American child and other cultural inventions, *American Psychologist*, 34(10): 815–20.

Lamb, M., Sternberg, K., Hwang, C.P., and Broberg, A. (eds) (1992) *Childcare in Context*. Hillsdale, NJ: Lawrence Erlbaum.

Lancy, D. (1996) *Playing on the Mother Ground: Cultural Routines for Children's Development.* London: The Guilford Press.

Lave, J. and Wenger, E. (1991) *Situated Learning: Legitimate Peripheral Participation.* Cambridge: Cambridge University Press.

LeVine, R., Dixon, S., LeVine, S. *et al.* (1994) *Childcare and Culture: Lessons from Africa.* Cambridge: Cambridge University Press.

Moss, P. (1998) *Training and Education of Early Childhood Education and Care Staff.* Report prepared for OECD, May 1998.

Ngugi Wa Thiong'o (1993) *Moving the Centre: The Struggle for Cultural Freedoms.* Portsmouth: Heinemann.

Palacios, J. and Moreno, M.C. (1996) *Parents' and Adolescents' Ideas on Children: Origins and Transmission of Intracultural Diversity,* in S. Harkness and C. Super (eds) *Parents' Cultural Belief Systems: Their Origin, Expressions and Consequences.* New York: The Guilford Press.

Penn, H. (1997a) Inclusivity and diversity in early childhood services in South Africa, *International Journal of Inclusive Education,* 1(1): 101–14.

Penn, H. (1997b) *Review of Early Childhood Services in Developing and Transitional Countries.* London: Department of International Development.

Penn, H. (1998a) Children and Childhood in the Majority World. Paper presented to conference paper, Childhood Research and Policy Centre, University of London Institute of Education, June 1998.

Penn (1998b) Comparative research – a way forward?, in T. David (ed.) *Researching Young Children: A European Perspective.* London: Paul Chapman.

Rabain, J. (1979) *L'enfant du Lignage.* Paris: Payot.

Riesman, P. (1992) *First Find Your Child a Good Mother: The Construction of Self in Two African Communities.* New Jersey: Rutgers.

Rogoff, B. and Chavajay, P. (1995) What's become of research on the cultural basis of cognitive development? *American Psychologist,* 50(10): 859–75.

Scheper-Hughes, N. (ed.) (1987) *Child Survival.* The Netherlands: D. Reidel Publishing.

Serpell, R. (1993) *The Significance of Schooling: Life Journeys in an African Society.* Cambridge: Cambridge University Press.

Shweder, R.A. (1990) Cultural psychology: what is it?, in J.W. Stigler, R.A. Shweder and G. Herdt (eds) *Essays on Comparative Human Development.* Chicago, IL: Chicago University Press.

Thomas, E. (ed.) (1994) *International Perspectives on Culture and Schooling,* proceedings of a symposium. London: Institute of Education, London University.

Thorpe, R. (1994) Intergroup differences amongst native Americans in socialization and child cognition: an ethnographic analysis, in P. Greenfield and R. Cocking (eds) *Cross Cultural Roots in Minority Child Development.* Hillsdale, NJ: Lawrence Erlbaum.

Tobin, J.J., Wu, D.Y.H. and Davidson, D. H. (1989) *Preschool in Three Cultures.* New Haven: Yale University Press.

Woodhead, M. (1998) 'Quality' in early childhood programmes – a contextually appropriate approach, *International Journal of Early Years Education,* 6(1): 5–17.

1 Towards a global paradigm for research into early childhood

Martin Woodhead

The case for a global perspective on early childhood is clear enough, although globalization is full of contradictions. A few examples will suffice. Firstly, we are constantly reminded that we live in a global economy, yet we witness gross economic inequalities between richest and poorest childhoods. Secondly, universal schooling is a global right for childhood, according to the United Nations Convention on the Rights of the Child (1989). Education is generally regarded as one of the most powerful tools for enhancing children's quality of life. Yet millions of the world's children are unable to attend school, and even where they do attend the resources can be mediocre, the teaching inappropriate and the benefits unclear. Thirdly, we are witnessing a global technological revolution, such that children throughout the world can watch the same satellite television channels, and their thoughts and aspirations are shaped by the same media images and marketing pressures. When people talk glibly about globalized childhoods I am torn between competing images: on the one hand an image of acute and highly visible social inequalities, and on the other hand an image of standardized childhoods regulated on the same technically regulated mass production principles as the fast food industry!

What does all this have to do with early education? Firstly, early education is now part of the process of globalization. Diverse programmes of family support, childcare and early education can now be found throughout the world, very often strongly influenced by models that originate in Europe or North America (Lamb *et al.* 1992). Moreover, research evaluations increasingly take a cross-national perspective, comparing quality in different country contexts (see, for example, Olmsted and Weikart 1989). Secondly, global trends are relevant even to those whose work is firmly rooted in European contexts. They are an antidote to parochialism, the main symptom of which is a persistent and often dogmatic belief that there is only one way forward where quality is concerned. Setting

European quality issues in global context (as well as in historical context) encourages a broader perspective on the particular issues, constraints and priorities that determine what counts for early childhood quality in specific economic, cultural, educational and political contexts. Finally, although focusing here mainly on contrasts between European and non-European early childhood contexts, many of the same arguments apply to the diversity to be found within Europe, in terms of the social, ethnic and cultural experiences of our very youngest citizens.

Early childhood quality issues – Henry's experience

I've come to these themes through two recent international projects on child development. The first was specifically on quality issues in early education programmes: a Bernard van Leer Foundation project that included case studies in Kenya, France, India and Venezuela. I will introduce this project by briefly describing the situation of one child.

I met 4-year-old Henry at a preschool I visited in Nairobi. He lives in one of the poorest and most overcrowded districts of the city. His home is a one-room hut that he shares with his mother and sisters; the same living conditions as most of the other children in his preschool. His mother is a single parent and, like many of the women in the community, ekes out a living by helping out in the market, or by trading her own body in the local sex industry. Henry is fortunate to attend what is widely regarded as a high quality preschool, run by a local nongovernmental organization (NGO).

Quality for Henry means sharing a classroom with 50–60 other children, much of the time with just one adult. There are no play equipment and learning materials to speak of. There are some benches, and the children sit obediently in rows. As a visitor, this picture reminded me of the photographs I have seen of British elementary school classrooms at the end of the nineteenth century, which were so strongly condemned by many of the pioneers of early childhood education. But how should I react? Should I apply the same quality principles to Henry's preschool as might be used to judge a nursery school in Britain? To do so would logically entail condemning perhaps the majority of the world's early childhood centres. Leaving aside the resourcing and political dimensions of the issue, I wasn't even sure that such condemnation would be appropriate from an educational point of view.

Much of the curriculum and pedagogy of Henry's preschool was based on wall charts of the English alphabet. The teacher led the group, and the children recited the words and letters in unison. Discipline was strict; children didn't risk speaking out of turn. Clearly, many different factors were shaping Henry's early childhood experience. One of the most powerful was to do with the elementary schooling, which is highly competitive and very formal, and later grades are dominated by the English language.

Looking at Henry's preschool within the broader context of schooling helped me to understand respects in which it might be 'contextually appropriate', even if from other points of view it might not be recognized as 'developmentally appropriate'. From these and other experiences I went on to elaborate a more ecological framework for thinking about quality issues in *In Search of the Rainbow* (Woodhead 1996, 1999a).

Children's working lives – Moni's experience

The topic for the second project was on the face of it very different. I co-ordinated a project about child labour for Radda Barnen (Swedish Save the Children) in Bangladesh, Ethiopia, the Philippines and Central America.

Moni is a 'brick-chipper' in Dhaka, Bangladesh. She works with her mother, breaking up bricks by hand, with a hammer, to provide chippings for road-building. Moni has already finished with school. In fact, she only attended for a few months, but the costs became too high for her parents to afford, and in any case they needed her meagre wages to help pay for medicines for her brother, who had been very sick.

There is now a strong international movement to eliminate exploitative and harmful child labour, spearheaded by UNICEF and the International Labour Office (ILO). The UN Convention on the Rights of the Child, Article 32 is targeted to situations like Moni's: 'States Parties recognise the right of the child to be protected from economic exploitation and from performing any work that is likely to be hazardous or to interfere with the child's education, or to be harmful to the child's health or physical, mental, spiritual, moral or social development'.

In order to implement this article of the Convention, appropriate indicators for child development are required, which can be used to determine degrees of 'harm'. In many ways, identifying harm is the flip side of promoting quality. Physical injuries are clear enough, but 'mental, moral and social development' are much less readily operationalized in universally appropriate ways. Also, any interventions designed to liberate children from harmful work must be planned within a more comprehensive understanding of the context of their lives. Otherwise there is a danger that they will be 'liberated' into circumstances that may be even more prejudicial to their development and well-being. This was the starting point for the study *Children's Perspectives on their Working Lives*, which has tried to look at the impact of work in children's lives from their own point of view (Woodhead 1998b, 1998c).

Child development research and policy

What both of these studies drew to my attention is the central role that child development beliefs, knowledge and research play in informing standard setting in childhood policy and practice. What also became clear were the serious knowledge imbalances where young children's development and learning is concerned (Woodhead 1999b). The vast majority of studies of early child development and education have been carried out in very narrow socioeconomic and cultural contexts, mainly in Europe and in North America. Yet Europe only constitutes 12 per cent of the world's population, and North America a further 5 per cent (Penn 1998). The partiality of research emphasis is in many ways inevitable. As researchers, we have to make choices about which contexts are studied, which children included, which questions asked, which indicators selected and which instruments used, and how data is recorded, analysed, interpreted and so on. The problems arise when that partiality is not acknowledged, both in terms of the generalizability of research contexts and outcomes, and more subtly in terms of the generalizability of the interpretive frame of beliefs and values that shape all social scientific research (Hwang *et al.* 1996). At worst, context-specific, cultural accounts masquerade as universal statements about what is 'natural', 'normal' or 'developmentally appropriate' (Kessen 1979; Burman 1994).

In the past, these problems have frequently been exacerbated by the universalist aspirations of the foundation discipline of the field: child development. The science of psychology has constructed powerful normative models of development, based on a fundamental belief in the psychic unity of humankind (Stigler *et al.* 1990). Shared features of childhood have been emphasized. At best, differences have been treated as 'variations on a theme': at worst, as 'noise in the system'. Fortunately, cross-cultural studies go some way to redressing the balance, rendering problematic some of the more ethnocentric assertions that have been made about the needs of young children (Segall *et al.* 1990).

Super and Harkness's concept of the developmental niche is a helpful starting point (Super and Harkness 1986). It draws attention to three features of early childhood environments in particular:

• the physical and social setting;
• the culturally regulated customs and child-rearing practices;
• the dominant beliefs or 'ethnotheories' about childhood.

Super and Harkness originated this concept from their research in rural Kenya. But I think it is a salutary lesson to turn the social scientific lens on to the developmental niches occupied by modern European children, including the early childhood programmes they attend, and especially to recognize the way they are mediated by the more sophisticated belief systems and cultural practices we elevate to the status of theories of learning.

I will give some examples of what I mean in relation to both early childcare and children's work.

Textbook images of early care and development

Traditional textbook accounts of early development have been based very largely on studies carried out in Europe and North America. Studies of children's early attachments and social interactions have mainly been focused on mother–infant relationships, even though from a global perspective it has long been recognized that multiple caregiving arrangements are widespread, and sibling care has been a very important source of security and learning for infants and young children (Weisner and Gallimore 1977). Studies have also conveyed a particular image of a 'normal' mothering style, marked by close maternal attention to infant interests, and early initiation into playful exchanges anticipating verbal communication. Fortunately, cross-cultural studies have periodically challenged the ethnocentric biases of research. A classic example comes from a cross-cultural study in 12 societies. Whiting and Edwards (1988) concluded that the caregiving style observed in the USA was exceptional in terms of the extent of mothers' sociability with their children, and in the number of playful interactions in which children were treated as equals. Yet, this style of interaction has become part of child development orthodoxy as the normal, and indeed healthy way for parents to relate to their children.

The point is made most clearly for language and communication. Close observation of Euro–American families has revealed the subtle parental strategies through which infants are encouraged to become partners in 'proto-conversations'. Their language learning is facilitated by caregiver's adoption of so-called 'motherese', in which intonation is exaggerated, vocabulary and sentence structure are simplified, and the child's utterances are repeated and expanded (Snow 1976). By contrast, a cross-cultural study amongst the Kaluli of Papua New Guinea, revealed that caregivers rarely engaged their infants in dyadic communicative exchanges, and when they did they tended to be directive rather than reciprocal. Yet these infants acquired their mother tongue quite 'normally' (Schieffelin and Ochs 1983). It may be that Euro–American caregiving patterns are the exception rather than the norm.

I give the next example not merely to emphasize the existence of different cultural practices, but to draw attention to the very different interpretations that can be put on the same issue; the way different beliefs mediate what counts as appropriate or 'quality' care. Joseph Tobin and colleagues carried out a cross-cultural study of preschool settings (Tobin *et al.* 1989; see also Tobin *et al.* 1998). When they were observing in Komatsudani, a Japanese kindergarten, one little boy called Hiroki seemed to be stepping out of line. Asked to interpret his behaviour an American specialist felt that the problem might arise because he was intellectually gifted but easily bored. The Japanese teachers couldn't accept this view at all; they couldn't see how a gifted child could fail to work harmoniously, because this attribute was part of their definition of intelligence. These observers then turned to another line of explanation, to do with Hiroki's emotional relationships. Whereas a Western commentator might draw on the con-cept of 'attachment', and talk about the growing capacities for autonomy and self-control expected in preschool age children, Japanese teachers drew on the concept of '*amaeru*', emphasizing dependency as something that children have to learn during infancy. At root this example draws attention not only to different views of developmental process, but differ-ent views about the development of a sense of self.

Work in child development

As part of the project on child labour, I asked the question, 'Is there a place for work in child development?' (Woodhead 1998b, 1998c). Two kinds of answer are possible. In terms of children's lived experience the answer is that at least 190 million children aged 10–14 are working, according to UNICEF estimates. Three quarters of these children work for six days a week or more (UNICEF 1997). This figure does not include the domestic help and casual work carried out by many millions of children, including very young children, throughout the world. But textbook accounts of child development convey a different story. Textbook authors do not write about the child development experienced by the world's children. They construct an image of a very particular kind of childhood, as a period of life spent almost entirely in the contexts of family and school, where the emphasis is on care, play, learning and teaching, at least until adolescence, when self-esteem and social relationships within peer groups assume importance. Ironically, this is called 'normal' childhood.

Table 1.1 summarizes index entries for eight child development textbooks published between 1987 and 1995. This is only a very crude

Table 1.1 Some child development textbooks (1987–1995): number of index entries for 'work', 'play', 'school', 'family' and 'friends'*

Textbooks	Family	School	Friends	Play	Work
Clarke-Stewart and Friedman 1987	20	15	3	26	0
Cole and Cole 1989	10	16	4	8	1
Berger 1991	16	8	5	5	0
Smith and Cowie 1991	1	5	5	26	0
Shaffer 1993	57	14	9	9	0
Dworetzky 1993	0	7	1	10	0
Berk 1994	36	26	13	34	0
Bee 1995	17	17	5	8	0
Total	157	108	45	126	1

*I am grateful to Rachel Reynolds for preparing the data in this table

indicator of the relative emphasis given to various topics. The striking thing is the consistent neglect of the formative influence of work in children's lives, with only one entry across all eight textbooks: a brief account (Cole and Cole 1989) of the effects of part-time work on adolescents' school performance in the USA.

In defence of these eight textbooks, it could be argued that the selective treatment of child development topics reflects childhood realities in the European and North American contexts. But the exclusion of work as a significant influence in child development cannot be justified even within these minority world contexts. While paid work has been marginalized by universal compulsory schooling for nearly a century, child employment remains widespread in the UK (McKechnie *et al.* 1996) and the USA (Pollack *et al.* 1990). Family based domestic work for children is also quite normal (Morrow 1994). Yet work is not part of the textbook writer's definition of childhood, despite its impact on their skills, identity, self-esteem, social relationships and school experience.

This example is a further illustration of the ways in which 'child development' is an idealized construction, which not only underrepresents the diversity of Western childhoods, but also seriously misrepresents childhoods within a wider global context. Children themselves may have a different view. For them, work is not only normal, it is a core part of growing up. As one boy fishing in the Philippines put it, 'to work is a natural thing to do. Our friends do it. My parents work, my brothers work so why shouldn't I work? Even schooling is not an excuse not to work' (cited in Woodhead 1998c: 35).

Part of the problem is that even where children are engaged in work activities in the West, the dominant construction of childhood as work-free means that these are relabelled as play or learning or taking social responsibility. Rheingold (1982) drew attention to this issue in her study of US toddlers helping their mothers carry out domestic chores. 'All the children, even those as young as 18 months of age, promptly and for the most part without direction participated in some everyday housekeeping tasks performed by adults' (Rheingold 1982: 122).

Wanting to contribute is as much a feature of early childhood as wanting to learn or wanting to play. This even applied to some of the children in the Radda Barnen study, whose working lives are harsh and potentially dangerous. One of Moni's friends (brick-chippers in Bangladesh) identified strongly with her family's work.: 'when I was a child I used to cry for a hammer. So my mother bought me a hammer and I started to break bricks' (cited in Woodhead 1998c: 35).

Dominant expectations of what is 'normal' child development can be seen as reflecting features of a very particular developmental niche (Super and Harkness 1986). The danger lies in these features being taken to be a standard for all. From our perspective (as minority world professional educators and researchers), we may view particular styles of adult interaction, ways of teaching and approaches to play and learning, as appropriate for early childhood. We may not feel that work has any place at all in a quality childhood, but that it can interfere with children's education, and so on. But this does not justify excluding other childhood experiences and influences as outside the range of 'normal' or 'healthy' child development. The consequence is that other people's childhoods too readily become labelled as deprived, deficient and damaging. A paradigm is needed that still recognizes where young children may be at risk of harm, injury or abuse, but at the same time is more inclusive of diversity of contexts beliefs and practices. As I mentioned earlier, adopting a more inclusive, globally appropriate paradigm can also enable early childhood theories and practices that have evolved within familiar contexts to be understood within a wider framework.

The potential of a sociocultural approach

In terms of a theoretical framework on early child development, I believe research within the growing field of sociocultural developmental psychology has greatest potential (Woodhead 1999b). This theoretical view originates in the work of L.S. Vygotsky. Vygotsky was working in Soviet Russia during the early decades of the twentieth century and his inspiration was to recognize that child development is a social process, historically and culturally relative:

> The fundamental aspiration of the whole of modern child psychology . . . [is] the wish to reveal the eternal child. The task of psychology, however, is not the discovery of the eternal child. The task of psychology is the discovery of the historical child . . . The stone that the builders disdained must become the foundation stone.
>
> (Vygotsky, cited by Rogoff 1990: 110)

Michael Cole has elaborated this idea that child development is a cultural process, in a very profound sense that is not just about cultural variation:

> the capacity to inhabit a culturally organized environment is the universal, species-specific characteristic of *homo sapiens*, of which particular cultures represent special cases. A full understanding of culture in human development requires both a specification of its universal mechanisms and the specific forms that it assumes in particular historical circumstances.
>
> (Cole 1992: 731–2)

According to this view, child development is naturally cultural. Briefly, every child is born into a social–cultural–historical context. Infants are by nature attuned to engage with the social and cultural environment of activities and meanings. There is nothing fundamentally natural about environments for childcare, either at home or within a preschool setting.

All environments are culturally constructed, shaped by generations of human activity and creativity and mediated by complex belief systems, including about the 'proper' way for children to develop. The most significant features of any child's environment are the humans with whom they establish close relationships. These individuals (usually family) are themselves cultural beings. They are the product of cultural history and circumstance, which structure their lives and give meaning and direction to their experiences of their offspring, as they introduce them to cultural practices and symbol systems. The way parents care for their children is shaped in part by their cultural beliefs (or ethnotheories) about what is appropriate and desirable, in terms both of the goals of child development and the means to achieve those goals.

Colwyn Trevarthen (1998) has argued from studies of newborn babies that one of the human infant's most fundamental needs is to become part of a culture. Babies actively engage with their social environment from the start; pre-adapted to social relationships, they strive to make sense of their surroundings by sharing with others in a process of intersubjectivity on which joint activity, cooperation and communication is built. Judy Dunn (1988) has worked with an older age group, revealing the way preschool children achieve social understanding in family contexts; negotiating disputes; teasing and joking with adults and siblings; and sharing in conversations about social and moral issues from a very early age. While these studies have been carried out in Euro–North American settings they can be the starting point for elaborating the way children become initiated into features of their sociocultural niche, including the range of settings and relationships, and opportunities for sibling and peer interaction, through which they learn about social rules, rituals and meanings. A feature of early learning is young children's capacity to engage in a repertoire of different interactive styles according to context and relationship, acknowledging that in complex, changing pluralistic contexts, children may encounter multiple, competing and even conflicting developmental niches as a normal part of everyday life.

Barbara Rogoff has perhaps gone furthest in elaborating a sociocultural model with direct applicability to early childhood education. She has proposed a model of 'guided participation' as a framework for examining the way children are initiated into cognitive and social skills perceived as relevant to their community (Rogoff 1990). Comparing mother–child dyads in India, Guatemala, Turkey and the USA, Rogoff *et al.* (1993) found that 'guided participation' was a feature in all these settings, but that the goals and processes of learning and teaching varied, which in turn was linked to the extent to which children's lives were segregated from the adult world of work.

For example, while US mothers were often observed to create teaching situations, the Guatemalan mothers relied on the child's engagement with activities of the community. In one sequence of Rogoff's research video, there is a fine illustration of these mothers' different orientation to communication. In the US context, the dominance of verbal communication is taken for granted. But when a Guatemalan mother wishes her toddler to hand over a toy, she says not a word, but merely touches the toddler's elbow, a simple direct communicative device whose symbolic meaning is already well understood by the child.

Taking a sociocultural approach to children's development breaks away from universalistic assumptions, about both the process and the products of development. Rogoff makes the point clearly in respect of children's intellectual development:

> The developmental endpoint that has traditionally anchored cognitive developmental theories – skill in academic activities such as formal operational reasoning and scientific, mathematical, and literate practices – is one valuable goal of development, but one that is tied to its contexts and culture, as is any other goal or endpoint of development valued by a community . . . Each community's valued skills constitute the local goals of development . . . In the final analysis, it is not possible to determine whether the practices of one society are more adaptive than those of another, as judgements of adaptation cannot be separated from values.
>
> (Rogoff 1990: 12)

Acceptance of this view – that children's behaviour, thinking, social relationships and adaptation, are culturally as much as biologically constituted – has profound implications for the way we conceptualize and research early years education. Early childhood programmes can be understood for what they are: highly specialized environments with quite distinctive characteristics linked to their goals and priorities for children's learning. Comparing a modern preschool in Europe with a preschool like the one Henry attends in Kenya, or the work based childhood of Moni in Bangladesh, draws attention to taken-for-granted features of the range of developmental niches of modern European childhoods.

A sociocultural perspective alters frameworks of quality evaluation too. The 'developmental appropriateness' of children's experiences, and the 'harmfulness' or 'benefits' of their environment, cannot be separated from the cultural context in which they are developing, the values and goals that inform their lives, their prior learning experiences and future prospects. Unlike frameworks that emphasize supposedly normal and natural criteria for judging the quality of child development, cultural approaches argue that these criteria are constructed and contextual. In due course, human societies may come to share beliefs about what is 'normal' and 'natural' for children. The implication of accepting that early child development and learning has to be understood as a social and cultural process is that benchmarks of quality are not intrinsic, fixed and prescribed. They are extrinsic, historically specific and negotiable within a framework of promoting children's rights and welfare.

Towards a more inclusive framework for early childhood education

A 'contextual' approach offers a more inclusive starting point for understanding a range of perspectives on the goals and processes of child development, as well as the contexts that can sustain child development in global contexts (Woodhead 1996, 1998a). In particular, we need to ensure that 'top-down' generalizations are balanced by 'bottom-up' studies about what harms and what promotes development in the context of children's developmental niches, including the issues that confront caregivers, teachers and children themselves. Figure 1.1 summarizes a cycle of quality development, founded on an ecological model of the various contexts that shape children's lives. One of the first steps is to make explicit the perspectives of all those with a stake in the these issues, including ourselves. Figure 1.2 suggests a procedure for doing just this, based on asking three key questions.

- *Who has a perspective on 'quality'?* Numerous different interest-groups (or stakeholders) are involved in any early childhood programme, each with their own perspective on quality; for example, programme managers, teachers, parents, community leaders and child development experts, and not forgetting children themselves.
- *Who do these stakeholders perceive as beneficiaries from 'quality'?* While programmes are first and foremost for children, most stakeholders would recognize other beneficiaries, notably parents, who are freed of care responsibilities, the care-workers or teachers, who gain employment, and the community leaders, who gain prestige. For some care programmes, older children are seen as major beneficiaries, because they are no longer required to care for their youngest siblings.
- *What do they take to be indicators of 'quality'?* Judgements about quality can focus on any number of things. Indicators range from basic standards (for example, physical space, staffing ratios, hygiene and nutrition), and resources for play activities and learning (for cxample, toys and materials), to the quality of adult–child relationships, flexibility to parents' working patterns, notions of cost-effectiveness and many more.

This framework accommodates diverse perspectives on the quality of an early childhood programme. It can be a vehicle for making explicit profound differences in perspective on quality in early childhood that might otherwise remain submerged. It can be the starting point for negotiating a shared understanding amongst key stakeholders in a particular community, notably between parents, and teachers or care-workers.

In presenting this framework I am aware that some critics might argue that it is far too open-ended, far too relativistic, which risks undermining the essential process of standard setting. At worst it could be viewed as endorsing some traditional childcare and education practices that are

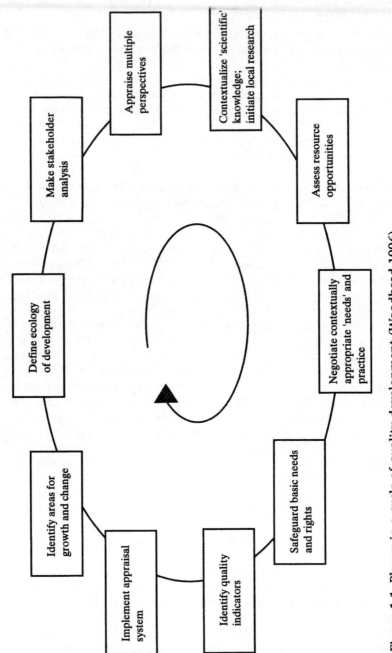

Figure 1.1 Phases in a cycle of quality development (Woodhead 1996)

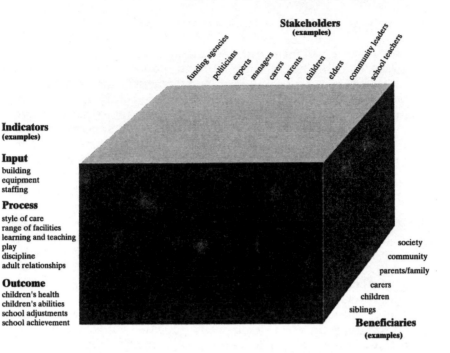

Stakeholders
(examples)

funding agencies politicians experts managers carers parents children elders community leaders school teachers

Indicators
(examples)

Input
building
equipment
staffing

Process
style of care
range of facilities
learning and teaching
play
discipline
adult relationships

Outcome
children's health
children's abilities
school adjustments
school achievement

society
community
parents/family
carers
children
siblings
Beneficiaries
(examples)

Figure 1.2 Three dimensions for examining the quality of early childhood programmes

ineffective, maladaptive or even harmful (Evans and Myers 1994). So it is important to emphasize that adopting a more inclusive, contextual framework does not undermine efforts to improve quality in the lives of young children. Acknowledging diverse contexts and multiple perspectives is not the end of the story: it is the starting point for debate and for research, including carrying out rigorous evaluations, in ways that make much more explicit the criteria on which one feature or another of children's environment, teaching or behaviour is taken to be an indicator of 'quality'. This is especially important in the context of social change (in economic, social, cultural and educational systems), which is one of the features of global childhoods.

Numerous criteria can shape quality indicators in early childhood education. Some may be identified at local programme level; others at regional or national level. Some will be internationally agreed, setting the boundaries of adequacy on any early childhood environment. In the final analysis, international instruments like the UN Convention on the Rights of the Child (1989) set global standards for early childhood quality (Verhellen 1997). There is much work to be done at every level, from the day-to-day goal setting of a preschool teacher to the international enforcement of children's rights.

Status of the child in research and practice

So far, I have argued for an early childhood quality paradigm that is more inclusive of childhood diversity. I have proposed that a sociocultural approach to children's learning and development is most appropriate, and suggested some implications for the process of identifying quality criteria that are both developmentally and contextually appropriate. I ended the last section by acknowledging globally applicable principles in the UN Convention on the Rights of the Child. While the Convention is not unproblematic in terms of the cultural images of childhood it presumes (Boyden 1997; Woodhead 1998d), potentially it has profound implications. I want briefly to consider just one Article, about children's status and participation in the issues that shape their lives, including questions about quality. 'States Parties shall assure to the child who is capable of forming his or her own views the right to express those views freely in all matters affecting the child, the views of the child being given due weight in accordance with the age and maturity of the child' (UN Convention on the Rights of the Child 1989: Article 12).

This Article of the UN Convention sets one of the strongest challenges for child development work, which cuts across some aspects of the cultural variability in child development urged in earlier sections of this paper. It is especially significant for those contexts dominated by hierarchical authority relationships where children's voice is not heard. Article 12 reminds us that children have their own perspective on the issues that concern parents, teachers, psychologists and child rights workers, which has legitimacy in its own right. In their own way, children are also trying to understand about their development, and their own place within it, as they interpret the behaviour, demands and expectations of adults and other children, and as they construct a repertoire of ways of acting and reacting. To put it bluntly, respect for children's rights to participation demands that children be viewed not just as the subjects of concern, care, teaching, research and study, but also as young citizens with concerns of their own.

Early childhood practitioners are already beginning to progress the implementation of this principle in their practice, enabling young children to take responsibility and make decisions (for example, Miller 1997). Initiatives are also required that support children's participation in other areas of public life (for example, Johnson *et al.* 1995; Davie and Galloway 1996; Hart 1997). I want to draw attention to the ways the principle applies also to the way we carry out research into early childhood: our use of intervention, observation or psychometric paradigms. It also applies to the way we conceptualize the child in theories about how they learn and develop. The question is about the status we accord the child through the methodologies we adopt and the conclusions we draw, and about whether we allow children space to alter our agenda of presuppositions.

Allison James offers a very useful tool for thinking about these issues

(James 1998; see also James *et al.* 1998). James distinguishes four models or images of 'the child' constructed by social scientists through the research methods they adopt, and the way they interpret their observations.

The model comprises two dimensions: the extent to which childhood is seen as a 'world apart' from adulthood; and the status accorded to children's expressions of competence.

Within a 'developing child' paradigm, competence is an achieved status. Development is a long journey to mature, adult status. As Verhellen (1997) puts it, within the developmental paradigm children are in a state of 'not yet being'. They are a set of 'potentials', a 'project' in the making. The child constructed by conventional psychological research is closely observed, tested and differentiated in terms of ways of thinking, playing and learning. The 'developing child' is researched within an evaluative frame that is mainly interested in their position on the stage-like journey to mature competence.

This image was neatly captured in the title of a collection of key articles

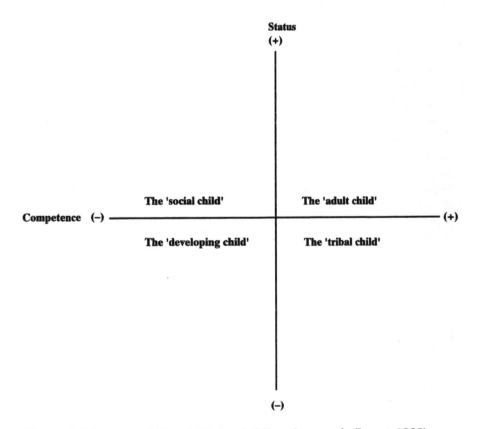

Figure 1.3 Images of 'the child' in childhood research (James 1998)

on early development, which I co-edited as recently as 1991 under the title *Becoming a Person* (Woodhead *et al.* 1991). With hindsight, this title clearly denigrates children's status as persons from the beginning of life, but at the time it appeared to reflect the growing research literature on the social processes through which young children construct skills and identity. And we should note in passing that this issue does not only relate to the theoretical frameworks of developmental research. It has also been implicit in the treatment of children as objects of research, who were until recently subjected to experimental procedures with insufficient account taken of ethical considerations (Alderson 1995; Morrow and Richards 1996; Woodhead and Faulkner 1999).

It is essential to keep firmly in mind that 'child development' is a body of knowledge constructed by adults for other adults, and used in order to make sense of, regulate and shape children's lives and learning. Piaget's (1952) theory is the most influential example of this paradigm (see Donaldson 1978 for an overview). To be fair, one of Piaget's goals was to encourage greater respect for young children's ways of thinking and behaving.

> It is of paramount importance [. . .] to play your part in a simple spirit and to let the child feel a certain superiority at the game [. . .] In this way the child is put at ease, and the information he give as to how he plays is all the more conclusive. [. . .] The interrogatory, moreover, requires extremely delicate handling; suggestion is always ready to occur, and the danger of romancing is ever present. It goes without saying that the main thing is simply to grasp the child's mental orientation.
>
> (Piaget 1932/75: 14–16)

Instead of dismissing their words and deeds as due to ignorance, he wanted to reveal the underlying 'logic' of children's reasoning at various ages. The value of the paradigm was in encouraging teachers and parents to provide learning opportunities that were seen as developmentally appropriate. The problem is that respecting developmental stages is a double-edged sword. It can also be used to justify taking actions on children's behalf, or avoid exposing them to difficult issues on the grounds that they are too young and too innocent to understand what is going on (Short 1998).

The 'tribal child', is associated with different research traditions, especially ethnographic research. Studying children at play, in the home, the playground and the street, this approach recognizes children's separateness from the adult world but (in the style of anthropology) celebrates their competence in their own cultural terms. William Corsaro's work on peer cultures is a good example of this tradition (Corsaro 1997).

The 'adult child' is a relatively rare paradigm of childhood research, and especially early childhood research. James argues that research images of the 'adult child' most often emerge when researchers encounter children living outside the protected space of modern childhoods. James illustrates the 'adult child' through studies of children coping with multiple hospital operations. In these circumstances the children's superior understanding of their situation places an obligation on the researcher to listen to their perspective.

We adopted a similar framework in embarking on the Radda Barnen study of working children. The study was designed to inform the debate about eliminating hazardous child labour with the views and feelings of those most affected by childhood work, and most affected by any interventions taken 'in their best interests'. By studying children's perspectives, we wanted to give voice to the principal stakeholders, whose concerns were in danger of being overlooked by interventions designed to protect their 'development' (Woodhead 1998c, 1999a).

Finally comes what James calls the 'social child'. Displacing an image of the developing child with an image of the competent child must not result in the neglect of differences between younger and older human beings. We must not throw out the baby with the developmental bathwater. The 'social child' accords children status within society as well as within the research process. Children are social actors with their own abilities and interests, who should be respectfully researched within relationships that enable them genuinely to participate in the process.

The difference between 'developmentalism' and the 'social child' is in the status accorded children as social actors. Instead of being about how children become competent to participate, the 'social child' emphasizes the way children can be enabled to grow in competence through participation. Respect for children's competence as rights bearing citizens does not diminish adult responsibilities. It places new responsibilities on the adult community to respect their status as stakeholders, structure their environment, guide their behaviour and enable their social participation in ways consistent with their understanding, interest and ways of communicating, especially in the issues that most directly affect their lives.

Conclusion

In this chapter I have looked at the issue of promoting early childhood quality in global context. I started by considering the knowledge imbalances that risk creating a distorted picture of what is normal and appropriate for young children, and argued for a sociocultural approach, spelling out some of the implications of taking account of diverse contexts and multiple perspectives on children's development. I also acknowledged the boundaries of any global quality debate, notably in respect for children's rights. I argued that the UN Convention poses a challenge for early childhood work, offering the example of children's right to participation. Finally, I argued that these issues don't just affect the way quality issues are resolved in the design of programmes for young children. They also have implications for researching these issues. Overall, I have argued for an inclusive framework of thinking, which acknowledges the actual and potential diversity in perspectives on young children's education and welfare, and which asserts their own central status as principal stakeholders in the process.

I believe it is important to assert these principles on academic, moral and pragmatic grounds. Theoretically, a sociocultural framework opens the way to a more complete understanding of the factors that shape children's lives. It is also a positive framework: recognizing that childhoods are socially constructed means that they can also be reconstructed. Pragmatically, an early childhood intervention, childcare programme or early education initiative is much more likely to be effective if it builds on the human and physical resources, beliefs, goals and experiences of those who participate in it. Morally, it seems to me that as teachers, students and researchers we have a responsibility to be attuned to how the tasks of childhood are perceived, felt and understood by those children, their parents and other carers who have to solve the problems of living and growing up, in circumstances that may be vastly different from those that shape our own personal and academic priorities.

Acknowledgements

This chapter was originally presented as a paper at the European Early Childhood Education Research Association Conference, Santiago de Compostela, September 1998.

I want to thank the Bernard van Leer Foundation (The Hague) and Radda Barnen (Stockholm) who commissioned the work referred to in the paper.

References

Alderson, P. (1995) *Listening to Children*. London: Barnardos.
Bee, H. (1995) *The Developing Child*, 7th edn. New York: Harper Collins.
Berger, K.S. (1991) *The Developing Person through Childhood and Adolescence*, 3rd edn. New York: Worth Publishers.
Berk, L.E. (1994) *Child Development*, 3rd edn. London: Allyn and Bacon.
Boyden, J. (1997) Childhood and the policy-makers: a comparative perspective on the globalization of childhood, in A. James and A. Prout (eds) *Constructing and Reconstructing Childhood*, 2nd edn. Brighton: Falmer Press.
Burman, E. (1994) *Deconstructing Developmental Psychology*. London: Routledge.
Clarke-Stewart, A. and Friedman, S. (1987) *Child Development: Infancy through Adolescence*. New York: Wiley.
Cole, M. (1992) Culture in development, in M.H. Bornstein and M.E. Lamb (eds) *Human Development, an Advanced Textbook*. Hillsdale, NJ: Lawrence Erlbaum.
Cole, M. and Cole, S. (1989) *The Development of Children*. New York: Scientific American Books.

Corsaro, W. (1997) *The Sociology of Childhood*. Thousand Oaks, CA: Pine Forge Press.

Davie, R. and Galloway, D. (eds) (1996) *Listening to Children in Education*. London: David Fulton Publishers.

Donaldson, M. (1978) *Children's Minds*. London: Fontana Press.

Dunn, J. (1988) *The Beginnings of Social Understanding*. Oxford: Blackwell.

Dworetzky, J.P. (1993) *Introduction to Child Development*, 6th edn. St Paul, MA: West Publishing Company.

Evans, J.L. and Myers, R.G. (1994) Childrearing practices: creating programs where traditions and modern practices meet, *Coordinators' Notebook*, No. 15: 1–21.

Hart, R.A. (1997) *Children's Participation: The Theory and Practice of Involving Young Citizens in Community Development and Environmental Care*. London: UNICEF/ Earthspan Publications.

Hwang, P., Lamb, M. and Sigel, S. (eds) (1996) *Images of Childhood*. Hillsdale, NJ: Lawrence Erlbaum.

James, A. (1998) Researching children's social competence: methods and models, in M. Woodhead, D. Faulkner and K. Littleton (eds) *Making Sense of Social Development*. London: Routledge.

James, A., Jenks, C. and Prout, A. (1998) *Theorizing Childhood*. Cambridge: Polity Press.

Johnson, V., Hill, J. and Ivan-Smith, E. (1995) *Listening to Smaller Voices: Children in an Environment of Change*. London: Actionaid.

Kessen, W. (1979) The American child and other cultural inventions, *American Psychologist*, 34(10): 815–20.

Lamb, M.E., Sternberg, K.J., Hwang, C. and Broberg, C. (eds) (1992) *Child Care in Context: Cross-Cultural Perspectives*. Hillsdale, NJ: Lawrence Erlbaum.

McKechnie, J., Lindsay, S. and Hobbs, S. (1996) Child employment: a neglected topic?, *The Psychologist*, 9(5): 219–22.

Miller, J. (1997) *Never too Young*. London: Save the Children.

Morrow, V. (1994) Responsible Children? Aspects of children's work and employment outside school in contemporary UK, in B. Mayall (ed.) *Children's Childhoods Observed and Experienced*. London: Falmer Press.

Morrow, V. and Richards, M. (1996) The ethics of social research with children, *Children and Society*, 10: 90–105.

Olmsted, P. and Weikart, D. (eds) (1989) *How Nations Serve Young Children*. Ypsilanti, MI: High/Scope Press.

Penn, H. (1998) *Children and Childhood in the Majority World*. Paper presented to conference, Childhood Research and Policy Centre, University of London Institute of Education, June 1998.

Piaget, J. (1932/75) *The Moral Judgement of the Child*. London: Routledge & Kegan Paul.

Piaget, J. (1952) *The Origin of Intelligence in the Child*. London: Routledge & Kegan Paul.

Pollack, S.H., Landrigan, P.J. and Mallina, D.L. (1990) Child Labor in 1990: Prevalence and Health Hazards, *Annual Review of Public Health*, 11: 359–75.

Rheingold, H. (1982) Little children's participation in the work of adults, a nascent prosocial behaviour, *Child Development*, 53: 114–25.

Rogoff, B. (1990) *Apprenticeship in Thinking: Cognitive Development in Social Context*. Oxford: Oxford University Press.

Rogoff, B., Mistry, J., Göncü, A. and Mosier, C. (1993) Guided participation in cultural activity by toddlers and caregivers, *Monograph of the Society for Research in Child Development*, 58(8): 236.

Schieffelin, B.B. and Ochs, E. (1983) A cultural perspective on the transition from prelinguistic to linguistic communication, in R.M. Golnikoff (ed.) *The Transition from Prelinguistic Communication*. Mahwah, NJ: Lawrence Erlbaum.

Segall, M.H., Dasen, P.R., Berry, J.W. and Poortinga, Y.H. (1990) *Human Behaviour in Global Perspective: An Introduction to Cross-cultural Psychology*. New York: Pergamon.

Shaffer, D.R. (1993) *Developmental Psychology*, 3rd edn. Pacific Grove, CA: Brooks/Cole Publishing Company.

Short, G. (1998) Children's grasp of controversial issues, in M. Woodhead, D. Faulkner and K. Littleton (eds) (1998) *Making Sense of Social Development*. London: Routledge.

Smith, P.K. and Cowie, H. (1991) *Understanding Children's Development*, 2nd edn. Oxford: Blackwell.

Snow, C.E. (1976) The language of the mother child relationship, in M. Woodhead, R. Carr and P. Light (eds) (1991) *Becoming a Person*. London: Routledge.

Stigler, J.W., Shweder, R.A. and Herdt, G. (1990) *Cultural Psychology: Essays in Comparative Human Development*. Cambridge: Cambridge University Press.

Super, C. and Harkness, S. (1986) The developmental niche: a conceptualisation at the interface of child and culture, *International Journal of Behavioural Development*, 9: 545–69.

Tobin, J.J., Wu, D.Y.H. and Davidson, D.H. (1989) *Preschool in Three Cultures*. New Haven, CT: Yale University Press.

Tobin, J.J., Wu, D.Y.H. and Davidson, D.H. (1998) Komatsudani: a Japanese preschool, in M. Woodhead, D. Faulkner and K. Littleton (eds) *Cultural Worlds of Early Childhood*. London: Routledge.

Trevarthen, C. (1998) The child's need to learn a culture, in M. Woodhead, D. Faulkner and K. Littleton (eds) (1998) *Cultural Worlds of Early Childhood*. London: Routledge.

UNICEF (1997) *The State of the Worlds Children*. New York: UNICEF.

Verhellen, E. (1997) *Convention on the Rights of the Child*. Leuven: Garant Publishers.

Weisner, T. and Gallimore, R. (1977) My brother's keeper: child and sibling caretaking, *Current Anthropology*, 18(2): 169–90.

Whiting, B. and Edwards, C. (1988) *Children of Different Worlds: The Formation of Social Behaviour*. Cambridge, MA: Harvard University Press.

Woodhead, M. (1996) *In Search of the Rainbow: Pathways to Quality in Large Scale Programmes for Young Disadvantaged Children*. The Hague: Bernard van Leer Foundation.

Woodhead, M. (1998a) Quality in early childhood programmes: a contextually-appropriate approach, *International Journal of Early Years Education*, 6(1): 15–18.

Woodhead, M. (1998b) *Is There a Place for Work in Child Development?* Conceptual paper on children, work and development. Stockholm: Radda Barnen.

Woodhead, M. (1998c) *Children's Perspectives on their Working Lives: A Participatory Study in Bangladesh, Ethiopia, The Philippines, Guatemala, El Salvador and Nicaragua*. Stockholm: Radda Barnen.

Woodhead, M. (1998d) Children's rights and children's development: rethinking the paradigm, Paper presented at international interdisciplinary course, Ghent, June 1998.

Woodhead, M (1999a) Combating child labour: listen to what the children say, *Childhood,* 7(1): 7.

Woodhead, M. (1999b) Reconstructing developmental psychology: some first steps, *Children and Society,* 13(1): 1–17.

Woodhead, M. and Faulkner, D. (1999) Subjects, objects or participants: dilemmas of psychological research with children, in A. James and P. Christensen (eds) *Conducting Research with Children.* London: Falmer Press.

Woodhead, M., Carr, R. and Light, P. (eds) (1991) *Becoming a Person.* London: Routledge.

Two sides of an eagle's feather: University of Victoria partnerships with Canadian First Nations communities

Alan Pence and Jessica Ball

Introduction

The First Nations[1] of the Meadow Lake Tribal Council believe that a child care program developed, administered and operated by their own people is a vital component to their vision of sustainable growth and development. It impacts every sector of their long-term plans as they prepare to enter the twenty-first century. It will be children who inherit the struggle to retain and enhance the people's culture, language and history; who continue the quest for economic progress for a better quality of life; and who move forward with a strengthened resolve to plan their own destiny.

(Meadow Lake Tribal Council Vision Statement 1989)

The above statement, adopted by the Meadow Lake Tribal Council, served as the starting point for an innovative approach for co-constructing a programme of culturally appropriate Early Childhood Care and Development (ECCD) training. The model evolved through a series of pilot partnerships, first with the Meadow Lake Tribal Council, and subsequently with six other tribal organizations in rural areas of western Canada. Although distributed across vast distances, and in very different cultural and institutional contexts, this participatory approach has thrived.

The Generative Curriculum Model (GCM), as the approach came to be called, represents a radical departure from the established and familiar paths of training and education in ECCD in North America, which promote knowledge transmission and prescribed practices based on assumptions of their universal validity and desirability.

After seven pilot partnership projects with First Nations tribal organizations, we have become convinced that the popular demand for programmes to be 'culturally sensitive' cannot be met through established education and professionalization practices. In order to respond meaningfully to the goals and practices that define cultural communities and the children and families within them, we must acknowledge the cultural specificity of mainstream research, theory and professional practices, and forge new understandings of how we might better prepare ECCD practitioners for work in specific cultural communities.

We hope to encourage and support the elaboration and extension of an alternative discourse to the largely exclusionary, Western, modernist agenda of ECCD. Our First Nations partners have initiated partnerships with us at the University of Victoria with an understanding that the ways to enhance conditions for the well-being of children in their communities might not match either the best practices of the West or the traditional practices of their aboriginal forebears. Starting with the training of ECCD practitioners, rather than with programmes for children, our partnerships with First Nations communities highlight the many entry points that can be used to advance alternative discourses.

Context of the partnerships

In Canada, First Nations people have been subject to every kind of colonial assault, ranging from overtly genocidal practices to assimilationist requirements and practices (McMillan 1995; Ross 1997). Reams of poignant testimony have been collected describing the suffering of parents, children and communities as a result of the infliction of Western best practices – including enforced residential schooling, child welfare practices that undermine extended family support systems, and other helping services – all deemed, at the time, to be in the best interests of the subjected children and families. As the First Nations have begun to regain greater political control over their futures, they have adopted a path of caution in considering best practices and improvements from the dominant society. Many First Nations people seek training that enables practitioners to understand and contribute both to mainstream and to aboriginal settings, using approaches that have multiple roots and traditions but that are controlled by their own agency and actions. Unfortunately, even the history of partnerships has been problematic for aboriginal people, with more and less dominant cultures attempting to work together and, over time, the less dominant being required, implicitly or explicitly, to accommodate the more dominant culture and to act as if assimilated. This dynamic is one that neither the First Nations with whom we have partnered nor we at the university have wanted to repeat.

As expressed in a 1992 Aboriginal Committee Report on Family and Children's Services Legislation in British Columbia, many First Nations are prioritizing ECCD training and services as a prerequisite for economic development and as a way of protecting and enhancing the physical and psychosocial health and cultural identities of children and families: 'Our main goals are to preserve and strengthen our culture; to support and maintain the extended family system; to promote the healthy growth and development of our children and to develop community based programs conducive to the realization of these goals' (Aboriginal Committee, Community Panel 1992: 9).

The Assembly of First Nations (1989), representing aboriginal peoples across Canada has urged that caregivers be trained to deal with the burgeoning population of aboriginal children needing comprehensive care in a culturally appropriate manner (1989: Recommendation 39). The need for childcare facilities and trained community members to staff them is particularly urgent in First Nations communities located on federal reserve lands.

Grounding ECCD training in culture and community

The GCM involves communities in mutual learning, sharing of skills and collaborative construction of concepts and curricula needed to initiate new programmes that foster the well-being of children and families within their communities. Theories and methods of ECCD offered by most universities and colleges in North America are predominantly grounded in Euro–North American developmental theory and research. First Nations people are increasingly vocal about the many aspects of mainstream programmes that they see as not transferable or perhaps simply not desirable within their cultural value systems and circumstances (Pence *et al.* 1993). Some postsecondary institutions providing ECCD training take pride in producing culturally sensitive curricula by introducing pan-aboriginal information, wherein generalizations are made about the ways of life and beliefs of a conglomerate of aboriginal peoples. Such a homogeneic picture belies the diversity and complexity of aboriginal societies.

When administrators at the Meadow Lake Tribal Council reviewed available ECCD programmes, they were dissatisfied with such superficial reflections of difference, asking, in essence, What of us – our Cree and Dene cultures – is in these programmes? How are the particular needs and circumstances of our remote communities going to be addressed in these programmes? These questions were the original stimulus for initiating a collaborative approach to constructing curricula that relies on significant input from community members who can help to ensure that students' training is informed by the culture, spirituality and history of specific First Nations communities.

When the Meadow Lake Tribal Council proposed the first partnership, they sought an innovative ECCD training programme that would reflect themselves, incorporating and advancing cherished aspects of their Cree and Dene cultures, languages, traditions and goals for children: 'We must rediscover our traditional values – of caring, sharing, and living in harmony – and bring them into our daily lives and practices' (Ray

Ahenakew, Executive Director of Meadow Lake Tribal Council, personal communication)

The importance of letting each constituent community involved in the programme at Meadow Lake speak for itself, bringing in its own unique sets of priorities and practices, was a guiding principle: 'The prime focus of this project was ultimately to develop child care services at the community level which would be administered and operated by the communities. As Tribal Council staff, we could not make the error of walking into any of the communities to show them the correct and only way of doing things' (Opekokew and McCallum, personal communication).

In the initial stage of each of the seven partnership projects, no one could anticipate exactly what the generated curriculum would include. Few practitioner training models in the human services invite students, much less communities, to engage in an activity of co-construction wherein the outcome is not predetermined. Yet, reflecting on the evolution of the GCM, what was perhaps most critical was an acceptance of the powerful potential of not knowing: not knowing where exactly the work of the partnership would lead; not knowing what aspects of mainstream theory and research on child development would fit and what would need to be reconstructed by community participants; not having the answers for what would constitute quality care in the context of First Nations communities; and not being poised with vats of knowledge to be poured into the empty vessels of ECCD trainees' minds.

Guiding principles

While agreeing that there is no need to achieve consensus on what is of value in curriculum content or activities, our First Nations partners and we have agreed on a set of general principles that can serve as navigation points in uncharted waters:

- support and reinforcement for community initiative in a community based setting;
- maintenance of bi/multicultural respect;
- identification of community and individual strengths as the basis for initiatives;
- ensuring a broad ecological perspective and awareness of the child as part of family and community;
- provision of education and career laddering for students such that credit for this coursework will be fully applicable to future study and practice;
- awareness that while the immediate focus is on early childhood care and development, this training should provide the basis for broader child, youth, family and community serving training and services.

These principles articulate the belief shared among partners that the cooperative and co-constructionist approach is not only desirable, but

necessary. Through these principles we commit ourselves to the position that multiple truths must be respectfully represented in this programme and that such knowledge is not disembodied but must come through the people who live that truth.

There are some constraints within which the partnerships operate, for example the need for the programme to be viewed as academically credible and rigorous, and the need to meet provincially legislated licensing and accreditation criteria. Meeting these expectations without reverting back to the mainstream road to formalizing a pre-emptive, prescriptive, pan-aboriginal curriculum has provided one of several reasons to make the GCM highly process oriented, using an open architecture capable of incorporating input from different cultures and communities.

Co-constructing quality through dialogue and praxis

A key characteristic of the GCM is that it is open to and respectful of information from the community, from academia and potentially from other sources as well. The elaboration of curriculum for each course in the training programme involves members of the community and the university working together to incorporate knowledge from the mainstream of theory, research and practice pertaining to early childhood, and from the communities represented by the First Nations tribal organization. A student in the programme at Mount Currie, in southwest British Columbia put it succinctly: 'Being in this program is like having the best of both worlds. We love to learn about what researchers have found about child development and such from our textbooks, and we love to learn more about our own culture and how we can use it to help the children of our community.'

By contrast, most post-secondary education requires two bodies of participants to commence the activity: students and representatives (instructors, administrators) of the post-secondary institution. The approach envisioned in our partnerships with First Nations requires the addition of a third participating body: the students' community(ies). In contrast to the assumptions of community deficiencies that underlie many expert-driven approaches to professional training and service delivery, an empowerment approach assumes that 'All families have strengths and that much of the most valid and useful knowledge about the rearing of children can be found in the community itself – across generations, in networks, and in ethnic and cultural traditions' (Cochran 1988: 144).

The principles of respect and voice that guide the work of the partnership within a caring, supportive and inclusive educational environment approximates to Benhabib's conditions of universal moral respect and egalitarian reciprocity (Benhabib 1992: 105).

A basic assumption of the GCM, consistent with recent critiques of

developmental psychology by Nsamenang (1992), Burman (1994) and Cole (1996), is that there are no empirical or logical bases to assume the validity of theories and research findings about child development across cultures, sociopolitical conditions or geographic contexts. Thus, we cannot presume the goodness of fit of strategies for promoting the growth and development of children that may have been demonstrated as effective in settings very different from First Nations communities on reserves. As Woodhead (1996) contends, 'It seems to me that trying to pin down 'quality' is a bit like trying to find the crock of gold at the end of the rainbow . . . the "crock of gold" exists only as a cultural myth' (1996: 9).

A growing number of leaders in ECCD in various countries have argued that the objectives and methods of childcare embody and reproduce or change the culture in which children and caregivers live and work (Pence and McCallum 1994; Bernhard 1995; Woodhead 1996; Penn 1997; Dahlberg *et al.* 1999; Lubeck and Post, in press). Hence, there may be significantly different, equally useful and valued ways of encouraging and responding to children across diverse communities and cultural groups. Pence and Moss (1996) have argued that definition of quality must be arrived at through an inclusionary process.

Although students in a training programme using a GCM learn about mainstream theories, research and practice pertaining to early childhood care and development, the curriculum does not rest on modernist assumptions about universally shared goals for children or caregivers or about common pathways towards optimal developmental outcomes. Rather, in the manner called for by postmodernist educators and psychologists (for example Kessler and Swadener 1992; Green 1993; Scheff and Gayle 1995; Lubeck 1996), students explore diverse possibilities regarding the meaning and implications of development for caregivers within the context of their own histories, cultures and communities (Cook 1993). They are routinely asked to engage with questions of goodness of fit of various conceptualizations of ECCD throughout the programme, rather than necessarily to adopt the best practices and criteria for determining quality provided by outside agents, who are unfamiliar with the exigencies and goals of students First Nations communities.

Illustrating the construction of distributed knowledge elaborated by Lubeck and Post (in press), students in the training programme, their instructors, community supporters and the university based team work collaboratively, and in the context of each community's particular visions for children, towards the goal of elaborating curricula and programme designs that address the community's particular needs and goals for nurturing children. Thus, rather than reducing variation, as quality control experts advise or imply, the GCM celebrates variation. As Kofi Marfo remarked in 1993 when asked to review critically the programme at Meadow Lake, 'The curriculum model acknowledges the limits of the knowledge base the principal investigators bring to the project, while appropriately respecting and honouring the tremendous contributions that Elders, students, and community members at large can make to the program'.

The GCM focuses on building an open curriculum that sits between the two cultures, allowing both the message and the medium from each to enter the training process. One community based instructor of the programme at Mount Currie noted, 'We don't have all the answers. In a generative program, we can enjoy learning about what research on child development has shown and what methods seem to be helpful in certain situations. And we can delve further into our own history and traditions, and see how these can help us with our children.'

One of the Elders at Meadow Lake described the bicultural, community specific features of the curriculum as *two sides of an eagle's feather*, pointing out that both are needed to fly.

The University of Victoria brings to the training programme a representative sample of theory, research and practical approaches to ECCD from the largely middle-class, Euro–North American mainstream. But as partners, the First Nations community brings their knowledge of their own unique culture, values, practices and sometimes their language, and their vision about what optimal child development looks like and how to facilitate healthy development. One community based administrator of the programme pointedly remarked:

> We can consider what mainstream theories say and if we choose to believe them and use them in our work, that doesn't make us less Indian. And if we choose to assert the importance of our cultural traditions and ways of raising children, that doesn't make us wrong. This program recognizes and encourages this give and take, pick and choose. It doesn't cage us and expect us to act like Europeans.

By bringing together the different worlds of Western academia and tribal communities, plausible alternatives to Euro–North American, modernist ways of conceptualizing child development and childcare have surfaced or been created, some of which build on each other, stimulating additional changes and new directions throughout the generative curriculum process. It is the process, the recursive consideration of these different views, the seeking out of what Friere (1997: 192) would call 'new knowledge', that represents the heart of the GCM. The goal is not to progress forward towards a state of group consensus, with the risk of formalizing an ossified curriculum similar to those on offer in most educational institutions.

Rather, the ongoing, dialogical, process-driven approach of participatory praxis that is the essence of the GCM has the potential for creating a new generation at each delivery – a living, responsive, evolving curriculum.

Culturally grounding curriculum through Elders contributions

In the seven partnership training programmes to date, Elders and other respected community members have played a particularly significant role in bringing cultural content, historical knowledge and years of experience with generations of the community's children and families into the classroom on a regular basis. Each tribal organization identifies a number of Elders in its constituent communities. Elders are older people who are venerated carriers of cultural knowledge and historical experiences, and often of traditional language as well. They help to reinforce and extend students' positive identifications with their cultural heritage and roles as caregivers (Pence and McCallum 1994). In the words of one student in the partnership programme at Mount Currie:

> This program is unique in giving me the chance to learn from my Elders what I need to know about who I am and about my cultures' ways of being with children. I couldn't learn this from any textbooks, but I couldn't reach out to the children in my community and help them to become who they are without knowing what the Elders can teach me through this program.

An Elder who participates regularly in the programme at Mount Currie noted that, 'Our weekly meetings with students help us all to remember and pass along the knowledge of our culture before the White Man came, and reminds us of the ways of our culture in raising our children and how we want them to grow and who they will become'.

The Elders and other respected community members become participatory conduits between the classroom experience and the community experience, and they themselves, as participants in both worlds, become part of the transformational process. One student from the programme at Meadow Lake remarked, 'Students who took this program have learned a lot about how our cultures think about children, and what they have learned will make a difference to our children and grandchildren. I believe our children, our future, are going to get back on the right track.'

Rekindled intergenerational relationships – between Elders and students, and between Elders and young children – have been consistently reported in the communities where this programme has been delivered (Riggan and Kemble 1994). A student in the programme at Tl'azt'en Nation in North Central British Columbia remarked, 'Having the Elders coming to the program on a regular basis is really a good idea because we are learning their knowledge and we are also getting to know them. Now I can walk with the Elders and we can continue to talk about the old ways and how these can still be used to help us with our children today.'

The Elder Coordinator in the programme at Meadow Lake observed an enhanced role of Elders at a systemic level: 'The students, recognizing the special wisdom of the Elders, began to consult them on personal as well as course-related matters . . . Today we have Elders involved in most community programs. In the past we seldom involved Elders. The child care training program is where it all started.'

Learning all ways

One of the attributes of the GCM approach is that learning occurs all ways, with university based partners positioned to learn as much as community based partners in programme delivery. Instructors in the community and the curriculum resource team at the university hear about experiences and viewpoints they may not have previously heard and are often similarly challenged and stimulated. Hearing diverse voices and views from Elders, other community members, instructors, classmates and texts, the students in the programme become more fully aware of their own voices, their own views and how these relate to the views of others. Thus, like Rogoff's description of a community of learners, all become active in an ongoing process of learning and teaching. One community based administrator succinctly stated a sentiment often expressed by the First Nations community partners: 'I hope you people at the university are learning as much from us as were learning from you. It's important for university lecturers and theorists to listen and learn what they don't know about what being Indian means – in this case, what being Indian means for parents and children growing up in our communities.'

From the outset, the First Nations Partnerships Team at the University of Victoria has seen its role as developing a model for generating curricula in collaboration with communities in a way that could be used in partnerships with other communities around the globe. The ECCD programme using the GCM currently exists as 18 university-level courses that are equivalent to those offered in the mainstream university courses, but they are delivered in and by communities, where they are uniquely enriched by the cultural teachings and experiential wisdom of Elders and other community based resource people. Each course includes a structure of activities and assignments, including weekly sessions in which students meet with Elders and other carriers of the First Nations culture and experience, to discuss specific areas related to child and youth care and development.

Because it is a process that is deeply contextual, valuing variable understandings emerging from community, rather than laid on it, in no two partnerships has the programme delivery or the curriculum generated looked exactly the same. As one of the programme administrators at Meadow Lake asserted, 'Curricula that are not respectful of cultural diversity, that do not acknowledge that there are many trails that lead up the mountain, cannot expect to generate the pride and self-respect necessary to develop caring caregivers'.

Evaluation: generating ECCD curriculum, developing communities

Three formative evaluations of both the curriculum aspect of the project and the community services component of the project have been conducted to date (Cook 1993; Jette 1993; Riggan and Kemble 1994). Across all of these reviews, positive impacts of the partnership initiative upon community life as a whole have been recorded. For example, because of the high level of involvement by community members in the programme as it was being delivered right on their own doorsteps, communities have shown heightened awareness of the challenges faced by children and families and increased motivation to meet their needs. As a programme administrator at Meadow Lake observed, 'There's much more talk in the community these days about improving the environment for children. There's definitely a ripple effect. And it took a program like this to get things rolling.'

Leaders in the constituent Cree and Dene communities around Meadow Lake reported a revitalization of the roles of Elders in all aspects of community affairs as a result of their pivotal and effective roles in the ECCD training programme (Jette 1993).

> The involvement of the Elders in the Indian Child Care Program and subsequently into all community events and undertakings has led to a revitalization of cultural pride and traditional value systems. These individuals are those that hold the fabric of community life together. They have increased the awareness of the need to work together, to have self respect and respect for others. Unless there is a healthy community environment there cannot be healthy community members. Traditional values and ceremonies have a rightful place in the modern world.
>
> (Jette 1993: 58, 59)

Our explorations of the GCM of co-constructing ECCD curricula in partnership with communities support the view that when we really do grasp the full significance of responding to community needs and being sensitive to culture, we can no longer engage in the business as usual of delivering mainstream early childhood education programmes, no matter how adequately they respond to research and theory reported in mainstream literature and lecture halls about the developmental needs of children studied by Western psychologists and educators. Being responsive to communities and being sensitive to culture means more than letting community members voice their concerns or preferences; more than acknowledging diversity. It means opening up the very foundations of how training programmes are conceived, and how optimal developmental outcomes are defined, to let communities co-construct programmes of training and services that will further their own, internally identified goals. It means engaging in dialogic construction of curricula, sharing the floor in delivering courses and moving over to let communities determine the desired end products of training. It means transforming our training from a pre-packaged, didactic process to an open-ended, participatory process. As the Meadow Lake Tribal Council Programs and Policy Director, Vern Bachiu, put it, 'What we are trying to do is turn the world upside down'.

Note

1 First Nations are among Canadian aboriginal peoples, who also include Inuit, Aleut and Métis. Groups of First Nations are often organized for administrative purposes into Band or Tribal Councils representing several communities that are usually clustered together geographically. Constituent communities may or may not share the same cultural and migration history, language and customs.

References

Aboriginal Committee, Community Panel (1992) *Liberating our Children, Liberating our Nation*. British Columbia: Family and Children's Services Legislation Review.

Assembly of First Nations (1989) *Report of the National Inquiry into First Nations Child Care*. Summerstown, ON: Assembly of First Nations National Indian Brotherhood.

Benhabib, S. (1992) *Situating the Self*. Cambridge: Polity Press.

Bernhard, J. (1995) The changing field of child development: cultural diversity and the professional training of early childhood educators, *Canadian Journal of Education*, 20(4): 415–36.

Burman, E. (1994) *Deconstructing Developmental Psychology*. London: Routledge.

Cochran, M. (1988) Parental empowerment in family matters: lessons learned from a research program, in D. Powell (ed.) *Parent Education as Early Childhood Intervention: Emerging Directions in Theory, Research, and Practice*. Norwood, NJ: Ablex.

Cole, M. (1996) *Cultural Psychology: A Once and Future Discipline*. Cambridge, MA: Belknap Press/Harvard University Press.

Cook, P. (1993) Curriculum Evaluation for the MLTC/SCYC Career Ladder Project. Unpublished manuscript, School of Child and Youth Care, University of Victoria, Canada.

Dahlberg, G., Pence, M. and Moss, P. (1999) *Beyond Quality in Early Childhood Education and Care: Postmodern Perspectives on the Problem of Quality*. London: Falmer Press.

Friere, P. (1997) *Pedagogy of Hope*. New York: Continuum.

Green, M. (1993) The passions of pluralism: multiculturalism and the expanding community, *Educational Researcher*, 22(1): 13–18.

Jette, D.I. (1993) Meadow Lake Tribal Council Indian Child Care Program Evaluation. Unpublished manuscript, Meadow Lake Tribal Council, Saskatchewan.

Kessler, S. and Swadener, B. (eds) (1992) Introduction: reconceptualizing curriculum, in S. Kessler and B. Swadener (eds) *Reconceptualizing the Early Childhood Curriculum: Beginning the Dialogue*. New York: Teachers College Press.

Lubeck, S. (1996) Deconstructing child development knowledge and teacher preparation, *Early Childhood Research Quarterly*, 11(2): 147–67.

Lubeck, S. and Post, J. (in press) Distributed knowledge: seeing differences in beliefs and practices as a resource for professional development, in L.D. Soto (ed.) *Rethinking Childhood*. New York: SUNY Press.

McMillan, A.D. (1995) *Native Peoples and Cultures of Canada: An Anthropological Overview*, 2nd edn. Vancouver: Douglas and McIntyre.

Nsamenang, A.B. (1992) *Human Development in Cultural Context*. London: Sage.

Pence, A. and McCallum, M. (1994) Developing cross-cultural partnerships: implications for child care quality, research, and practice. In P. Moss and A. Pence (eds) *Valuing Quality in Early Childhood Services: New Approaches to Defining Quality*. London: Paul Chapman.

Pence, A. and Moss, P. (1994) Towards an inclusionary approach in defining quality, in P. Moss and A. Pence (eds) *Valuing Quality in Early Childhood Services: New Approaches to Defining Quality*. London: Paul Chapman.

Pence, A., Kuehne, V., Greenwood-Church, M. and Opekokew, M.R. (1993) Generative curriculum: a model of university and First Nations cooperative postsecondary education, *International Journal of Educational Development*, 13(4): 339–49.

Penn, H. (1997) Inclusivity and diversity in early childhood services in South Africa, *International Journal of Inclusive Education*, 1(1): 101–14.

Riggan, R. and Kemble, A. (1994) The Cowichan Tribes Early Childhood Education/Child and Youth Care Career Ladder Project. Unpublished report to the Centre for Curriculum and Professional Development, Victoria, BC.

Ross, R. (1997) *Dancing with a Ghost: Exploring Indian Reality*. Markham, ON: Octopus Books.

Scheff, L. and Gayle, J.E. (1995) *Constructivism in Education*, NJ: Lawrence Erlbaum.

Woodhead, M. (1996) *In Search of the Rainbow: Pathways to Quality in Large Scale Programmes for Young Disadvantaged Children*. The Hague: Bernard van Leer Foundation.

Part two
What should children learn?
Approaches to the curriculum

The first two chapters explored the values that different communities hold about the place of learning and the experiences the authors had in applying conventional Western, or minority world ideas about child development and learning in such diverse situations. If learning is, above all, local, particular and contextual, and shaped by and reflective of culture and community, what does that mean for the curriculum, the set of domains in which a child is expected to become a skilled practitioner?

Deciding what gets taught in schools and in early childhood settings is a political act, although the degree to which governments centralize control and specify detail varies considerably between countries. In some countries early years education is more or less ignored, and the curriculum begins only with statutory schooling. In the UK the early years curriculum in nursery schools and classes was relatively open (when compared, for example, with the 18 volume early years curriculum in China). It was left to informed professional opinion to decide what was appropriate, within very broad guidelines. But in the past ten years the early years curriculum has become increasingly a matter of government concern. For preschools outside the education system there is a standardized set of learning outcomes, and there is an inspection system based on these outcomes. On arriving at school, there are 'baseline assessments', involving a check-list that covers reading, letter recognition and phonological awareness, writing, speaking and listening, understanding of mathematics and what is loosely called 'personal and social development': ability to play collaboratively; concentration; ability to express opinions; and keenness to contribute to the class, and try out new things.

There is currently discussion as to whether children should be graded into ability groups – at age 4 or 5 – on the basis of these baseline assessments. There is a national curriculum for children of statutory school age, in which the content and sequences of knowledge areas are clearly set out and on which children are tested at ages 7 and 11. (There are, however, as yet, no repeat years, which is a common requirement in many countries where children fail to pass tests.) Most recently literacy and numeracy 'hours' have been introduced into schools, and teachers must precisely follow instructions of how these compulsory hours must be conducted. Teachers in the UK, as under the Communist systems of Eastern Europe and China, are becoming performers of set Government scripts, ironically at the time when those Communist systems are abandoning instruction in order to promote child-centredness (*The Economist* 1998).

Schools that do not achieve the required standards in the tests are put on a 'hit list' of failing schools and the worst of these have been 'named and shamed'. This curious procedure assumes that public humiliation is a necessary spur to improvement for schools that have poor results. The dunce's cap and the cane are no longer permitted as a punishment for individual children in schools, but schools themselves can be labelled as 'failing', which almost inevitably results in lower uptake of places, and therefore reduced income. But conversely, schools, including nursery schools, that improve or perform well are publicly congratulated and designated as 'beacon schools'. Ministers and officials deny vigorously that social class and poverty directly affect performance, or that such early pressures on children to succeed may deter many children and inadvertently teach them that they are failures.

Early childhood services in the UK are inevitably shaped by this prescriptive, competitive and more punitive approach to education. Their traditional 'child-centredness' and 'holism' and their emphasis on 'play' are under threat. The effect of various funding initiatives, as well as the competitive educational climate, mean that most 4-year-olds in England are now in school reception classes, two or three years earlier than most of their European contemporaries who will have had a much more relaxed and liberal regime before starting school aged 6 or 7.

The following two articles on the curriculum illustrate how differently the issue has been approached in other countries. In New Zealand there have been many educational policy changes at a national level, some of them adverse, yet Margaret Carr and Helen May show how they were able to develop, argue for and retain an innovative early years curriculum. Their curriculum was crucially informed by and supported by a diverse early years community. The process in which they engaged attempted to reconcile major cultural dichotomies between traditional minority worldviews of childhood and those of Maori and Pacific island communities. At the same time the authors also wanted to draw upon the most recent theory and research in the international community, and particularly sociocognitive ideas of learning. Their success in getting a radical curriculum implemented is partly because of its insistence on theoretical context, partly because of the widespread local support of diverse communities, and last, but certainly not least, because of their political adroitness.

In Spain the situation has been very different. Under the Fascist regime of Franco, education had been narrow, didactic and rigidly functional. Once Franco died, the socialists attempted to undertake a major overhaul of the system, to liberalize it at every level, and to decentralize it and make it sensitive to regional and local concerns. This was done through a ten-year process of discussion, experimentation and research at every stage from preschool to tertiary, culminating in the passing of the Education Reform Act (LOGSE) in 1989. The LOGSE, on paper at least, is one of the most comprehensive and coherent pieces of education legislation in Europe and is widely quoted in many contexts. For instance the Spanish work on the inclusion of children with disabilities has culminated in a worldwide statement, the Salamanca Agreement, which has been adopted as a guideline by international agencies such as UNESCO and UNICEF.

Marta Mata y Garriga played a key political role in launching the new educational reforms. She was a member of the first elected Spanish parliament, the chairwoman of the Education and Culture Committee in Barcelona for many years, and subsequently a member of the Spanish Senate or upper house. A teacher herself, a long-standing activist within the early years teachers' organization 'Infancia', and a staunch Catalan, she wrote and spoke in many places, inside and outside parliament, about early childhood services. She recognized the need to articulate these ideas simply and straightforwardly to diverse audiences; I have heard her give an address about young children to an Olympic stadium full of people attending a political rally for the then Prime Minister, Felipe González.

As a politician, she expounded a socialist rhetoric that stressed socialization, sociability, solidarity and equality as underpinnings for an education system. Above all she has had a transcending vision of the importance of an educational approach to very young children. She insisted that education and learning are seamless, and that it is artificial to distinguish between the needs of children under 3 and those over 3. As a result of her efforts, and those of the alliances she represented, the first stage of the education cycle is defined by LOGSE as 0–6 years. The Act contains an outline curriculum, which can be and is expected to be adapted regionally, locally and in each nursery. Teacher training is organized to reflect the curriculum, and teachers are trained specifically to cover the age group 0–6.

Marta Mata y Garriga, in explaining her work, takes a historical perspective, and traces her commitment to earlier movements in Spain agitating for change; and she describes the persistence needed to keep liberal ideas alive in the years of dictatorship. (In her spare time, she founded a library of publications, posters and other artifacts on infant education, which is open to early years workers and to scholars.)

At the same time she has been concerned with the practical implementation of her broad policy stance, and as chairwoman of the Education and Culture Committee of the Barcelona City Council she oversaw and contributed to the expansion, in quality and quantity, of provision for children under 3 in the city. This is described in more detail in the book *Comparing Nurseries* (Penn 1997).

Chapter 4 combines two short talks that she gave in London. Also included in this section is a brief extract from the LOGSE, the Spanish Education Reform Act, which formally states the objectives of the Act for children under 3; and a brief account of the implementation of the LOGSE from Irene Balaguer, who was the Director of Infant Education in Barcelona whilst Marta Mata y Garriga was the chairwoman of the Education and Culture Committee.

References

The Economist (1998) Plowden's Progress, *The Economist*, 20 June.
Penn, H. (1997) *Comparing Nurseries*. London: Paul Chapman.

3 | *Te Whāriki:* curriculum voices

Margaret Carr and Helen May

Introduction

In 1996 the Prime Minister of New Zealand launched the final version of Te Whāriki Matauranga mo ngā Mokopuna o Aotearoa: Early Childhood Curriculum (Ministry of Education 1996a). From August 1998, early childhood services receiving funding from the Ministry are required to demonstrate that their programmes are operating according to the four principles, five strands and eighteen goals outlined in *Te Whāriki* (Ministry of Education 1996b).[1]

The writing of the curriculum began in 1991 when we were contracted by the Ministry of Education to coordinate the development of a national early childhood curriculum that would: make connections with the new national curriculum for schools; embrace a diverse range of early childhood services and cultural perspectives; and articulate a philosophy of quality early childhood practice. The story of the development of *Te Whāriki* illustrates debate and negotiation between three voices: the voice of government interests at a time of political and curriculum change (a voice that by 1991 had become focused on the role of national curriculum and assessment policies in creating an efficient and competitive economy); the voice of early childhood practitioners and families from a diversity of services and cultural perspectives (a voice that took a local, situated and often *personal* view of early childhood curriculum – and sometimes rejected the term 'curriculum'); the national and international early childhood voices advocating for equitable educational opportunities and quality early childhood policies and practices (voices that have taken an increasingly sociocultural view of curriculum and childhood, but frequently rejected a totally relativist view of curriculum).

The political voices

The late 1980s and early 1990s, the period when the early childhood curriculum was being proposed and written, were a time of political change
in New Zealand. In 1990 the Labour Government was replaced by a
conservative National government. The Labour Government had in
1987 instituted widespread curriculum interest and debate in relation
to schools with a public discussion document, *The Curriculum Review*
(Department of Education 1987). *The Curriculum Review* emphasized aims
for individual growth and development, with 'learning to learn' seen as
'an essential outcome' (Department of Education 1987: 10). It received
over 20,000 submissions from individuals and groups (McGee 1997: 53),
and the follow-on discussion document, the *National Curriculum Statement*
(Department of Education 1988), retained a view of curriculum as more
than traditional school subjects, and emphasized the continuity of education from age 5 through secondary schooling.

In the second half of the Labour Government's term, the *National Curriculum Statement* framework and philosophy were put to one side as
administrative reforms (Lange 1988a) to create 'self-managing' schools
were introduced: '(T)he rhetoric of the late 1980s was focused upon devo-
lution, democratisation of schooling and parental empowerment and it
came from both educators and the business sector . . . but the latter had a
different ideology, as the 1990s would show' (McGee 1997: 61).

School trustees, elected from the community, were given new administrative responsibilities, although these responsibilities did not include curriculum. Early childhood was not part of *Tomorrow's Schools* or the *National
Curriculum Statement*, but the philosophy of the statement was compatible
with an influential early childhood document that was commissioned at
the same time as part of the Labour Government's planned social policy
reform: *Education to be More* (Department of Education Early Childhood
Care and Education Working Group 1988), also called the Meade Report.
Education to be More argued for an enhanced role for government in early
childhood and the benefits for the nation of quality early childhood
experience, and called for an institutional structure that would protect
quality and give a voice to parents. It did not include curriculum suggestions, although an 'illustrative charter' (Department of Education Early
Childhood Care and Education Working Group 1988: 52) included a set of
15 curriculum principles that had been developed at a government sponsored working group in February 1988 attended by representatives from
the Department of Education, early childhood services and Colleges of
Education.[2]

By 1991 the new Conservative Government had abandoned the
National Curriculum Statement and introduced a discussion document: *The
National Curriculum of New Zealand* (Ministry of Education 1991). It
emphasized the need to 'define a range of understandings, skills and
knowledge that will enable students to take their full place in society and

to succeed in the modern competitive economy' (1991: 1). It set out seven principles, three of which were explicitly to do with education needed for work, or for the needs of the economy. After scant public consultation (McGee 1997: 61), the final 1993 *New Zealand Curriculum Framework* (Ministry of Education 1993a) emerged very little changed from the 1991 document. It defined nine principles, three of which mention the economy or preparation for the 'world of work', seven traditionally subject-based learning areas (health and physical well-being, the arts, social sciences, technology, science, mathematics, language and languages) and eight groupings of essential skills (one grouping is described as 'self-management and competitive' skills, although the list of sub-skills for this grouping does not mention the word 'competitive'). This curriculum covered both primary and secondary schooling, and included policy proposals for national assessment at key transition points: school entry (age 5); at the start of year 7; and at the start of year 9 (the first year of secondary school). Finally, the new curriculum framework included the principle 'the New Zealand Curriculum recognises the significance of the Treaty of Waitangi' (Ministry of Education 1993a: 7): a landmark treaty that in 1840 set out rights and responsibilities for the relationship between Māori (the indigenous people of New Zealand) and the British Crown. In response to the perceived responsibility to Māori curriculum, Māori versions of the subject based curriculum statements were subsequently developed: these came after the English text was developed and tended to be translations rather than cultural alternatives (McKinley and Waiti 1995). It was against this backdrop that in 1990 the government decided there would also be a national early childhood curriculum.

Governments had not previously been concerned with curriculum in the early childhood sector. Each of the different early childhood services had their own approaches to curriculum, although the term curriculum itself was rarely used (Carr and May 1993a). In 1989 policy reforms that followed from *Education to be More*, known as the *Before Five* policy (Lange 1998b), established a common formula for funding, administration and regulations across all early childhood services. With government funding now reaching an average of 50 per cent of operating costs of early childhood centres, alongside an emerging espoused policy of 'seamless' education from birth to tertiary (Ministry of Education 1994), there was sufficient rationale for government to justify an interest in the early curriculum itself. In 1990 the Ministry announced that a national early childhood curriculum would be developed.

The local and national early childhood voices: the writing of *Te Whāriki*

Early childhood organizations and practitioners, including ourselves (with backgrounds including experience as kindergarten and childcare practitioners), were originally wary of the idea of a national early child-hood curriculum; we were concerned that it might constrain the sector's independence and diversity. But the alternative strategy of *not* defining the early childhood curriculum, was now becoming a potentially danger-ous one for the early childhood organizations, since the developing national curriculum for schools might start a 'trickle down' effect, par-ticularly as the government was also proposing more systematic national assessment during the early school years. Our curriculum project at the University of Waikato won the early childhood curriculum contract with the Ministry of Education; the project began in 1991 and a draft curricu-lum was delivered to the Ministry at the end of 1992 (Carr and May 1992).

By 1991 and 1992 the national government curriculum themes so far had included: curriculum decisions at the national level; educational con-tinuity leading to a competitive and efficient workplace (education as a branch of economic policy); an interest in national assessment and levels of achievement; a subject based school curriculum, and curriculum docu-ments that would be later translated for Māori. We wondered, given this context, what an early childhood curriculum might look like. A brief sum-mary outlines the main features of what eventuated; the detail is in Min-istry of Education (1993a, 1996a) and earlier overviews of the philosophy and early implementation are in Carr and May (1993b, 1994, 1996, 1997).

Firstly, a set of four principles underpins the aims and goals for children. These principles are as follows, with the English text elaborated:

Whakamana   *Empowerment*: the early childhood curriculum empowers the child to learn and grow;
Kotahitanga   *Holistic development*: the early childhood curriculum reflects the holistic way children learn and grow;
Whānau tangata   *Family and community*: the wider world of family and community is an integral part of the early childhood curriculum;
Ngā hononga   *Relationships*: children learn through responsive and reciprocal relationships with people places and things.

The principles and aims of the curriculum are expressed in both Māori and English languages, but neither is an exact translation of the other. They were negotiated early in the curriculum development process as equival-ent. Secondly, a set of five aims (later to be renamed 'strands', to fit in with the language of the school curriculum documents) provided the frame-work for goals (and later, learning outcomes) for children:

Mana atua	Well-being
Mana whenua	Belonging
Mana tangata	Contribution
Mana reo	Communication
Mana aotūroa	Exploration

Once again, neither is a translation of the other: an acceptable cross-cultural structure and the equivalence were discussed, debated and transacted early

Guiding principles

Whakamana The early childhood curriculum will empower the child to learn and grow	Kotahitanga The early childhood curriculum will reflect the holistic way children learn and grow	Whanāu Tangata The wider world of family, Whanāu and community is an integral part of the early childhood curriculum	Ngā Hononga Young children learn through responsive and reciprocal relationships with people, places and things

Aims for children

Mana Atua	Well-being
Mana Whenua	Belonging
Mana Tangata	Contribution
Mana Reo	Communication
Mana Aoturoa	Exploration

Goals for learning and development

Well-being	Belonging	Contribution	Communication	Exploration
The health and well-being of the child is protected and nurtured	Children and families feel they belong here	Opportunities for learning are equitable and each child's contribution is valued	The languages and symbols of children's cultures are promoted and protected	The child learns through active exploration of the environment
Their health is promoted	Connecting links with the family and the wider world are affirmed and extended	There are equitable opportunities for learning irrespective of gender, disability, age, ethnicity or background	They develop non-verbal communication skills for a range of purposes	Play is valued as meaningful learning and spontaneous play is important
Their emotional well-being is nurtured	They know that they have a place here	They are affirmed as individuals	They develop verbal communication skills for a range of purposes	Confident in and control of one's body is developed
They are protected and safe from harm here	They feel comfortable with the routines, rituals and regular events	Opportunities to learn with and alongside others are encouraged	They experience the cultures' stories and symbols	They learn strategies for active exploration
	They know the limits and boundaries of acceptable behaviour		They discover different ways to be creative and expressive	They develop working theories for making sense of their living physical and material world

Figure 3.1 Te Whāriki; national early childhood curriculum guidelines in New Zealand

in the curriculum development process. The conceptualization of early childhood curriculum therefore took a very different approach to either the subject based framework of the school curriculum, or the more traditional developmental curriculum map of physical, intellectual, emotional and social skills. Instead, the strands defined an interpretation of the major interests of infants, toddlers and young children: emotional and physical *well-being;* a feeling that they *belong* here; opportunities to make a *contribution;* skills and understandings for *communicating* through language and symbols; and an interest in *exploring* and making sense of their environment. In the original version (Carr and May 1992; Ministry of Education 1993a) each aim (strand) was elaborated into goals for learning and development, which were further expanded to illustrate what they might mean in practice in a variety of contexts, such as: Māori immersion programmes; including children with special needs; home based programmes; Tagata Pasefika (Pacific Island) programmes. The 1992 document also included the implications of the framework for adults and management. In a final document, edited by the Ministry (Ministry of Education 1996b), this contextual elaboration was considerably reduced: government favoured a more universalist approach.

In other words, in conceptualizing the early childhood curriculum in this way, the Early Childhood Development Team motored upstream to resist the philosophical principles of the early 1990s. In our opinion, a major reason for this was the capacity by 1991 for local and national early childhood interests to speak strongly and loudly, and, when necessary, with one voice. The articulation of this voice in the new curriculum domain was certainly facilitated by setting up a Curriculum Development Team with a broad representative base, and insisting on wide consultation throughout the process. But history was on our side. During the 1980s, as well as the *Education to be More* document and the *Before Five* reforms, some very significant events happened in early childhood in New Zealand.

- In 1982 the first Māori immersion early childhood centre, Te Kōhanga Reo (Māori language immersion early childhood programmes, literally translated as the language nest), was established. The Kōhanga Reo movement, transmitting, revitalizing and protecting Māori language and culture, grew rapidly during the 1980s (Royal Tangaere 1996). By 1998, there were 704 Kōhanga in New Zealand (Ministry of Education 1998). In 1995, 46 per cent of all Māori children enrolled in early childhood services were attending Ngā Kōhanga Reo and 18.7 per cent of all children enrolled in early childhood programmes in 1995 were Māori (Early Childhood Education Project 1996: 11).
- In 1986 the administrative responsibility for the licensing and support of a broad range of early childhood services, somewhat arbitrarily labelled 'childcare', moved from the Department of Social Welfare to the Department of Education, to join with kindergartens (sessional programmes for 3 – and 4-year-olds) and play centres (parent cooperatives).

- In 1988 the colleges of education began teaching a national three-year integrated (childcare and kindergarten) Diploma of Teaching (early childhood), parallel and equivalent to primary teacher education.
- In 1990 the two major early childhood unions, the Early Childhood Workers Union and the Kindergarten Teachers Association, amalgamated to form a more powerful combined union, the Combined Early Childhood Union of Aotearoa.

New Zealand is a small country of 3.7 million people. The early childhood network, although fiercely parochial in some matters, could speak together when they saw a united purpose and the structures gave them the platform and the power to do so. Each of the above events created debate and challenge to the status quo, but resulted in some collective 're-weaving' of the fabric of the institutions supporting early childhood provision.

By 1991, the curriculum development process could build on this increasing integration and strength. In particular, before any curriculum framework was decided upon, four decisions were made. The first was to establish a broadly based Curriculum Development Team with links into the diverse early childhood networks. Six specialist working groups of four practitioners with a coordinator were established: infant and toddler; young child; te Kōhanga reo; tagata pasefika (representing Pacific Island language groups); home based services; and children with special needs. Each group consulted with their own networks, and argued their case in the smaller Curriculum Development Team of coordinators. The second was to write a series of 'position papers' and use these as a focus for consulting widely with the early childhood community. During the fourteen months of curriculum development the authors travelled to seminars of practitioners throughout the country. The third decision was to negotiate a bicultural framework from the beginning. The fourth decision was to use a weaving metaphor to define the curriculum: Te Whāriki refers to a traditional floor mat woven from harakeke (flax).

The weaving metaphor

The title of the curriculum, Te Whāriki, is a central metaphor. Firstly, the early childhood curriculum is envisaged as a Whāriki, a woven mat 'for all to stand on' (Carr and May 1992: 6). The principles, strands and goals defined in the document provide the framework that allows for different programme perspectives to be woven into the 'fabric'. There are many possible 'patterns' for this, as individuals and centres develop their own curriculum pattern through a process of talk, reflection, planning, evaluation and assessment (Carr and May 1994). Secondly, the metaphor describes a 'spider web' model of curriculum for children, in contrast to a 'step' model (Eisner 1985: 143). The 'step' model conjures up the image of a series of independent steps that lead to a platform from which the child exits and at which point measurable outcomes can be identified. The Te

Whāriki model views the curriculum for each child as more like a spider web or weaving than a series of steps, and emphasizes the notion that developing knowledge and understanding for young children is like a tapestry of increasing complexity and richness. This is in tune with the idea that:

> The developmental potential of a setting is enhanced to the extent that the physical and social environment found in the setting enables and motivates the developing person to engage in progressively more complex molar activities, patterns of reciprocal interaction, and primary dyadic relationships with others in that setting.
> (Bronfenbrenner 1979: 163)

Te Whāriki defines three age groups – infants, toddlers and the young child – but, consistent with the idea of the curriculum for each child as being more like a tapestry than a flight of stairs, these age groups were not defined as self-contained stages. The document included a 'developmental continuum' of learning and growing during the early childhood years, linked to age but recognizing that development will vary for individual children in unpredictable ways. In tune with the principle that children learn through responsive and reciprocal relationships with people, places and things, where they are, who they are with, and what the children perceive as the agenda, will all make a difference. Te Whāriki emphasizes that curriculum for the early childhood years must be able to embrace the everyday realities of rapid change, leaps and regressions, uneven development and individual differences, and recognize that learning is distributed across people places and things (Salomon 1993).

The national and international voices on learning, curriculum, and quality early childhood

It is interesting to look back at the development of Te Whāriki from the vantage point of the late 1990s. By the 1990s the national and international education and early childhood education literature was more loudly acknowledging diverse rather than universal viewpoints and taking an increasingly sociocultural and poststructural view of learning, childhood and curriculum (Metge 1990; Rogoff 1990; Lave and Wenger 1991; Kessler and Swadener 1992; Burman 1994; Tobin 1995; Bruner 1996; Morss 1996; Smith 1996; Woodhead 1996, 1998). Writers like Noddings (1994, 1995) had been arguing for some time for an ethic of 'care' in education; a theme taken up more recently in mathematics and science education (Taylor 1998). The ideas in Te Whāriki came primarily from local and cultural voices: they were, however, substantially in tune with these national and international voices on learning, childhood and curriculum.

The authors of the 1992 document wrote from the local and cultural voices, but added ten pages of annotated footnotes and references from the national and international literature to provide the documented and researched trail that supported these voices, and elaborated on ideas for practitioners. These pages included reference to Bronfenbrenner (1979), Bruner (1990), Metge (1990), Penn (1991), Royal Tangaere (1991), Pere (1991). They also however included reference to Erikson (1950) and Honig and Lally (1981), taking a traditional developmental view of infants' needs for trustworthy environments and relationships in early childhood programmes. They also ensured that the currently available research on quality was evident in the document (Howes 1987, 1991; Whitebook *et al.* 1989). For example, the sections on the management and organization of the environment drew strongly on research on structural indicators of quality (deemed at the time to be universal): staff ratios, group size, training and parent involvement and staff stability.

The principle of a 'holistic' curriculum, a mantra in everyday early childhood language, has now been supported by arguments in the education literature for: portfolio and diverse approaches to assessment (McGinn and Roth 1998); integration of the emotional, social and cognitive in joint attention episodes (Moore and Dunham 1991; Ratner and Stettner 1991; Smith in press); narrative frameworks for education (Bruner 1990, 1996) and assessment (Carr 1998a); and dispositions as outcomes (Resnick 1987; Katz 1993; Carr 1998b). The weaving metaphor, together with the cross-cultural structure, tried to set up a curriculum that was not dominated by one worldview of the child and childhood, a point more recently made cogent in his discussions of the culturally specific nature of 'quality' early childhood by Martin Woodhead (1996, 1998).

This is not, however, a 'universal curriculum, will travel' document. It belongs in bicultural Aotearoa–New Zealand, and it has attempted to set down the values of that community about children, learning and early childhood. These values include the special needs and characteristics of infants and toddlers, and arguments for primary caregiving: 'an adult who is consistently responsible for, and available to, each infant' in the final document (Ministry of Education 1996a: 22). They include an emphasis on the value and importance of spontaneous play (one of the eighteen goals – the consultation included heated discussions about whether play is children's work and therefore should be called 'work') and a goal about children knowing 'the limits and boundaries of acceptable behaviour' in an early childhood setting. They also include an emphasis on 'belonging', and a goal on equity, which makes reference to the United Nations Convention on the Rights of the Child and includes as outcomes for children: an understanding of their own rights and those of others; the ability to recognize discriminatory practices and behaviour and to respond appropriately; some early values of appreciating diversity and fairness; and the self-confidence to stand up for themselves and others against biased ideas and discriminatory behaviour. The framework is a celebration of this country's biculturalism (Reedy 1993, 1995).

Survival

Te Whāriki has so far depended on all three communities for survival and support: the local early childhood community; the international early childhood community; and the will and priorities of decision makers in government. It will continue to do so.

The voice of the local early childhood community

The early childhood community was relieved and somewhat surprised that the integral philosophy and framework of Te Whāriki survived the long complex political process from draft to final document. A collaborative and consultative process was a key to gaining unified support for the document from all organizations and constituent groups. A 1993 document (Ministry of Education 1993b), an edited version of the 1992 document, was sent out for consultation to all early childhood centres. The Ministry commissioned a survey of early childhood practitioners from centres (Murrow 1995) as well as inviting responses from anyone who had read Te Whāriki. The response from the profession was overwhelmingly positive. The summary report from the centre survey concluded that. 'Support for *Te Whāriki* as a whole was . . . very high, with the vast majority of the respondents supporting the document in principle or without reservation . . . Comments made were often highly supportive of the document' (Murrow 1995: 28).

Some of the acclaim might have been a sense of relief that Te Whāriki was no 'takeover' by the school national curriculum; that it respected the existing diversity; that it affirmed some strongly held beliefs about early childhood practice; that it was very much a New Zealand statement and not another import from abroad. On the other hand it soon became apparent that the document was complex, partly because it resisted telling practitioners what to do: it asked each programme to 'weave' its own curriculum pattern. As Nuttall and Mulheron wrote:

> With the introduction of Te Whāriki many early childhood practitioners are going to be thrown headlong into a major learning curve. Although the principles of Belonging, Communication, Exploration, Well-being and Contribution have long been accepted in early childhood, the way they have been defined and, if you like, packaged will be new. It is a challenge for centres now to try them out . . . Te Whāriki resists the temptation to provide specific 'recipes' for centres.
>
> (Nuttall and Mulheron 1993: 1)

The Murrow (1995) report added, 'Reservations expressed by respondents tended to focus on physical aspects such as wording, presentation and binding, however, some respondents were concerned with philosophical or practical difficulties of implementation' (Murrow 1995: 28).

Two research trials were also commissioned (Dunedin College of

Education 1994; Haggerty and Hubbard 1994). These trials confirmed a high degree of support but revealed some disquiet at centre level regarding the process of implementing something new and conceptually different. Lack of time and resources was already a pressure on staff and a new curriculum requiring considerable debate was an added burden. These trials made it clear that for Te Whāriki to really make a difference for children there would need to be a considerable level of ongoing professional development in a sector that still had large numbers of untrained or poorly trained staff. Similarly, it was apparent that government funding levels affecting such issues as staff turnover, ratios, group size and qualifications were a significant factor in implementing Te Whāriki. Since 1994 the Ministry of Education has awarded contracts for professional development to a range of organizations to mount programmes to support the new curriculum (Nally 1995); within the short timeframe of these contracts much innovative work has been done, especially in those programmes that have provided professional development and support to a centre over a sustained period (Gould 1998). But not all centres receive professional development.

The unified support from the early childhood profession overcame initial political resistance because Te Whāriki didn't 'look like' a curriculum. The Minister of Education would not allow the 1993 draft of Te Whāriki to be called a 'curriculum' (it was called 'draft guidelines for developmentally appropriate programmes') because it looked so different to the national school curriculum documents. The final version of *Te Whāriki* however, is called a 'curriculum', and the definition of 'curriculum' in the 1992 version is retained: 'The term "curriculum" is used in this document to describe the sum total of the experiences, activities, and events, whether direct or indirect, which occur within an environment designed to foster children's learning and development' (Ministry of Education 1996: 10).

A number of the major training institutions that teach New Zealand qualifications in early childhood have begun to use Te Whāriki as a framework and a resource. At the University of Waikato the early childhood curriculum courses have for some years been matched up with the five strands, and there is also a progression of courses that build upon each other in the professional strand of the degree:

- Learning through *exploration* and play
- Growth and *well-being*
- Language and *communication*
- *Belonging* and *contribution*
- Making sense of the world

In 1995 an equivalent Māori immersion programme began at the University of Waikato, the *Ki Taiao* three-year degree, establishing in the early childhood teacher education programme at the university a parallel to the bicultural and bilingual framework in *Te Whāriki* (Ritchie and Walker

1995). In both programmes, students combine study with time spent working with children in centres; coming to understand child development knowledge and research in its historical and cultural context and to assess its relevance to the respective curriculum strands; learning to plan programmes using the principles, strands, goals and outcomes of the curriculum; and coming to understand the links between practice and theory, curriculum and research. In 1998 a new joint degree at Victoria University of Wellington and the Wellington College of Education began. Like Waikato, the curriculum papers are also structured around the framework of *Te Whāriki*. The national integration of curriculum and qualifications has begun. We hope that this will benefit children in early childhood programmes, embed the curriculum into teacher education and ensure the local critique and debate that will keep the curriculum alive.

Not all voices, however, support initiatives that will increase the level and status of early childhood qualifications, often because of the cost implications, but also because historic attitudes to early childhood teachers take time to change. In 1998, government started the development of two policy initiatives that are causing both disquiet and support among early childhood groups: to increase the qualification levels required for regulatory purposes (Meade *et al.* 1998); and to introduce another tier of funding for centres meeting some (yet to be defined) process criteria of high quality (Meade and Kerslake-Hendricks 1998). From our perspective, both are important for strengthening the government commitment to implementing Te Whāriki. Some voices of dissent against these initiatives are already being heard from within the early childhood community, whose collective voice, so important for the early support of Te Whāriki, has only ever been occasional. There is already a campaign underway from mainly privately owned childcare centres who view the costs of any changes to minimum regulations as a reduction of profit (Sobstad 1998): this is the new, market driven, voice of the late 1990s.

The international early childhood community

There has been considerable international interest, particularly in Europe and especially in Great Britain, in the philosophy and structure of *Te Whāriki*. Cathy Nutbrown (1996) highlights the emphasis in Te Whāriki on children's rights as a source of curriculum, the respect for children as learners and the importance of emotional and social development in contributing to intellectual growth. The Early Childhood Forum in the United Kingdom acknowledged the model of *Te Whāriki* when they developed their own curriculum framework, which they called 'foundations for early learning' (Early Childhood Forum 1998). Tina Bruce has urged her British colleagues to speak out and clarify for the politicians, 'what we want for our children in early childhood. This has been done in New Zealand . . . the radicals have been allowed to speak' (Bruce 1996: 11). In Denmark *Te*

Whāriki has been translated, and a book written on New Zealand's approaches to school and early childhood curricula (Olsen 1996). Frode Sobstad, who held a parallel position to the authors in the development of the Norwegian curriculum framework (Ministry of Children and Family Affairs 1996), has written that:

> The most interesting aspect of the New Zealand curriculum is that the name of the curriculum and the profile is taken from the minority culture, the Maori people. We have not given the Sami culture a chance to influence our national program for day care institutions in Norway. Instead they have been given their own chapter. But is this enough?
>
> (Sobstad 1997: 11)

The government takes notice of this international interest, and it has been of importance for the editorial process: from the 1992 document to the 1993 draft document, which was sent to all centres and, finally, to the 1996 version.

The political community

The survival of Te Whāriki is not due only to the vigilance and support of local and external pressures. There has been governmental support as well, notably with funding for professional development; but the impact of other political policies and swings has impacted on both the shape and implementation of Te Whāriki.

Universalist assumptions by government

The 1992 and 1993 Te Whāriki included extensive footnotes and bibliography. During its development and testing phase we wanted to show that the ideas and suggestions had a research base that provided sound arguments to support Te Whāriki through the political process. We also wanted to provide practitioners with a rationale for the curriculum principles and goals, and the trail of evidence – local, national, and international – for the values and detailed learning outcomes. The references also provided further reading for practitioners who wanted elaboration of a document that had to be, by its very nature, somewhat peremptory, brief and authoritarian. These footnotes and references were deleted from the final 1996 curriculum, setting up an assumption that it is one authority; universal and timeless. We regret the loss. A further example of the universalist assumptions of the government is that in an attempt to integrate difference the emphasis in the draft documents on specialist curriculum contexts such as home based curriculum, Pacific Island contexts and children with special needs disappeared. Maggie Haggerty has argued that the Ministry of Education's final version of Te Whāriki is more prescriptive and wonders how well the 'multiple curricula' approach articulated in the earlier drafts will fare in the longer term (Haggerty 1998: 34).

Transition to school

Although the curriculum is a radical departure from describing an entry level of achievement for children as they approach Level 1 of the school curriculum, the document makes clear links with the New Zealand school curriculum. By 1992, the mathematics and science school documents had been completed, and the authors made the connections with those; in the 1996 final version of Te Whāriki, links were made between the five early childhood strands and both the 'essential skills' and the 'essential learning areas' in the school curriculum framework. The government has a vision for a seamless education system from early childhood through to tertiary level (Ministry of Education 1994), and this rhetoric suggests that the early childhood curriculum development is seen as an important part of this process. Words in *Te Whāriki* outline the connections between early childhood and school, but in reality there is a mismatch and disruption for children at age 5 as they move from early childhood programmes into the early school years. Play based programmes in new entrant classes appear to be an historic relic from the past as teachers seem less able to articulate the value of play, or see play as a fill-in between the subject based areas of the new curriculum. While these new learning areas of the school curriculum can be taught holistically and through play, many teachers are finding the complexities and requirements of measuring objectives and assessment for each child for each learning area a reason for a more timetabled and subject-driven approach. It is a dilemma for teachers in school, and the demands of the more content based school curriculum may override (and run counter to) the demands of a curriculum like *Te Whāriki* that focuses on well-being, belonging, contribution, communication and exploration. Both are necessary.

Assessment and evaluation

We take the view that this curriculum could be destroyed by poorly considered assessment, and agree with Bredekamp and Rosegrant when they say, 'Assessment is the tail that wags the curriculum dog. If we want to see real curriculum reform, we must simultaneously achieve reform of assessment practices' (Bredekamp and Rosegrant 1992: 29).

In the final version of Te Whāriki the 1992 and 1993 'knowledge skills and attitudes' were retitled 'learning outcomes', but remained much the same. (The Ministry did add 'positive and constructive attitudes to competition' to a goal that reads 'they are encouraged to learn with and alongside others'!) But in spite of the current political climate of national assessment and accountability, the government has not so far pursued early plans for subject based national assessment at school entry. However, the climate makes more demands than previously on early childhood practitioners in relation to curriculum, assessment and evaluation (Ministry of Education 1996b). Much of this is a new language for early childhood practitioners, some of whom are volunteers, and/or are poorly paid and/or have low levels of training; many of them have got to grips with the notion of 'curriculum', but find 'assessment' another hurdle. There is so far little extra resourcing to support centres to manage the extra work that implementing assessing and evaluating a new curriculum involves. Early childhood charter guidelines, the mandatory document for early childhood services, state that 'educators should implement curriculum and assessment practices which (a) reflect the holistic way that children learn, (b) reflect the reciprocal relationships between the child, people and the learning environment, (c) involve parents/guardians and, where appropriate, *whanau*, and (d) enhance children's sense of themselves as capable people and competent learners' (Ministry of Education 1996a). Given a curriculum model that sees learning as the development of more complex and useful understanding, knowledge and skill attached to cultural and purposeful contexts rather than as a staircase of individually acquired skills, the assessment and evaluation of children and programmes becomes a complex matter. The research literature on assessment in early childhood is enormous, much of it spearheaded by researchers in the UK (such as Blenkin and Kelly 1992; Drummond 1993; Pascal and Bertram 1998), and researchers search for alternative ways to assess learning in early childhood that draw on both early childhood curriculum imperatives and the research literature in the wider education arena (for example, Crooks 1993; Black 1994; McGinn and Roth 1998). Following on from the development of Te Whāriki, we have initiated research projects on assessment and evaluation, funded by the Ministry of Education (Carr 1998a, 1998c; May and Podmore 1998; Podmore and May 1998). These projects have attempted to respond to a new conception of curriculum with a matching approach to assessment and evaluation: 'learning and teaching stories' that see learning as distributed across people places and things, and take a narrative rather than a skills approach to assessment and evaluation.

Resources for early childhood
Curriculum developments such as Te Whāriki sit in a wider political and educational context for achieving quality experiences for children. Issues such as funding, regulations, accountability and training policies are also part of the fabric. Te Whāriki was developed on the assumption that early childhood centres would have the funding and the trained staff to operate quality programmes. Cullen (1996) highlights the tensions between the developmental and sociocultural perspectives inherent in *Te Whāriki* and expresses concern that much of the current professional development and training is being conducted by educators unfamiliar with the theoretical underpinnings of the latter. To Cullen the issue of training is a crucial one:

When providers of pre-service training and professional development contracts themselves have a restricted knowledge base it is unlikely that the theoretical richness of Te Whāriki will be conveyed effectively

. . . For the busy practitioner, implementation of *Te Whāriki* is likely to be constrained by a superficial understanding of its rationale and implications for practice.

(Cullen 1996: 118)

Underlying Cullen's concern is the difficulty in achieving a balance between rigour and accountability for children's learning and the realities of an under resourced and ill trained sector, which has historically been more *laissez-faire* in its approach. Cullen is uncertain whether what she perceives as perhaps the 'soft' approach of Te Whāriki can deliver on the former (quality provision), given the realities of the latter (resources and training).

It will not be possible for the strands and goals to work for children in a satisfactory way under current levels of funding and minimal regulatory and accountability requirements. The early trials of *Te Whāriki* highlighted this issue. The original Early Childhood Charter developed with the Before Five policy required centres receiving government funding to demonstrate how they were moving towards defined quality measures (Smith and Farquhar 1994). These measures have since disappeared. Since the National Government took office in 1990 there has been a gradual erosion of the Before Five 1989 education reform policies (May 1992; Dalli 1993). Most devastating was the halting after one year of a four-year staged funding plan, which left most centres unable to balance the equation of low fees, reasonable wages and quality for children. The 1995 budget, however, introduced a new tier of funding for early childhood programmes, again using quality criteria as the basis (Ministry of Education 1995). We have already commented on new government policy initiatives to increase the qualification levels required for regulatory purposes and to introduce new criteria of high quality, initiatives that have so far found little favour in the private sector and may yet be abandoned by government as too controversial, too difficult and too expensive.

In summary, making a difference for children through curriculum will depend to a large extent on the commitment and energy of staff and management in centres and programmes, but unless the structural fabric is in place (adequate funding levels, quality staffing and training requirements) Te Whāriki will remain a document only. That structural fabric is the responsibility of the government; not of staff and management in centres. Without it, the new curriculum will not make the difference for children that was intended. The majority of centres are now using Te Whāriki, albeit with some variety of interest interpretation and insight. But the feedback available suggests that to implement Te Whāriki fully requires a larger and bolder investment by government to support the infrastructure of early childhood than is currently available. Small increases in funding have not been sufficient to offset the costs of new quality criteria, and of concern are the number of centres that are not prepared to begin to climb the ladder of quality. Developing and mandating a national statement that protects and values well-being, belonging, communication, contribution and exploration in early childhood settings is only a beginning.

Notes

1 Te Whāriki is pronounced 'te (as in ten) fa (as in far) re (as in reap) key', with an emphasis on the '*fa*'.
2 'The charter will state the service's curriculum objectives and methods. Until national objectives are finalised, boards should work to the objectives formulated by the members of the February 1988 Lopdell course: "The curriculum will enable all children to experience an environment in which: 1 – They learn who they are. 2 – They are safe. 3 – They are healthy. 4 – They relate positively to others. 5 – They enjoy themselves. 6 – They learn in appropriate ways. 7 – They respect the natural environment. 8 – There are goals for children. 9 – Learning is not limited by gender. 10 – Learning is not limited by race or colour. 11 – Decision making is shared. 12 – Conflict is resolved peacefully. 13 – The importance of home and family is recognised. 14 – Adults are learners. 15 – People are accountable" ' (Department of Education Early Childhood Care and Education Working Group 1988: 52).

References

Black, P. (1994) Can teachers use assessment to improve learning?, *British Journal of Curriculum and Assessment*, 6(2): 7–11.

Blenkin, G.M. and Kelly, A.V. (eds) (1992) *Assessment in Early Childhood Education*. London: Paul Chapman.

Bredekamp, S. and Rosegrant, T. (1992) Reaching potentials through appropriate curriculum: conceptual frameworks for applying the guidelines, in S. Bredekamp and T. Rosegrant (eds), *Reaching Potentials: Appropriate Curriculum and Assessment for Young Children*, vol. 1. Washington DC: National Association for the Education of Young Children.

Bronfenbrenner, U. (1979) *The Ecology of Human Development*. Cambridge, MA: Harvard University Press.

Bruce, T. (1996) Weaving links between New Zealand and the United Kingdom. Paper presented at the seminar, Beyond Desirable Objectives, Pen Green Research, Development and Training Base, November.

Bruner, J. (1990) *Acts of Meaning*. Cambridge, MA: Harvard University Press.

Bruner, J. (1996) *The Culture of Education*. Cambridge, MA: Harvard University Press.

Burman, E. (1994) *Deconstructing Developmental Psychology*. London: Routledge.

Carr, M. (1998a) *Assessing Children's Experiences*. Final report to the Ministry of Education. Hamilton, University of Waikato.

Carr, M. (1998b) Taking dispositions to school, *Children's Issues*, 2(1): 21–4.

Carr, M. (1998c) A project for assessing children's experiences in early childhood settings. Paper presented at the eighth European Conference on Quality in Early Childhood Research, Santiago de Compostela, Spain, September.

Carr, M. and May, H. (1992) *Te Whāriki*. Early Childhood Curriculum Development

Project Final Report to the Ministry of Education. Hamilton: University of Waikato.

Carr, M. and May, H. (1993a) The role of government in early childhood curriculum, in New Zealand Council for Educational Research invitational seminar, *What is Government Role in Early Childhood Education?* Wellington: New Zealand Council for Educational Research.

Carr, M. and May, H. (1993b) Choosing a model: reflecting on the development process of *Te Whāriki*, National Early Childhood Curriculum Guidelines in New Zealand, *International Journal of Early Years Education*, 1(3): 7–22.

Carr, M. and May, H.(1994) Weaving patterns: developing national early childhood curriculum guidelines in Aotearoa–New Zealand, *Australian Journal of Early Childhood Education*, 19(1): 25–33.

Carr, M. and May, H. (1996) Te Whāriki, making a difference for the under fives? The new national early childhood curriculum, *Delta*, 48(1): 101–12.

Carr, M. and May, H. (1997) Making a difference for the under-fives? The early implementation of Te Whāriki, the New Zealand national early childhood curriculum, *International Journal of Early Years Education*, 5(3): 225–36.

Crooks, T. (1993) Principles to Guide Assessment Practice. Keynote address to the Assessment and Learning in New Zealand: Challenges and Choices Conference at Palmerston North College of Education, September 5–8.

Cullen, J. (1996) The challenge of Te Whāriki for future development in early childhood education, *Delta*, 48(1): 113–25.

Dalli, C. (1993) Is Cinderella back among the cinders? A review of early childhood education in the early 1990s, in K. Sullivan (ed.) *New Zealand Annual Review of Education*, vol. 3. Wellington: Victoria University Press.

Department of Education (1987) *The Curriculum Review*. Wellington: Government Printer.

Department of Education (1988) *National Curriculum Statement: A Discussion Document for Primary and Secondary Schools*. Wellington: Government Printer.

Department of Education Early Childhood Care and Education Working Group (1988) *Education to be More* (the Meade Report). Wellington: Government Printer.

Drummond, M.J. (1993) *Assessing Children's Learning*. London: David Fulton.

Dunedin College of Education (1994) *Te Whāriki Curriculum Trial*. Wellington: Ministry of Education.

Early Childhood Education Project (1996) *Future Directions. Early Childhood Education in New Zealand*. Wellington: New Zealand Institute for Education.

Early Childhood Forum (1998) *Quality in Diversity in Early Learning, a Framework for Practitioners*. London: National Children's Bureau, Goldsmith' College.

Eisner, E. (1985) *The Educational Imagination: On the Design and Evaluation of School Programmes*. New York: MacMillan.

Erikson, E. (1950) *Childhood and Society*. New York: Norton.

Gould, K.E. (1998) A study of early childhood educators' experiences on one professional development programme, unpublished MEd thesis, University of Waikato.

Haggerty, M. (1998) Sighting, Citing and Siting Te Whāriki: exploring the use of video feedback as a tool for critical pedagogy, unpublished MEd thesis, University of Wellington, Victoria.

Haggerty, M. and Hubbard, P. (1994) *Te Whāriki Trial*. Wellington: Ministry of Education.

Honig, A. and Lally, R. (1981) *Infant Caregiving: A Design for Training*. New York: Syracuse University Press.

Howes, C. (1987) Quality indicators in infant and toddler care: the Los Angeles study, in D. Phillips (ed.) *Quality in Childcare: What Does the Research Tell Us?* Washington: National Association for the Education of Young Children.

Howes, C. (1991) Children's experiences in childcare: does age of entry or quality of care matter? in M. Gold, L. Foote and A.B. Smith (eds) *Proceedings of the Fifth Early Childhood Convention*. Dunedin: University of Dunedin.

Katz, L.G. (1993) *Dispositions: Definitions and Implications for Early Childhood Practices*. Perspectives from ERIC/ECCE: a monograph series. Urbana, IL: ERIC Clearinghouse on ECCE.

Kessler, S. and Swadener, B. (eds) (1992) *Reconceptualizing the Early Childhood Curriculum: Beginning the Dialogue*. New York: Teachers College Press.

Lange, D. (1988a) *Tomorrow's Schools: The Reform of Education Administration in New Zealand*. Wellington: Government Printer.

Lange, D. (1988b) *Before Five*. Wellington: Government Printer.

Lave, J. and Wenger, E. (1991) *Situated Learning: Legitimate Peripheral Participation*. Cambridge: Cambridge University Press.

May, H. (1992) After Before Five: Early Childhood Policy into the Nineties, *NZ Women's Studies Journal*, 8(2): 83–100.

May, H. and Podmore V. (1998) Project for Developing a Framework for Self Evaluation of Early Childhood Programmes. Paper presented at the Eighth European Conference on Quality in Early Childhood Research, Santiago de Compostela, Spain, September.

McGee, C. (1997) *Teachers and Curriculum Decision-Making*. Palmerston North: The Dunmore Press.

McGinn, M.K. and Roth, W.-M. (1998) Assessing students' understanding about levers: better test instruments are not enough, *International Journal of Science Education*, 20(7): 813–32.

McKinley, E. and Waiti, P. (1995) Te Tauākī Marautanga Pūtaiao: He tauira – the writing of a science curriculum in Māori, in A. Jones (ed.) *SAMEPapers 1995*. Hamilton: CSMTER, University of Waikato.

Meade, A. and Kerslake-Hendricks, A. (1998) *Preliminary Ideas about Quality Improvement Systems and Indicators*. A discussion paper. Wellington: New Zealand Council for Educational Research.

Meade, A., Podmore, V., May, H., Te One, S. and Brown, R. (1998) *Options paper: Early Childhood Qualifications and Regulations Project*. Final Report to the Ministry of Education. Wellington: New Zealand Council for Educational Research.

Metge, J. (1990) *Te Kohao o te Ngira: Culture and Learning*. Wellington: Learning Media.

Ministry of Children and Family Affairs (1996) *Framework Plan for Day Care Institutions*. Oslo: Norwegian Ministry of Children and Family Affairs.

Ministry of Education (1991) *The National Curriculum of New Zealand: A Discussion Document*. Wellington: Learning Media.

Ministry of Education (1993a) *The New Zealand Curriculum Framework*. Wellington: Learning Media.

Ministry of Education(1993b) *Te Whāriki: Draft Guidelines for Developmentally Appropriate Programmes in Early Childhood Services*. Wellington: Learning Media.

Ministry of Education(1994) *Education for the 21st Century*. Wellington: Learning Media.

Ministry of Education(1995) *Criteria for Funding Rate from 1st March, 1996*. Wellington: Ministry of Education.

Ministry of Education(1996a) *Te Whāriki. He Whāriki Matauranga mo nga Mokopuna o Aotearoa: Early Childhood Curriculum.* Wellington: Learning Media.

Ministry of Education(1996b) Revised Statement of Desirable Objectives and Practices (DOPs) for Chartered Early Childhood Services in New Zealand. *The New Zealand Gazette*, 3 October.

Ministry of Education(1998) Kōhanga Reo: Te Tapaetanga Korero. *Update 27*, 9 March.

Moore, C. and Dunham, P.J. (eds) (1991) *Joint Attention: Its Origins and Role in Development.* Hillsdale, NJ: Lawrence Erlbaum.

Morss, J.R. (1996) *Growing Critical: Alternative Views to Developmental Psychology.* London: Routledge.

Murrow, K. (1995) Early Childhood Workers' Opinion on the Draft Document Te Whāriki, Research Section Report Series No. 5, Ministry of Education, New Zealand.

Nally, P. (1995) Professional development for the implementation of new curriculum in the early childhood sector, *Proceedings of the Sixth Early Childhood Convention*, vol. 2. Auckland: University of Auckland.

Noddings, N. (1994) Postmodern musings on pedagogical uses of the personal, *Journal of Curriculum Studies*, 26(4): 355–60.

Noddings, N. (1995) Teaching themes of care, *Phi Delta Kappan*, 76(9): 675–9.

Nutbrown, C. (ed.) (1996) *Respectful Educators – Capable Learners: Children's Rights and Early Education.* London: Paul Chapman.

Nuttall, J. and Mulheron, S. (1993) What's for pudding? Curriculum and change for staff of childcare centres in Aotearoa/New Zealand, paper presented to the CECUA Early Childhood Curriculum Conference, Christchurch, June.

Olsen, S.O. (1996) *Verdens Bedste Folksole! – vi kan lære af det New Zealandske Skolesystem.* Denmark: Dafolo Forlag.

Pascal, C. and Bertram, A. (1998) The AcE project: accounting for life long learning, in L. Abbott and H. Moylett (eds) *Early Childhood Reformed.* London: Falmer Press.

Pascal, C., Bertram, A., Ramsden, F. *et al.* (1998) *Evaluating and Developing Quality in Early Childhood Settings: A Professional Development Programme.* Worcester: Worcester College of Higher Education.

Penn, H. (1991) Quality in services to young children: the European approach, in M. Gold, L. Foote and A.B. Smith (eds) *Proceedings of the Fifth Early Childhood Convention.* Dunedin: University of Dunedin.

Pere, R.R. (1991) *Te Wheke.* Gisborne: Ako Global Learning New Zealand.

Podmore, V. and May, H. (1998) *Evaluating Early Childhood Programmes Using Te Whāriki. Final Report on Phases One and Two to the Ministry of Education.* Wellington: New Zealand Council for Educational Research.

Ratner, H.H. and Stettner, L.J. (1991) Thinking and feeling: putting Humpty Dumpty together again, *Merrill-Palmer Quarterly*, 37(1): 1–26.

Reedy, T. (1993) I have a dream, in *Proceedings of the CECUA Early Childhood Conference.* Wellington: Institute for Education.

Reedy, T. (1995) Knowledge and power set me free. Keynote address, in *Proceedings of the Sixth Early Childhood Convention*, vol. 1. Auckland: University of Auckland.

Resnick, L.B. (1987) *Education and Learning to Think.* Washington DC: National Academy Press.

Ritchie, J. and Walker, R. (1995) Development of a Māori immersion education programme, in *Proceedings of the Sixth Early Childhood Convention*, vol. 11. Auckland: University of Auckland.

Rogoff, B. (1990) *Apprenticeship in Thinking: Cognitive Development in Social Context*. Oxford: Oxford University Press.

Royal Tangaere, P. (1991) Kei hea te Komako e ko? Early childhood education, a Māori perspective, in M. Gold, L. Foote and A.B. Smith (eds) *Proceedings of the Fifth Early Childhood Convention*. Dunedin: University of Dunedin.

Royal Tangaere, P. (1996) Te Kōhanga Reo – more than a language nest: the future of te reo Māori, te iwi and a people's soul. Keynote presentation to the NZARE Conference, Nelson,

Salomon, G. (ed.) (1993) *Distributed Cognitions: Psychological and Educational Considerations*. Cambridge: Cambridge University Press.

Smith, A.B. (1996) The early childhood curriculum from a sociocultural perspective, *Early Child Development and Care*, 115: 51–64.

Smith, A.B. (in press) Joint attention and quality childcare, *International Journal of Early Years Education*,

Smith, A.B. and Farquhar, S. (1994) The New Zealand experience of charter development in early childhood services, in P. Moss and A. Pence (eds) *Valuing Quality in Early Childhood Services*. London: Paul Chapman.

Sobstad, F. (1997) National Program for the Kindergarten in Norway: a Framework for Reflection in Action. Paper presented at a Curriculum Seminar, Queen Maud's College of Early Childhood Education, Norway.

Sobstad, F. (1998) Swings and Roundabouts, *Person Responsible Campaign: Early Childhood Industry 7 Point Plan*, Spring.

Taylor, P.C. (1998) Constructivism: value added, in B.J. Fraser and K.G. Tobin (eds) *International Handbook of Science Education, Mythmaking and mythbreaking in the mathematics classroom*. Dordrecht: Kluwer Academic Publishers.

Tobin, J.J. (1995) Post-structural research in early childhood education, in J.A. Hatch (ed.) *Qualitative Research in Early Childhood Settings*. Westport, CN: Praeger.

Whitebook, M., Howes, C. and Phillips, D. (1989) *Who Cares? Child Care Teachers and the Quality of Care in America, Final Report National Child Care Staffing Study*. Oakland, CA: Childcare Employee Project.

Woodhead, M. (1996) *In Search of the Rainbow: Pathways to Quality in Large Scale Programmes for Young Disadvantaged Children*. The Hague: Bernard van Leer Foundation.

Woodhead, M. (1998) 'Quality' in early childhood programmes – a contextually appropriate approach, *International Journal of Early Years Education*, 6(1): 5–17.

4 | The future of infant education

Marta Mata y Garriga

The rationale for infant education

No one now disputes the importance of primary education for children, and the necessity for it to be obligatory and provided by the state. But in the nineteenth century, when the idea of primary education took root, the resistance to it was formidable. Families needed the income from child labour, and put that before schooling. Various vested interest groups, such as religious groups, opposed the intervention of the state.

The greatest resistances have now been overcome. Although in different countries there are different patterns of education, nobody now denies the right of the state to extend the education system, and to ensure its quality; on the contrary, they claim it.

The suitability and appropriateness of education is obvious. The laws, the powers, public opinion, all proclaim that the predominant note of quality in obligatory schooling is its educational character; the drive for the personal, social and intellectual development of the child. Teaching is valued now as it never was at the end of the nineteenth century. Nobody now challenges the place of education, primary and secondary schools and universities. On the contrary, they want the education system to be more effective in transmitting knowledge, and in helping form the personality of the child.

But preschool education, nearly a century and half after Froebel, and nearly a century after Montessori, does not have such a status. Although a majority of children over 3 now go to nursery schools because their preparatory value is recognized, only a minority of children under 3 benefit from such education.

The tradition of nurseries for children under 3 is distinct in different countries. Generally, these nurseries are lacking in quantity and quality, and are not usually integrated in the education system. Who should be responsible for them, economically or administratively? Should children be outside the home at this age? Should nurseries only be for social referrals? How should the needs of children under 3 best be met? Only when the mother is also present? Should the basic function of these nurseries also be educative? How old are children before they begin to learn: several months old; a year old; 3 years old?

Who should work in these nurseries? How should they be trained? How will the costs of nurseries be met? Who should administer them? It is difficult to talk of the future of infant education when the present contains so many unanswered questions. But one thing is certain in Spain, as in many other countries: infant education is the touchstone of the Spanish education system.

We must take advantage not only of scientific advances and pedagogic developments, but also of democratic progress, and the need for community participation in public life.

In talking about education quality, we have a conception of the school that 'educates' rather than instructs. From the moment of birth children are learning; human genes carry this capacity and recreation of experience. This capacity is the key to both education and socialization, which is a miraculous process of humanity. This process, mismanaged, is responsible for the terrible tension between war and peace, oppression and liberty, and misery and well-being. Well managed, it opens up the possibility of a peaceful, responsible humanity, egalitarian and diverse, reaping the tangible and intangible benefits of the world.

The history of education has fluctuated between the selection of a few and the promotion of all; between ideological indoctrination and liberty; between arbitrary discipline, competition and punishment and self-respect and cooperation; between doling out and sharing.

Traditional pedagogy is to impart knowledge, in a way that is always marked by the distance between teacher and pupil, and by what is a convenient outcome for administrators. This should never be mistaken for real learning and real education.

In working with the youngest children, education is of a different kind, and our doubts about the system fade away. For us it is about understanding: the natural rhythms and discipline of children; the development and strengthening of personality and self-respect; the enjoyment of discovery, through work and play, of the company of equals and of communication with adults. The spectre of inculcation, instruction and taming is refuted.

Infant education influences the mainstream with this perception of education. This is the message of Froebel and Montessori. Quality and capacity are key concepts in education; to describe the level or standard obtained, but *also* the individuality of each development. The levels of scientific and practical education propounded by Montessori and Froebel, have found different expressions in Italian nurseries and in German kindergartens.

It is precisely this distinction between quality and capacity in infant education that enables us to address the problem of unity and diversity of educational methods between babies of 3 months, and those of 5 year old children. When education is seen in this unified way, the logic of preschool is inevitable.

In rural, artisan or industrial life alike, home and work are separated, and the extended patriarchal family is a thing of the past. The school has taken over the job of social reproduction from the family and can extend it. Resistance to public intervention has now been replaced with respect for it. In each case the intensity of the struggle to develop education has given it a particular shape and character in different countries. In Italy, for example, much power is vested in local authorities and little in the state. In Spain there is a national network of development of preschool services. But throughout Europe there is a unity of effort to address these issues of quality and individuality in the early years.

Yet at the same time, how far we have travelled from the isolation of the private home, and from the imposition of it. The quality of the education we offer, and its recognition of individuality, open a way through political ideology and administrative bureaucracy.

For these kinds of reasons, public opinion is now favourable to infant education and the extension of the school system downwards. Infant education has been the object of profound study, and generous resourcing, a level of practical education and resourcing which the most loving mother or grandfather or aunt will never be able to match.

This educational impulse to share life, to create equality, with the help of professional educators, is something that no contemporary society would choose to neglect. For each child, in each environment and at each age, in the proportion that is desirable and possible, we can supersede the exclusive song of mother and child, and match ignorance with reason.

In infant education nevertheless we still need to work on this conception of quality. We need to consider more carefully what local authorities can do to promote it. The demand for infant education from the public and professionals has been so great that many local authorities in Spain have tried, sometimes without the necessary help and resources, to meet it.

We realize now in Spain that after six years of work and two more of discussion, we are near the point of considering infant education, for children from birth to 6 years old, to be a responsibility of the education department, at national and local level. All our diverse kinds of provision – day nurseries, nursery schools, community childcare projects – will now be supported by an educational administration that will ensure their quantity and quality.

We will benefit from all the research – medical, psychological, sociological and pedagogic – on infant development that has been undertaken in our institutions of higher education, which is being translated into the training of our teachers. We are also benefiting from the networks of parent organizations, and from the interest and participation of the ordinary citizen.

We recognize and also hope to learn from the work that is going on elsewhere in Europe; in France, Italy, Hungary, Scotland and Denmark. In the immediate future, we have to put into practice our new legislation on infant education, to include:

* the continuation of scientific research, and reconciliation of theory and practice in infant education;
* the development of training of teachers working in this sector;
* action research to highlight good practice and develop new and more sensitive forms of provision, such as play provision in parks and integrated services for children with disabilities;
* competent administration at local authority level;
* collaboration with parents in developing and refining the services;
* networks between local authorities in developing these services, and with the education Ministry, to resourcing these and new initiatives;
* a community conception of services, from the ordinary citizen to the education department.

What of the future? Our immediate future is opening up such possibilities so we can imagine a time, not so very far distant, when our fragile and vulnerable children are welcomed into this world by parents fully responsible for their paternity, and by a society that puts at their disposal all the resources necessary for the best possible education.

La Ley Orgánica de Ordenación General del Sistema Educativo (the LOGSE) applied to infant education, 0–6 years

In Spain, compulsory schooling was introduced very gradually between the mid nineteenth century, when the Public Instruction Act (1857) was passed and the introduction of the General Education Act (1970), which finally required all children aged 6–14 to undertake a basic, general education.

Generally speaking, the education Acts laid down objectives to be achieved, and from Madrid, the Ministry slowly and unevenly implemented their specific, quantitative requirements: compulsory age of schooling; construction of schools with a greater or lesser number of classrooms; number of children per class; teacher's pay; and ancillary services. Children below compulsory school age were mentioned to a greater or lesser extent in the Acts, but nothing was done in practice.

The quality of teaching in schools progressed more slowly and unevenly as a result of legislation and the intervention of the Ministry than as a result of the activities of professional groups like the Institución Libre de Enseña in Madrid (which was founded by Giner de Los Ríos and that stressed active, task based learning). Either on their own initiative or with the help of local authorities, these groups got involved with modern trends in active learning and teaching and they created their own models of schooling, beginning with the youngest children.

Only during the period of the Second Spanish Republic (1911–39) did the Ministry, using directives taken from the aforementioned Institución and the Catalan movement, extend this model and put into practice the first major plan for building schools and for appropriate teacher training in higher education. In addition to maintaining these policies, the first 'Escoles Bressol' (nursery schools catering for children from the first months of life) were created in Catalonia.

Franco put an abrupt and brutal stop to the progress made during the Republic and between 1939 and 1970 school building was frozen. Many classrooms set aside for nursery schooling were used by primary school classes, the length of primary teacher training was cut by three years and the old welfare model of nurseries for children aged 0–6 was reintroduced.

In opposition to Franco, the former models based on active education were reintroduced in a few independent primary schools in the 1940s and 1950s; the majority of these concentrated their efforts on nursery schooling for 3-, 4- and 5-year-olds. In the 1960s the first nurseries for children under 3 were established, as were a variety of professional groups that were committed to the reform of teaching practices. The 'Summer Schools' that they organized attracted hundreds, even thousands, of participants. In 1975 they drafted the *Declaration for State Schooling*, which advocated an educational policy programme based on the consecutive stages 0–3 years, 3–6 years, 6–12 years and 12–18 years, as well as the democratization and decentralization of the education system. It has served as a basis for subsequent legislation.

After the death of Franco, hand in hand with the democratic changes begun in 1977, a twin pronged advance in the reform of the education system was initiated. One flank opened up the legal route leading from the new Spanish constitution, which gradually handed over the administration and regulation of the education system to the 17 autonomous regions of Spain and established the guidelines for participation in the administration and development of educational programming and planning.

The other flank opened up the participation route, with the involvement of professionals and citizens, pressure groups for the reform of teaching practices and parents associations.

In 1984, a preliminary education law, *La Ley Orgánica Del Derecho de la Educación* (LODE) was passed. This laid down the conditions that governed education, and specified the levels at which it was to be administered, in order to maximize participation at local, regional and national levels. The resultant structures were as follows:

Consejo Escolar de Centro (CEC)	School Governing Body
Consejo Escolar Municipal (CEM)	Municipal Education Committee
Consejo Escolar Territorial (CET)	District Education Committee

Consejo Escolar de la Comunidad	
Autónoma	Autonomous Regional Committee
Consejo Escolar del Estado (CEE)	National Schools Council

The first is an organ of management and the other bodies are participatory bodies, whose function is to interpret the regulations, planning proposals or other measures that might affect education in their area.

In 1985 an important period for the education of the youngest children began, within the above framework.

The Ministry of Education and Science (MEC) supported a series of experimental programmes as part of the 'Experimental Plan', which involved bringing together educators working in nurseries catering for children aged 0–3 years (as well as those working in nursery education for children aged 3–6), the majority of whose staff were without formal qualifications. At the same time a training scheme was set up that enabled those working in the nurseries to undertake a three-year in-service course leading to the new qualification of Specialized Teacher in Infant Education 0–6. These pilots run by the MEC made it possible for the 1987 white paper on the future education reform Act to propose nursery education between the ages of 0–6 years, in two stages, and with specialized teachers.

The people and institutions of early childhood education participated in or knew about these pilots and were able to join in the debate at all levels, and contributed their opinions during the drafting by the National Schools Committee of the Bill on the Restructuring of the Education System.

The LOGSE, finally passed in 1990, is the first law to have arisen out of a long process – five years – of experimentation and discussion with all the advisory groups mentioned.

The LOGSE has designed an education system that guarantees the right to education for children from birth to 18 years old, in three educational levels and in three modes of school; infant education, 0–6 years; primary schooling, 6–12 years; and secondary school from 12–18 years. Moreover, the LOGSE integrates into the overall system all curricular and other issues in education, from artistic education to special education, in an overall framework of measures, which will be implemented over a ten-year period, up to the year 2000.

The LOGSE divides the infant level, which is not compulsory, into stages 0–3 years and 3–6 years, each with its own educational curriculum focusing on the development of the child's abilities. In the infant (0–3) school, the first stage goes beyond the simple carer model of the traditional nursery, and the second stage goes beyond the view of nursery schooling as merely preparation for the preschool stage. In both cases, teachers have to have specialized training, and have to submit to official inspection within the education system.

With regard to the quality of education the LOGSE stresses a requirement for a close relationship at all levels between school and family, and for links between the two stages of infant education and the primary phase.

Finally, the LOGSE proposes that infant education should be maintained locally and nationally if it is to meet demand.

A great deal of work remains to be done in order to fully implement the LOGSE.

Extracts from the LOGSE

FIRST CHAPTER: Infant Education

Article 7

1 Infant education, which is up to 6 years of age, shall contribute to the child's physical, intellectual, social and moral development. Infant schools shall work closely with parents or tutors, whose responsibilities at this educational stage are fundamental.
2 Infant education shall be voluntary. Public authorities shall guarantee the existence of a sufficient number of places to assure the schooling of those who request it.
3 Education authorities shall coordinate the supply of school places from the various public authorities, ensuring cooperation from educational psychologist teams in the various cycles at school.

Article 8

Infant education shall help to develop the following abilities in children. They will:

(a) become familiar with their own bodies and its possibilities of action;
(b) relate to others using different forms of expression and communication;
(c) observe and explore their natural, familiar and social environment;
(d) progressively acquire self-discipline in day-to-day activities.

Article 9

1 Infant education shall be divided into two stages. The first shall be up to 3 years of age and the second from 3 to 6 years of age.
2 During stage one, infant education shall concentrate on developing movement, bodily control, the first signs of communication and language, the elementary criteria of communal life and social relationships and the discovery of the immediate environment.

3 The second stage shall cover the use of language, discovery of the physical and social characteristics of the society in which we live, development of a positive, well balanced image of themselves and the acquisition of basic behavioural habits for elementary personal independence.
4 Educational subjects shall be organized into areas that coincide with the natural experience and development of the children and include general activities that are of interest and significance to them.
5 Educational material shall be based upon experiences, activities and games, within an atmosphere of affection and confidence.

Article 10
Infant education shall be taught by specialized teachers. During the first stage there shall also be other professionals with the appropriate educational qualifications to attend to the children.

1 Infant schools may teach the first, second, or both stages.
2 Education authorities shall develop infant education. For this end they shall determine the conditions in which to establish agreements with local councils, other public bodies and non-profit-making organizations.

The implementation of the LOGSE in infant education

Irene Balaguer

From the time when the LOGSE was put on the statute books in 1990 until today, there have been some important changes in institutional education for the youngest children in Spain.

Conceptual changes

The fact that the new law sees infant education as the first level of the education system has meant for society in general as much as for teachers and professionals in particular, a change in the way in which we understand and cater for children under 6 years old.

With the passing of the LOGSE it has been recognized that education for children under 6 has its own characteristics and intrinsic value deriving from the Act itself, which are put into practice at a basic level through the guidelines of the curriculum framework, but which must also be implemented in the organizational structures of each centre, in initial teacher training and subsequent professional development, through the organization of the services, and so on.

Changes in regulations

The general themes outlined in the LOGSE have led to the development of a new curriculum, which is constructed around three main ideas; identity and personal autonomy; discovery of physical and social worlds; and communication and representation. The content is open and allows each school and each teacher to develop and apply a curriculum plan to fit each group of children in their everyday reality. The two most relevant characteristics of the present curriculum are flexibility and responsiveness in terms of implementation; and the valorization of the activity of each child in relation to his or her abilities and current interests and not in relation to what might need to be learned at some point in the future.

The passing of a decree that lays down minimum requirements and that applies to the country as a whole and to all centres whether public or private, has meant the beginning of a qualitative change in many contexts. However, minimum standards have yet to be satisfied in terms of resources and staffing.

Part three
Where should children learn?
Space and segregation

Time and place are increasingly seen by sociologists concerned with childhood as a critical component in children's lives. Where children are defines them. Jenks goes so far as to define a child as someone in the wrong place (James *et al.* 1998). But both the conceptions of childhood and the conceptions of space in urban developed societies shift dramatically in many majority world countries. In pastoralist and in some agrarian societies for example (and probably, if poets like John Clare can be counted as witnesses, in an earlier rural England), landscape is a central and organizing feature of everyday life, and people orientate themselves to and continuously place themselves in the environment around them. Such societies are likely to possess a substantial mythology and ritual associated with that landscape, to see it in some way as sacred (Croll and Parkin 1992; Humphrey 1996). In some societies, the language itself may not discriminate between social and spatial concepts, but use the same words for both, so that to do something is described by the place in which it is done (Leach 1992). The ecological movements in the minority world sometimes refer to and try to reproduce some of the knowledge of and respect for the environment that is inherent and fundamental in other ways of thinking (Monbiot 1994).

In industrialized countries we rely on a narrow definition of space as the built space of the urban environment and we make a basic distinction between private or household space, and public or communal space. As Jenks noted, we have clear ideas about who should occupy which kind of space and when. We commonly experience generational segregation in public spaces, if not in private spaces. It is unusual for young children and older people to be an ever-present part of ordinary everyday life. By contrast Jaqueleine Rabain (1979) describes the communality of daily life in rural Senegal:

The insistent presence of infants in the times, places and rhythms of everyday life in African villages is astonishing. Babies are carried in the morning on the backs of their mothers to market, or on the paths to the fields, or on the way to the well; their sounds accompany the cadences of the pestle, or of the dance. Young infants are passed from one person to another on the family mat, part of the dialogue and social repartee.

(Rabain 1979: 20, author's translation)

In the UK, as in many industrialized countries, children are rarely seen in public spaces. Children are confined to the home or to institutions; partly because the external world of the street and other public places is deemed to be too dangerous and unsafe for them, and partly because, if they were allowed freedom to roam, they would constitute a nuisance to other occupiers of the public spaces. Unlike the communities described by Jacqueline Rabain, where children are an intrinsic part of the public arena, and where they are taught from their earliest moments to be a respectful part of that community, young children here are unaccustomed to the constraints of being in public, as opposed to private, spaces. Unaware of any wider obligations to others, they may behave badly and their exasperated or shamed parents either condone or ignore them; the intimate battles of the home continue in occasional fraught forays into public space – witness the confrontations in a supermarket! Conversely, no outsider can comment on the scene; to address someone else's child in public is usually to intrude unacceptably.

If young children leave their private home space, then either they go to another home setting, a carer or a relative, or else to a nursery, an institution exclusively designed to house them. In the UK such institutionalized buildings, deliberately or not, often reflect a sentimentalized view of children as doll-like, cute little creatures, not so far removed in kind from Mickey Mouse and other Disneyesque creatures whose pictures so frequently decorate their walls. Such vulnerable children need to be carefully protected and kept safe. Yet, as Tobin (1995) eloquently points out, at the same time children are also seen as miniature consumers whose right to individual choices must be safeguarded from the earliest opportunity, which is an approach embedded into the curriculum as well as in the design of the building.

Consumer desire is produced by the reality of our pre-schools. The variety of things and choices offered by middle class preschools are overwhelming to many children. We create cluttered, overstimulating environments modelled on the excesses of the shopping mall and the amusement park and then we complain that children are hyperactive and unable to focus on what they are doing.

(Tobin 1995: 232)

The American measurement scale for rating the quality of the environment,

Early Childhood Environment Rating Scale (ECERS), for example, assumes that a good environment will necessarily offer a child a generous display of choice of activity, and that this itself constitutes a reliable measure of the quality of the space. Yet as Goldschmied and Jackson comment about British nurseries, 'we are often content for children to spend their most formative years surrounded by ugliness and clutter . . . colours and textures which do not add up to any harmonious scheme . . . that most of us would not tolerate in our own homes' (1994: 17).

In the UK, outside the private sector, where some of the bigger nursery chains have invested in new properties, many of the buildings young children inhabit are less likely to be new than castoffs from elsewhere in the education or welfare system. All but a few of the 300 nurseries in the Strathclyde region, for example, whether in the education system or the previous social work system were hand-me-downs; buildings originally designed for other purposes and often poorly adapted for young children (Penn 1992). Playgroups traditionally have had to operate in shared and often unsuitable premises in their local communities, such as church halls or multipurpose community centres.

Because there is relatively little tradition of design for children in the UK, and a limited notion of space, there is rarely a shared vocabulary, an understanding of possibilities, between architects and local people if and when new buildings are commissioned (Dudek 1996). The language of the educational and welfare debate is a parsimonious one. In the UK the 1989 Children Act specified a minimal standard of accommodation to meet health and safety requirements, but this does not elaborate at all on the nature of the space in which the children will spend their time; if the number of lavatories and electrical sockets, the fire proofing, and so on are all correct, then no more is required to safeguard children's interests and nothing is done to guide their concept of aesthetics and design. For example, I was involved in the commissioning of an out-of-school building where local people, canvassed for their views, put security at the top of their list. The architects designed a building without windows, where the only daylight came from a small skylight on the heavily protected roof. The room had to be continuously lit by artificial lighting and had the appearance of a prison cell (Penn 1992). This curious result of 'consultation' was a reflection both of the lack of a shared vocabulary and discussion between architects and their clients, and a dearth of ideas about space and place for children.

There are many countries where there is a much stronger tradition in building and design for children. One of the most attractive examples quoted by Dudek (1996) is the Jardín de Niños project in Tijuana in Mexico, created by the American architect and designer James Hubble, who worked with local women from the *favelas* or slums to design the building using traditional Mexican patterns and designs. The programme discussed below, from Frankfurt in Germany, is chosen because it is one of the most coherent and comprehensive attempts to redefine the nature and the significance of the spaces that children occupy, and to give them a new prominence and meaning, although still within the conventional segregated boundaries that characterize modern industrialized societies.

Federal reforms in Germany after unification required Lande (local regions) to provide kindergarten places for all 3-, 4- and 5-year-olds, and there has been a major expansion in the number of kindergarten places. In addition there has also been a major expansion in out of school centres, or *Kinderhorts*. Although there is a considerable 'alternative' anti-institutional movement in Germany, in the form of parent cooperatives, and various self-help groups (Jaeckel 1992) the obligation to make universal provision lies firmly with the Lande; that is, it is perceived as a state obligation to publicly fund and publicly provide kindergartens.

Germany has a similar system to Scandinavian countries and kindergartens are staffed by social pedagogues not teachers, and administered as part of a universal welfare system, rather than as part of the education system. Because there are generous maternity schemes in Germany, very few kindergartens cater for children younger than 3; mostly they are for children aged 3 to 6. They offer a full morning session (four hours), and, for a small fee, children can stay on in the afternoon if their parents need to use the service. Generally the kindergartens have very liberal regimes, and children's freedom of expression and freedom of movement are encouraged. Although the children have group room bases, they are often allowed a great deal of liberty in when and where they move within the building, and the pedagogy allows children to pace themselves. There is no formal curriculum. Children do not go to school until they are 6; and school, like the kindergarten, is a long half-day, so that the Kinderhort facilities are necessary for children whose parents are at work. The kindergartens are open to everyone in the neighbourhood. However one feature of the German system is that children with disabilities are further segregated into separate provision; and one of the real shortcomings of the Frankfurt kindergarten programme from a UK point of view is that there is no attempt to consider disabled access or any other building features that reflect the needs of the disabled.

Briefly, the origin of the Frankfurt kindergarten programme was that after launching a very successful museum and gallery programme, the architect's department, the Hochbauamt, was asked to come up with another landmark building programme to commemorate the 1200th anniversary of the founding of the city. They suggested that, more than any other kind of public institution, kindergartens signified contemporary life and living. In devising the kindergarten programme, initially for 35 new kindergartens, they were anxious to understand the pedagogic and architectural constraints of kindergarten buildings that were put up in a routine way in the 1960s and 1970s and wanted to identify and avoid past mistakes; and at the same time they wished to create a truly innovative new programme, where the issues of design and development for children could be addressed in a new creative way. Buildings also had to reflect, echo or complement the local surroundings, most of which were not in the city centre, but in outlying estates and districts, and were mostly low cost or council housing estates.

According to the criteria set by the welfare department, each kindergarten had to accommodate at least four group rooms, for kindergarten age children, and a Kinderhort. Both facilities had to have spaces that were exclusive to children, where children could play or retreat away from adults. In most of the kindergartens the Kinderhort also has its own child-sized kitchen and workshop space. The kindergartens also had to include a large hall or communal space that could be used by the community as well as for indoor games or for sleeping arrangements. Given the expansion in kindergartens throughout Germany, a considerable number of manufacturers now specialize in furnishings, toys and even kitchen equipment for children, so it was possible to choose extremely well designed equipment for the kindergartens.

There are a number of key points to be made about the Frankfurt programme. Firstly the acceptance that kindergartens represent an important social function that should be publicly identified and celebrated is remarkable. If young children are absent from most public spaces, so the argument ran, at least the spaces they do use should be worthy of commemoration. Secondly, the programme was generously funded; it is not for nothing that Frankfurt is popularly known as 'Bankfurt'. Yet although the funding was generous – certainly by UK standards – it was not unlimited. The architect, Peter Wilson's, account of building the Kiefernstrasse kindergarten shows how the financial limits were ever present, and it became a challenge to work within them. The most expensive, and most flamboyant, kindergarten in the programme, the fairy-tale castle designed by the famous Austrian artist Hundertwasser, which does not have a single straight wall or corner, cost over £2 million, but some of this money, principally used to gild the turrets, was raised by Hundertwasser himself through public subscription, when he realized with indignation that the Hochbauamt would not pay for all his details.

Thirdly, the rationale of the Hochbauamt is that good architecture, good space as contemporarily defined, is as necessary for the poor as well as the rich. Many of these kindergartens, including both Peter Wilson's and Hundertwasser's, are located in low-cost housing estates, where many of the inhabitants are Turkish immigrant families. Hundertwasser's kindergarten was built on a reclaimed industrial factory site. Some of the sites available for the kindergarten programme were at first unpromising, and it is a constant theme of the programme that clever new solutions were necessary to make the most of the land constraints, even if this meant rethinking some of the welfare department's guidelines on kindergarten provision – the equivalent in the UK of challenging the regulations and specifications laid down in the 1989 Children Act. The emphasis throughout the programme was on flexibility and innovation.

Fourthly, all of the kindergartens incorporate some ecological features:

turf or other kinds of growing roofs; solar heating; recycled water; recycled wood; and reusable or decomposable materials. One ecological challenge not so far included is sewage disposal using reed beds, a point raised in the account of the programme. All of the kindergartens have outside space, even if, as in one case, it is a series of terraced gardens. None of the kindergartens have car-parking spaces, unlike the various regulations in the UK, where the space allocated to cars frequently exceeds that allocated to play space. Because the kindergartens offer a universal local neighbourhood service, and because bicycle transport is safe and reliable, and public transport is good, there is little need for car-parking space: in a densely inhabited city car-parks consume too much ground. This ecological concern is not limited to kindergartens. There is a widespread view in Germany, put forward by the Green movement, that the environment cannot be taken for granted and has to be carefully cherished. This conception is still a long way from the pastoralist beliefs, discussed above, that a person interacts with and is shaped by the wider landscape, the distinctive features within it and the very lie of the land.

Fifthly, and most importantly, the programme represents an attempt to define childhood and children's needs. Architects specialize in making built space, but what sort of space suits children best? Given that, except perhaps in the confines of our own homes, we are mostly spatially illiterate, and consider the nature of space – length, width, height, proportion, light, colour, contour, surface, and so on – as largely irrelevant, the Frankfurt kindergarten programme is challenging in forcing us to consider how children might use and think about the spaces in which they spend a large part of their waking time.

The impetus for the kindergarten programme clearly came from architects rather than from those in the welfare department working directly with young children, and, indeed, from the outside the dialogue between them seems a limited one. Also it is not clear to what extent there has been any rigorous observation or feedback from the users of the kindergartens, from children or adults, although, given the innovativeness of the programme, it would be hard to consider what conventional psychological measures could be used. How would one begin to describe the impact on children of, for instance, living in a building without corners? However, on a visit to the Kiefernstrasse nursery with an architect colleague, while waiting to talk to the coordinator, we watched a group of four exuberant children using the space exactly as Peter Wilson envisaged. Starting at the 'large' end of the building, they dressed up in robes and hats and assembled themselves into some kind of procession. They paraded, ran and skipped all the way down the long corridor, and ended up, with much giggling and laughing, at the coordinator's office, where they became a neat little group sitting at the desk, one pretending to telephone, another scribbling messages on a pad, and the other two watching earnestly. When the coordinator arrived, she absent-mindedly shooed them out, saying she needed the space now, and the children ran happily back down the corridor, their gestures more expansive as the space grew wider.

References

Croll, E. and Parkin, D. (eds) (1992) *Bush Base: Forest Farm – Culture, Environment and Development*. London: Routledge.

Dudek, M. (1996) *Kindergarten Architecture: Space for the Imagination*. London: E. and F.N. Spon.

Goldschmied, R. and Jackson, S. (1994) *People Under Three: Young Children in Day Care*. London: Routledge.

Humphrey, C. (1996) *Shamans and Elders: Experience, Knowledge and Power Among the Daur Mongols*. Oxford: Clarendon Press.

Jaeckel, M. (1992) Childhood today – a wide vision of the quality of childhood. Paper presented at the European Childcare Network Seminar on Quality, Barcelona, May 1992.

James, A., Jenks, C. and Prout, A. (1998) *Theorizing Childhood*. Cambridge: Polity Press.

Leach, M. (1992) Women's crops in women's spaces: gender relations in Mende rice farming, in E. Croll and D. Parkin (eds) *Bush Base: Forest Farm – Culture, Environment and Development*. London: Routledge.

Monbiot, G. (1994) *No Man's Land: An Investigative Journey through Kenya and Tanzania*. London: MacMillan.

Penn, H. (1992) *Under Fives: The View from Strathclyde*. Edinburgh: Scottish Academic Press.

Rabain, J. (1979) *L'Enfant du Lignage*. Paris: Payot.

Tobin, J.J. (1995) Post-structural research in early childhood education, in J.A. Hatch (ed.) *Qualitative Research in Early Childhood Settings*. Westport, CT: Praeger.

5 | The Frankfurt kindergartens

Roland Burgard

In the mid 1980s the city of Frankfurt came up with an ambitious programme to tackle the long neglected task of building kindergartens. The Hochbauamt (City architects department) had already gathered a wealth of useful experience in the field of ambitious and unusual design through its museum building programme, which had involved the most celebrated of international architects, and which were located not only in the city centre, but in outlying districts. The kindergarten programme was also intended to be prestigious, and to be located in unfashionable urban and suburban districts. As a rule, the Hochbauamt awarded the contracts directly. One important criterion in the selection process was the fact that architects had already made a name for themselves as independent personalities and conceptual thinkers.

Although high priority was given to a carefully considered architectural design, it was felt that the architecture should also appeal directly to children. The Hochbauamt formulated this specification as follows:

> The quality of the architecture must be directed towards children. The structural space should support the children in their social learning as well as in their sensory learning. By adapting the premises to the powers of sensory perception, a sense of spatial awareness should be transmitted . . . the contemporary kindergarten architect risks taking up the challenge of play. His spatial play should harmonize with the children's play.

Since the programme began in 1985, 12 kindergartens have been completed, nine are under construction, and plans have been drawn up for a further nine. What has been developed in Frankfurt during this time has been hailed enthusiastically in the world of architecture.

What is architecture for children?

Architects are far from unanimous in their concepts of the way architecture should be designed to accommodate the needs of children today. Christoph Mackler, for example, puts it concisely: 'There is no such thing as architecture for children'. Mackler designed his kindergarten as a small town with houses, bridge, street and square. He takes children seriously as small adults and provides them with a space in which they have a wide variety of opportunities to develop. The design also acknowledges the single-family houses opposite the kindergarten by reiterating the theme of the gable. At the same time, he sets the building apart from the monotonous external rendering of the surrounding housing estate by his use of warm-toned, dark-red clinker brick. A further contrast to the neighbouring buildings is achieved by cutting through the gabled structures with a white wall to render visible, from the outside, the corridor that links the group rooms.

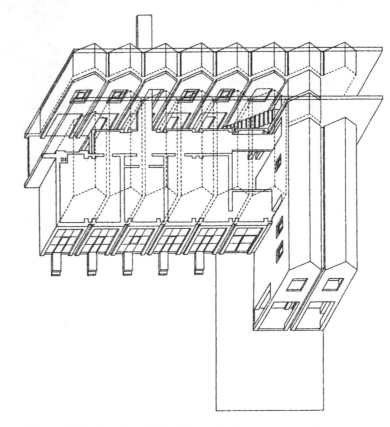

Figure 5.1 Christoph Mackler's kindergarten built as a series of terraced houses round a square

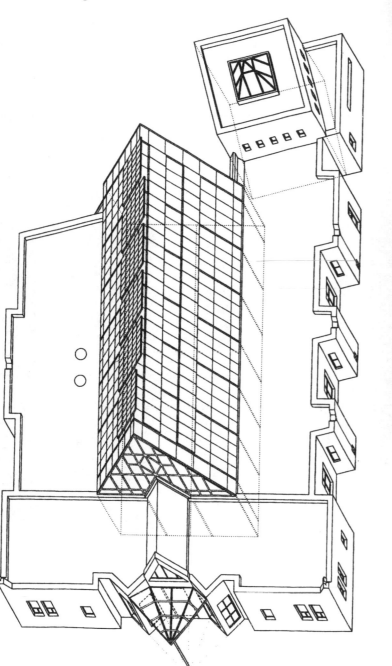

Figure 5.3 Solar heated kindergarten in a site at the back of a supermarket. The inside playspace is a tropical garden.

Andreas Keller in Rodelheim is similarly reluctant to use childlike forms. He has created a long, two-storey, bar-like structure. A hint of 1920s architecture is present in the references to the nearby estates built in that decade. With a completely glazed upper floor, the light opens out to the green space of the nearby park, thus achieving a fluid transition from architecture to nature. Keller has reduced any obvious pandering to children to a few details such as a low look-out window on the entrance floor. A distinctive feature of the building is the sunshade provided in the form of a cantilevered roof with aluminium sheathing reminiscent of the wings of a plane.

Fairytale castles and building bricks

Almost diametrically opposed to the concepts just mentioned are the kindergarten designs by the Austrian painter and ecologist, Friedensreich Hundertwasser. For him, creating architecture for children means making their wishes and dreams come true. In this sense the architect is merely an intermediary between the fantasies of children and the reality of the world. Hundertwasser has designed a kind of fairytale castle, whose onion domes and cosy corners make it seem very playful. He has pursued not only the aim of building for children, but also his concept of reconciliation between man and nature. The entire building is covered by a roof that is a meadow planted with trees. In this way the developed site (reclaimed industrial land) is returned to nature, the building having been gently 'slipped under its skin'.

Within the scope of this programme, a number of architects have interpreted 'architecture for children' as an architecture that takes up themes that hold a certain fascination for children: castles, towers, fire brigade, ship, cave, gallery and building blocks. Remembering their own former ideas and wishes, they have broken out of the restrictive mould of functionality to create an enormous diversity of spatial concepts. Of course, the reference to vivid childhood images neither constitutes architecture nor serves as a substitute.

In the same spirit, the firm of Worner and Partner designed their kindergarten as a 'building brick castle'. A sequence of building bricks is used to create an inner courtyard covered by a glass roof and forbiddingly closed to the outside world like a castle. The same motifs are repeated in the interior design. Another kindergarten designed by Uwe Laske defines itself as a large 'play object', with a round tower, oriels and gangway. This rich diversity is meant to encourage the children to act spontaneously, moving around and exploring. In spite of his attempts to accommodate the needs of children, the architect has not allowed himself to get bogged down in multiple design elements, preferring to give the long building a relatively clear form.

Michael Kleinert's concept for a kindergarten is similar to that of Uwe

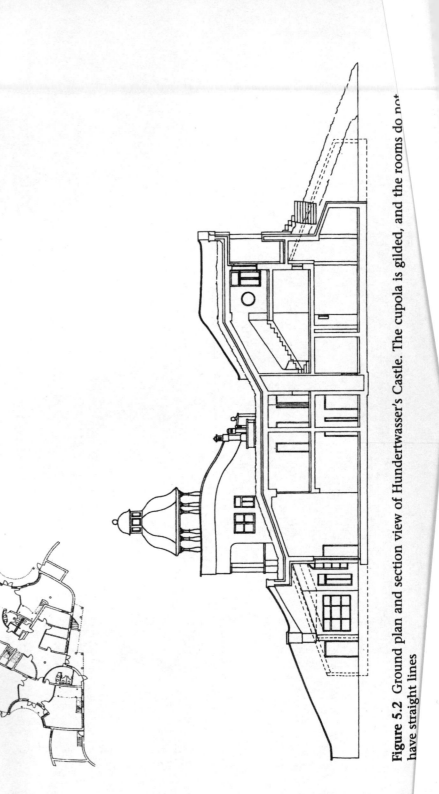

Figure 5.2 Ground plan and section view of Hundertwasser's Castle. The cupola is gilded, and the rooms do not have straight lines

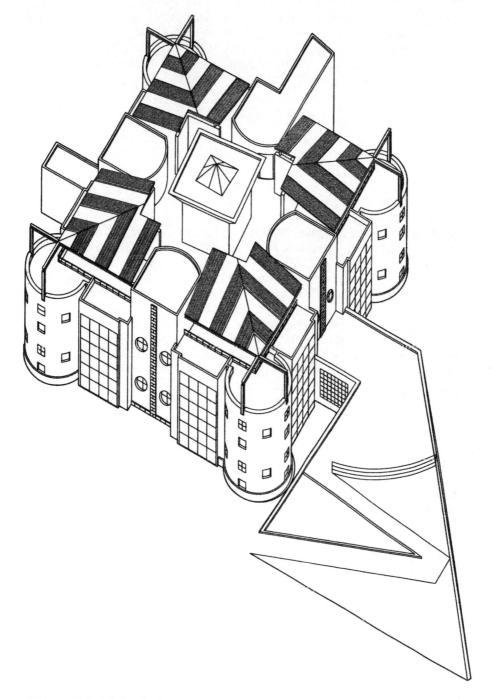

Figure 5.4 Michael Kleinert's turreted castle kindergarten

Laske. His house is intended as a 'plaything to be walked around and experienced'. At each of the four corners of the groundplan, the motif of the watchtower with relatively small windows is repeated. The building is, in part, a protective castle and, in part, a structure whose extensive glass oriels let the light and the surroundings flow in.

Shortage of space

The small and inconveniently shaped sites available for the programme are a further challenge to the versatility of the architects. Building sites are few and far between in Frankfurt. In the city centre, small buildings have been demolished and car-parks banished underground in a bid to eke out every available space for major office buildings. In an endeavour to step up the urgently required construction of housing, entire districts are being redeveloped on sites that were hitherto sparingly used. The kindergartens pose a different kind of challenge: the need for them to be inextricably linked with their respective district. Often, on the sites on which architects are expected to plan an entire kindergarten, there is barely room to swing the proverbial cat. Moreover, the sites themselves are often embedded in difficult development situations, the challenge being to serve the locality even when there is not enough space to meet planning guidelines or when the available space is poorly sited, for example very near a busy road.

Hans Kolhoff and Helga Timmerman, for example, had to build a four-storey kindergarten, in defiance of all accepted guidelines, in order to provide the required space. The lack of open spaces was compensated for by providing graduated terraces to the rear of the building. The closed structure screens the building from the noise and traffic of the busy main road, while at the same time lending it the air of a separate and public building. The design mediates between the line of the adjacent housing block on the one hand and the slightly recessed school on the other, by picking up the line and breaking it slightly. The material, a dark-red clinker brick, links the kindergarten to the neighbouring zoo wall.

Roland Burgard faced the difficult task of harmonizing his design with existing buildings while clearly articulating its function as a public building. What is more, the specifications also required that the extension should be built on a site within an otherwise enclosed block. This means that not only the dimensions, but also the general layout of the building were already predetermined. Burgard succeeded in stamping his own signature on the building by means of a few design elements such as a tunnel vaulted roof, uninterrupted rows of windows, and a row of columns on the ground floor. Moreover the public nature of the building was emphasized by an inviting corridor leading into the interior of the block.

Another example of making the most of a cramped site is the kindergarten designed by another member of the Hochbauamt team, Ulrich Kuhldahl. In this case not only was the site narrow, but the architect was

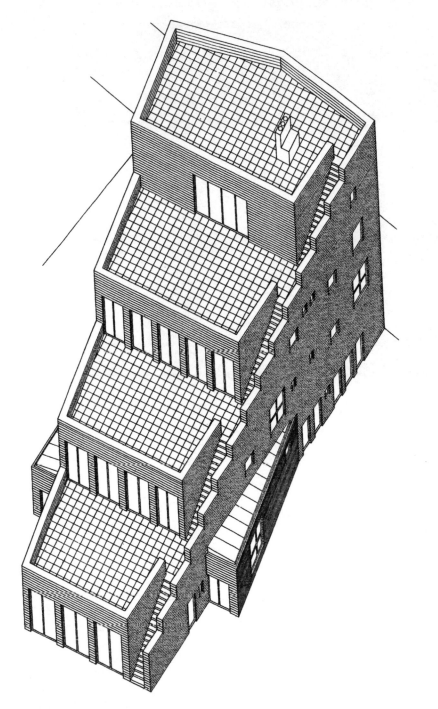

Figure 5.5 Timmerman and Kollhof's Ziggurat kindergarten, built to maximize the use of space

Figure 5.6 Light spaces inside Roland Burgard's kindergarten

also required to leave existing trees standing. The long building, its severity softened and structured by several protrusions and recesses, follows the outline of the site. The yard with the trees creates a break in an otherwise compact layout.

Experiments in ecological building

From an early stage, ecology has played an important role in the kindergarten programme. The possibilities of alternative energy sources have been examined in several projects in order to gain experience for their use on a larger scale. For example, one kindergarten has solar cells capable of generating 50 per cent of the electricity requirement. Solar collectors heat 800 litres a day, equivalent to normal daily needs. In yet another kindergarten, a thermally insulating core area, with subtropical plants, transforms sunlight into thermal energy, which is used to heat the building. Generally, the construction methods, operation and waste disposal had to fulfil ecological criteria. In addition to environmentally sound energy concepts, where possible low-pollutant building materials were to be used, which could later be recycled or harmlessly disposed of.

The Kiefernstrasse nursery

The Kiefernstrasse kindergarten is probably the most well known of the nurseries, and it is worth considering the architect's plans in more detail as an exemplar of the kind of detail and innovation pursued in the programme. Designed by Peter Wilson and his firm Bolles+Wilson, it was in a disadvantaged area of Frankfurt; a very narrow east–west site wedged in between a motorway, a low-income housing estate, a petrol station and a school. Many living in the area were one-parent immigrant families with a high rate of unemployment.

> Our job was to make of this barren site a safe place, an enclosure from the surrounding area and also a focus for it. We needed to shut out the noise from the motorway, and one of our first tasks was to make a decibel map, showing the directionality of the noise. As well as being noisy, the landscape at the back was tough and ugly.

The firm responded by designing a kind of ship, which they themselves refer to as a wedge, a 'growing object'. From the tip, where the entrance is located, the building develops in width and height, culminating in a relatively large hall at the other end. Wilson commented:

> The world is bigger for children because they are smaller. As they grow, the world shrinks. We wanted to use this as a metaphor, a theme for the building and vary the impressions of space, to have tight compressed spaces which open out and become bigger and bigger, so that moving through the building is a growing and shrinking process like Alice in Wonderland. We created a conical space. The smallest room, the principal's office was at one end of the building, the biggest room at the other, and the heights of the ceilings change as you move from one end to the other. The windows at the back of the building are at child height, so that children can see out, but not adults, unless they bend down.

As with the other nurseries in the programme the budget was finite, and by the standard of prestigious public works, modest.

> This was not a luxury budget, and our first design was rejected on the grounds of economy – we had originally suggested a roof garden, and the children's workshop as an extension to the main building. We tried to take these changes, the regulations and limits that were imposed, as positive incentives. For example, when we lost the workshop extension, we decided to create a blank cut-off wall for children's games. Our attitude to function was very flexible, and we made many changes during the building. For instance we originally planned a playhouse on the roof. When this was cut, we then thought of having an ivy covered green object on the roof but the staff did not want to water the plants; then we thought of using a floodlight light as the

Figure 5.7 Photograph of the entrance of Kiefernstrasse kindergarten

roof feature, but the electricians by accident wired up a different section of the building for the floodlight. In the end we used a sensor for
wind direction, part of the heating system, as the feature. These
changes are a paradigm for the design process – problems continually
occur, and the art is to make a virtue of the problems.

The out-of-school club, an important social feature for the neighbourhood, had to contain a homework area and a play area.

We made a vertical division with the older children on top, younger
on the bottom. The older children could filter off via the staircase. In
order to achieve the change in heights on the ground floor, we had a
little bridge on the upper floor from the main rooms to the children's
kitchen, a kind of little island.

All the nurseries had to have a large room, which could be used as a sports
hall or for public meetings, and for a variety of other purposes.

The general purpose room was essentially a big box. We had to put in
a second layer of detail to create its spatial quality. It had a big window
to the south. Small children slept in there after lunch, so we also had
a grid of glass bricks punctuating the other wall, to give the impression of stars shining through at night, a kind of rationalized heaven.
This general purpose room was another example of how we tried to
turn regulations to our advantage. There is a regulation which speci-
fies that the flooring cannot be of a single colour because it would

show up dirt too much; so we got round the regulation by inserting small patches of black lino into floor areas where there had been builders damage. (We even had a large black lino spot in the principal's office. We thought it might be a place where a child who had badly misbehaved could cool out, but unfortunately the black spot was placed right next to the console controlling the security of the building!)

In Kiefernstrasse, as in the other nurseries, every design feature was a matter of intense scrutiny.

Each of the group rooms had to have an exit on to the playground. We built a large door and a small door side by side. To make it obvious that there are scale jumps for children, we put the child handle and the adult handle at the same height on each door. On the stairway we integrated the crash barrier with the light switch – the kind of detail architects like. We had intended to make the staircase without a balustrade, but the regulations required it, but at the last minute we made one out of a panel crisscrossed with regular holes. We just squeezed past the regulations, by gearing the height of the wall between the group rooms and balcony on the bridge slightly lower than the required height, on the grounds that the children using it were smaller than adults. The upper balustrade was designed to include the children's lockers and shoeboxes.

The rooms at the bottom opened out on to the garden, so we used a horizontal timber window system so we could have long stretches of glass. In each of the rooms we built an 'object', a kind of architectural play area, for instance a staircase which takes on the theme of the children growing and shrinking. We put rubber cladding on the concrete pillars both as protection but also as a feature.

We used blue glass bricks, which have a curious light quality, in the storage rooms and in the bathrooms. In the bathroom they formed the window – we hoped to give the impression of being in a fishbowl under water – so the children would need no additional prompts to use the loo. The K-window on the front façade is a K for kindergarten. The blank end wall can be used as a surface for ball games. The back wall was mostly blank, but we tried to make incidents of the features it contained, like pieces of writing, for instance with the drainpipes and windows.

Because the programme was a collaborative one, it was important to consult throughout the design process.

It was a collaborative project, not an individual one. Our view is that the architect is a facilitator, and that once the building is in use, the architecture should disappear. Its success owes much to the coordinator of the nursery, who was able to fulfill the potential offered by the building. The Frankfurt programme required that we produce a scale model of 1:50; much larger than is usually the case, as a demonstration of how we proposed to develop the work. This working model was useful for discussion about the evolution of the building: it was a good working method.

Acknowledgements

The Frankfurt programme was discussed at a conference at the Royal Institute of British Architects in November 1996. Roland Burgard's paper was drawn from Archigrad, a review series produced for the Hauptbauamt, about architecture in Frankfurt. It is an edited version of the Archigrad version which is reprinted here, together with the illustrations from Archigrad and comments by Peter Wilson made at the conference.

Part four
Who should help children learn? A natural or unnatural profession

How, what and where children are perceived to learn determine who works with them. In many majority world countries children frequently learn their skills as apprentices helping out those who are experts in whatever is considered locally important: they learn musicianship and dancing, weaving and cloth-making, herding, food preparation, and even, as the anthropologist Pamela Reynolds (1996) vividly illustrates in her Zimbabwe sample, herbalism and traditional medicine. Local contexts matter a great deal in shaping how young children learn. As Shirley Brice Heath (1983) illustrates, the immediate environment not only affects the content of what is learnt but also shapes ways of behaving and performing and presenting oneself in public.

But in the minority world, just as children inhabit separate spaces from adults, teaching young children to learn has also become largely institutionalized. It requires people who have become trained in the processes of training young children to learn, rather than experts in their own right at a particular skill or trade. In the UK, training to work with young children is split between teachers, who are trained to teach curricular subjects to children aged 3–8 or 3–11 in a school setting; and those with vocational qualifications, where the emphasis is on child development and a highly specified understanding of what children at different ages and stages can do. But a central argument of this book is that child development is a problematic discipline for work in early childhood, since it relies very heavily on entirely Western or minority world assumptions about children and how and why they learn.

When I began teaching, in a very poor district of London, one of the two reception class teachers, Doris, was an artist who was supplementing her income by teaching. She insisted the children only painted with pure paint; she took them shopping to buy pigments, and she ground the pigments and blended subtle colours with them. She was very patient with the children, and treated them very seriously as apprentices in the highly technical business of producing art. Much of the school day was taken up with the preparation for and production of paintings. Painting was an activity that had to be done with reverence. Doris fortunately had a small class, but was given the most difficult children, who could not settle elsewhere. With her they appeared knowledgeable and competent and absorbed in what they were doing. This degree of idiosyncrasy in a teacher would not be tolerated now. Even then it was questionable, but in some way Doris transmitted her conviction to the children that making colourful pictures was an utterly worthwhile activity and that she could initiate them into its mysteries. I use this example because it seems to invert our understanding of appropriate teaching in early years; a teacher imposed on children exacting standards of performance in the practice of a highly specific skill.

The position of early years training in the UK has most recently been discussed by Abbott and Pugh (1998). They review recent developments, such as the possibility of extending teacher training, competence based qualifications and early childhood studies degrees. They are optimisic about the possibility of a 'climbing frame' of qualifications, as a means of uniting the very disparate trends in early childhood services in the UK.

In Chapter 6, originally a paper commissioned for the OECD, Peter Moss reviews training for early childhood workers in six countries: Denmark, France, New Zealand, Spain, Sweden and the USA. Moss argues that training generally reflects the nature of the early childhood system as a whole. In those countries where there are more coherent systems of early childhood services, this is matched by more coherent patterns of training, and where, as in the UK and the USA, the system is fragmented and much of the provision is located in the private sector, then much emphasis is put on competency assessments and regulation as a way of convincing or otherwise coercing private providers to provide a higher standard of care, even if this interferes with profits. In other countries, such as Denmark and France, where there are widespread publicly funded and publicly provided systems, the debate about competency and regulation is conspicuous by its absence, since it is assumed that standards will automatically be high.

I draw on my own research for the DfEE to argue that recruitment into childcare training in the UK is aimed at a particular group of women with low academic achievements and from mainly disadvantaged socioeconomic backgrounds. The nature of the childcare market means that those who complete training are most likely to find employment servicing more well-off families, either as nannies, or else working in private day nurseries. Childcare students in training tend to see themselves as 'naturals', building on their personal experiences in looking after children, and see their strength as lying in their everyday practice, rather than in the acquisition and application of knowledge about children. The nature of the training, and the childcare employment that is available to them, suggest that childcare workers in the UK have little in the way of career opportunities and are disadvantaged as workers in a competitive labour market.

References

Abbott, L. and Pugh, G. (eds) (1998) *Training to Work in the Early Years: Developing the Climbing Frame.* Buckingham: Open University Press.

Heath, S. Brice (1983) *Ways with Words: Language, Life and Work in Communities and Classrooms.* Cambridge: Cambridge University Press.

Reynolds, P. (1996) *Traditional Healers and Childhood in Zimbabwe.* Athens, OH: Ohio University Press.

6

The parameters of training

Peter Moss

Education and training of early childhood workers and the structuring of the workforce itself cannot be divorced from fundamental questions about early childhood services and work, to which different countries do, and will, come up with different answers. What are the purposes of early childhood institutions and the work they undertake? How do we conceptualize or construct the early childhood worker? It is clear that there are a variety of answers to these questions, reflected for example in the very different terminologies used to describe different groups of workers in different countries – pedagogue, teacher, nursery nurse, childcare assistant and so on. Oberhuemer and Ulich (1997), in their review of staff training in the European Union (EU), propose a number of different roles or constructions for early childhood workers, related to the purposes attached to early childhood institutions:

- as schoolteachers, in those countries (such as France) that train teachers to work with children from 3 or so through into primary school, where particular emphasis is placed on close relationships between nursery and primary school, with nursery school viewed very much in terms of preparing children for compulsory schooling;
- as early childhood specialists, in those countries (such as Spain) that train teachers or other workers to work with and across the whole early childhood age range; and
- as social network experts, especially in countries (such as Denmark and Sweden) whose training schemes:

  reflect an understanding of early childhood services as a framework both for educational work with children and for social support for families where the chief caregivers work or study . . . [I]nstitutions for children of preschool age are often seen to have a multipurpose role and are viewed as an integral part of the community infrastructure, liaising where necessary with local organisations and services and open to the needs of both children and parents.

(Oberhuemer and Ulich 1997: 21)

Dahlberg *et al.* (1999) have suggested fundamentally different under-standings of the early childhood worker in relation to learning, contrast-ing: (a) the idea of the worker as a transmitter of predetermined knowledge and culture to the child, and a facilitator of the child's develop-ment, ensuring that each milestone is reached and that the child's activi-ties are appropriate to his or her stage of development; with (b) the idea that the worker is a co-constructor of knowledge and culture, both the children's and their own, in a pedagogy that 'denies the teacher as neutral transmitter, the student as passive and knowledge as immutable material to impart' (Lather 1991: 15). Other understandings or constructions of the early childhood worker include: as a substitute parent or, more precisely, as a substitute mother, providing a close, intimate relationship with the children in her charge; as an entrepreneur, marketing and selling her prod-uct and managing the institution to ensure high productivity and con-formity to standards, in short an efficient production process; and as a researcher, seeking to deepen understanding of what is going on and how children learn, through documentation, dialogue, critical reflection and deconstruction.

Similarly, the structuring of the workforce, and therefore the structuring of training, reflects the structure of early childhood education and care services. Comparing six countries with very different service structures – Denmark, France, New Zealand, Spain, Sweden and the USA. This reveals three basic options for early childhood workers, at least in centre based services:

- *the pedagogue*, trained to work with children from birth to 6, or older, in non-school settings and having an equally important but different role to the school based teacher;
- *the early childhood teacher*, trained to work with children from birth to 6 within the education system, and viewed as occupying one branch/ specialism of the teaching profession;
- *a mixture of teachers working with older children in the early childhood age range within the education system and various types of 'childcare' workers*, employed in early childhood services in the welfare system.

Denmark and Sweden, each with a well established integrated system of early childhood services, follow the pedagogue option. France and the USA have a mixture of teachers and childcare workers, operating in two systems, one welfare based and the other education based. New Zealand and Spain are in the process of working towards greater coherence, as they move from a split to an integrated early childhood services system based on the early childhood teacher trained to work across the birth to 5 or 6 years age range.

There are two other related dimensions of the structuring of the workforce. Firstly, there is the complexity of the workforce, which is in part a product of the complexity of the services as well as the different types of worker and qualifications. Denmark has a very simple structure: a highly trained pedagogue and an untrained worker operating within a limited range of centres providing full-day provision. At the other extreme, New Zealand has a complex structure due to a diversity of different types of services, some full day and some part day, and a plethora of qualifications. Irrespective of the level of complexity, however, a common issue concerns the balance between the most highly qualified workers and other less qualified or untrained workers, such staffing hierarchies being present in all countries. Should the aim be, as in school, to move towards all staff having the highest level of training? Or should there be a group or groups of lesser trained auxiliary or assistant workers? If so, what should be the mix? And how should the roles of the different workers be defined?

Secondly, there is the age range of children with which workers are trained to work. In some cases, training covers the whole early childhood age range, and no more. In other cases, it covers part of the early childhood range, and no more. In yet other cases, it extends to include children of school age, although there is an important distinction here between teachers who are trained to work with part of the early childhood age group (usually 3 and upwards) as well as primary school children, and pedagogues who, as in Denmark, are trained to work across the whole childhood age range, from birth to 16 or older. An important issue here is whether and how early childhood workers should relate to services for other age groups of children. If, for example, you have teachers who are trained to work with children from 3 or 4 to 11, does this lead to early childhood education and care services being dominated by primary school perspectives and objectives? Does it lead to a closer and more harmonious relationship between nursery schooling and primary schooling? Does it create, at the other end, increased discontinuities between services for children under 3 and services for children from 3 upwards?

The content, entry requirements, level and length of training for early childhood work will depend on answers to the sorts of questions raised above. But although countries are taking a variety of different training routes, because they have come up with different answers, there is a widespread movement towards longer and higher level basic training for early childhood workers. Denmark, Sweden, Spain and New Zealand have all settled on a post-18 training of at least three years as the main or 'benchmark' training for workers *across the early childhood age range* (that is, from birth to 5 or 6); in all these cases, this training is similar to or not much lower than training for teachers in primary schooling. In France, there have been improvements in the training for teachers in *écoles maternelles* (who are also trained to work in primary schools) to the point where these teachers now have the highest formal academic level of training of any early childhood workers. However, in both France and the USA (and in most other countries with early childhood services split between welfare and education systems), different standards and types of training are applied to workers in the welfare and education systems, with the latter usually having higher levels of training than the former. One consequence is that in split systems younger children generally have workers with lower levels of training than older children. This 'two tier' system – between welfare and education – is a feature of all countries running a split system. It is apparent in New Zealand too, where moves towards an integrated system have still not eradicated different traditions and standards of staffing in kindergartens and childcare centres, as well as in Spain where only early childhood teachers can work with children over 3 years, whereas work with children under 3 includes a mixture of teachers and another group of workers with lower levels of qualification.

What distinguishes Denmark and Sweden from the other four countries is that these Scandinavian countries have reached a stage of having a workforce across the whole early childhood age range most of whose members (60 per cent or more) are relatively well trained, with relatively satisfactory pay and employment conditions. In contrast, the other four countries have substantial numbers of early childhood workers who have low levels of training and relatively poor pay and conditions. The question of how to get *to* a well trained and well paid workforce *from* a low baseline is a major issue for a number of reasons.

First and foremost there is the problem of funding. Good training costs, and well trained staff might expect higher earnings than staff with little or no training. Without substantial and sustained public funding, as there is in Denmark and Sweden, this is a difficult problem to resolve, if not impossible: the only alternatives are either for early childhood workers to subsidize improved training through paying the costs from their own pocket and accepting below average wages for their level of education and training, or to pass the costs on to parents through increased fees. (This is also one reason why issues of standards, credentialling and regulation seem to figure so high on the US agenda, as means of cajoling a market system to improve its performance, but hardly appear on the agenda in countries like Denmark and Sweden, where public funding enables and requires uniformly high staffing standards without jeopardizing affordability.)

Secondly, there is the issue of the position of existing members of the workforce during a transition period during which new and/or upgraded training are being introduced. Are they to be left behind, fated to occupy second-class jobs for the rest of their working lives? Or is there some way to offer them access to new qualifications, in a way that makes some recognition of their existing training and work experience? Both New Zealand and Spain have attempted to offer some special arrangements for this group and it should not prove an insuperable problem, if there is commitment to improve qualifications, if there are sufficient incentives to encourage existing staff to take further training, if there is adequate resourcing to enable retraining and if there is a carefully judged timescale – although all these are, in practice, as the experience of New Zealand shows, big 'ifs'.

Thirdly, upgrading training, and increasing the status of early childhood work, may cut off an important area of employment opportunities to people (at present, mainly women) with low educational qualifications, but often with a lot of experience with children and considerable potential. In short, the process of professionalization can serve to make early childhood work more exclusive, to the potential disadvantage of many women and children. At one level, it is difficult to see how this can be avoided; early childhood training and work should not be kept at a low level for these reasons. On the other hand, there are ways in which training can be made more open and inclusive. Denmark takes a relatively mature intake of students (the average age of pedagogue students is 27) and places some weight on prior experience of work with children; there are therefore opportunities for those who did not do so well academically at school. Modular training courses, which enable workers to go at their own pace and to their own choice of level, may also be important.

Competence based qualifications might also have a role to play. However, this is a very contentious area, involving different understandings of early childhood work, with many people arguing that a competence based approach to qualifications is incompatible with a conception of the early childhood worker as a reflective and critical practitioner. As already noted the issue is very live at present in New Zealand, where it has been argued that 'the crux of the debate is whether those people who work with young children in early childhood programmes are just competent technicians or reflective teachers and practitioners' (May 1997: 71). Another protagonist in this debate in New Zealand, Margaret Carr (Carr and May 1993), has contrasted the 'competency model' with what she calls the 'teacher change model', which she defines as to do with teaching pedagogical understandings that, she argues, are an essential part of the process towards the training of practitioners who are ongoing critical thinkers as they work with children. She characterizes the differences between the two models in the way shown in Table 6.1.

Education and training play a key role in determining the make-up of the early childhood workforce. For example, if entry requirements and/ or costs are high, then it may deter less advantaged groups; this will be particularly problematic in societies with high levels of inequality and material disadvantage. Similarly, training institutions can contribute to, or challenge, the gendered nature of early childhood work. The apparently successful drive in Danish colleges to recruit male students to train as pedagogues suggests what might be possible given a strong commitment and, perhaps also, a high standard of training, which is achieving increasing public recognition and status (Ærø 1998). However, policies adopted by training institutions with respect to recruitment, for example, of more male students, are likely to be most effective if part of a wider set of

Table 6.1

Competency model	Teacher change model
Teacher education is like adding layers and each layer represents a competency clearly separated	Teacher education is about challenging preconceptions and beliefs. The earlier layers are not left intact
The domains or units are clearly separated	The units are interconnected and influence each other
The competencies are measurable against a standard that can be precisely defined	The knowledge skills and attitudes are assessed by judgements and criteria cannot always be precisely defined
The units are developed from clusters of roles or jobs in the workplace	The units are developed from reflections on the problematic, the dilemmas of teaching and content knowledge
The units are portable from one domain to another	Most units are regarded as context-specific. Contexts are not just sites for technical competency, but have historical, cultural and sociological perspectives
Learning is sequential and cumulative	Learning may be sequential but is not necessarily so. It may also be in the form of networks of knowledge – a 'weaving' model rather than a 'steps' model

policies adopted by all organizations and institutions concerned with early childhood, from government through to individual centres (Jensen 1996).

Although the preceding discussion has been about centre based workers, it is important to remember the critical role played in many countries by family day carers. Family daycare raises very difficult and acute issues concerning training. Should family day carers be excluded from early childhood training, apart from a few limited and very basic courses (such as first aid)? Should a substantial but separate system of training be developed for them, geared to their particular needs and circumstances? Or should early childhood training be developed in such a way that it can encompass family day carers, alongside centre based workers, in short creating a common, basic training for all who want to work with children, albeit with some possibility of specialization? At present, family day carers have little possibility of moving into other early childhood work, but with a common, basic training this would become more feasible, as would moving on to further training. Attention also needs to be given to the training of people who supervise and support family day carers. It has been argued that supervisors should be specially trained for this work and preferably have personal experience of working as family day carers themselves.

Continuous training for early childhood workers can take various forms. It may mean providing opportunities for workers to take basic or further training on an in-service, part-time basis. It may mean providing training on particular subjects or skills through attending 'one-off' courses or other means. It may also be thought of as a continuous process of professional development that is built into the everyday work of the service. For example, the world-famous early childhood services in Reggio-Emilia place great emphasis on 'pedagogical documentation', a process of dialogue, confrontation and critical reflection about the pedagogical work in each centre that involves early childhood workers and others. This ongoing process of deepening understanding is part of the everyday life of each centre. Time is made for documenting the pedagogical work and for discussion and reflection on that work, with the assistance of *pedagogistas*, who work with a small group of centres and the workforces in those centres to develop a critical and reflective approach to pedagogical work (Dahlberg *et al.* 1999).

However defined, continuous training raises a number of issues. How much should be made available? In Spain (and parts of Italy), over 10 per cent of staff time is set aside for work not involving direct contact with children, including training. This example led the European Commission Childcare Network (1996) to propose 10 per cent non-contact time as a 'quality target' in early childhood services. What are the costs and who should meet them, not only of the training itself but to enable early childhood workers to have time to engage in such training? More broadly, the example of the *pedagogistas* in Reggio Emilia points to the need to consider the support systems for early childhood workers – whether in centres or family day carers. What opportunities do early childhood workers have to reflect critically and in relationship to others on their work? What means are available to enable early childhood workers to identify their needs for further training? Who can help ensure that early childhood workers get that training?

In summary then, the following issues – expressed below as a series of questions – appear to be particularly important and current in relation to training and education of staff in early childhood education and care services:

• How is early childhood work understood? How is the early childhood worker constructed? How do these understandings and constructions relate to constructions of the young child and early childhood institutions? Who do we think young children are? What do we think early childhood institutions are for? Who do we think early childhood workers are? Are they technicians, transmitters of knowledge, deliverers of pre-specified programmes and precise curricula, or co-constructors of knowledge, and reflective practitioners, critical thinkers and researchers about pedagogical practice?

- Should early childhood services be split or integrated? What are the implications of the structuring of early childhood services for the structuring of early childhood work? How are these different ways of structuring services and work justified?
- How can the process of reform – transition from a split to an integrated system, and from lower to higher levels of training – best be managed in relation to the existing early childhood workforce?
- How should the workforce be constituted? Should it be based on the pedagogue, the teacher or some other model? Should there be mainly or wholly one type of worker or should there be a variety of different types of worker, including workers with different levels of training?
- With what age range of children should workers be trained to work: birth to 3, 3 to 6, birth to 6, birth to 18 or some other combination? What should be the relationship between workers in early childhood services and in services for school-age children, including schools and services providing care and recreation (for example, with respect to training, salary, job description and status)?
- What should be the basic (benchmark) level of training for early childhood work? Should it be, as is increasingly the case, a three-year (or longer) post-18 training? Is there a role for competency based qualifications or should qualifications be based mainly or wholly on college or university based courses?
- How much continuous training should early childhood workers receive? What are the purposes of continuous training? What forms of continuous training are needed? What conditions are required to facilitate continuous training?
- Who pays for training, basic or continuous? What other conditions are needed to ensure the availability and access to training? How and over what period is it possible to get to a well trained workforce from a relatively low starting point?
- What is the position of family day carers with respect to training? Should their training be part of a broad training framework for all early childhood workers? Or should it be separate? What training is needed by people working with family day carers, and for people occupying support, management, regulatory and other positions that involve working with all early childhood workers?
- What information should be routinely collected on the early childhood workforce? How should this information be collected?

Acknowledgements

This article is reprinted with kind permission from OECD.

References

Ærø, L. (1998) Training and recruiting men to work in services for young children: is it possible to move towards a more mixed-gender workforce?, in C. Owen, C. Cameron and P. Moss (eds) *Men as Workers in Services for Young Children: Issues of a Mixed Gender Workforce*. London: Institute of Education University of London.

Carr, M. and May, H. (1993) Choosing a model: reflecting on the development process of Te Whäriki, National Early Childhood Curriculum Guidelines in New Zealand, *International Journal of Early Years Education*, 1(3): 7–22.

Dahlberg, G., Moss., P. and Pence, A. (1999) *Beyond Quality in Early Childhood Education and Care: Postmodern Perspectives on the Problem with Quality*. London: Falmer Press.

European Commission Childcare Network (1996) *Quality Targets in Services for Young Children*. Brussels: European Commission Equal Opportunities Unit.

Jensen, J. (1996) *Men as Workers in Childcare Services*. Brussels: European Commission Equal Opportunities Unit.

Lather, P. (1991) *Getting Smart: Feminist Research and Pedagogy with/in the Postmodern*. London: Routledge.

May, H. (1997) *The Discovery of Early Childhood*. Auckland: Auckland University Press.

Oberhuemer, P. and Ulich, M. (1997) *Working with Young Children in Europe: Provision and Staff Training*. London: Paul Chapman Publishing.

7

Is working with young children a good job?

Helen Penn

Introduction

Jobs are not what they used to be. The labour market is undergoing fundamental transitions. It is increasingly characterized by global competitive-
ness, and switching of work sites from country to country. Working hours
have to be more flexible, working conditions fluctuate, unions are less
powerful or non-existent and skills have to be continually upgraded. For
women, particularly women with children, these new jobs are problematic (Beck and Beck-Gernsheim 1995; Betcherman 1997). As more women
enter the workforce, the availability of informal family care diminishes.
Women need help in order to cope with their domestic lives. There is an
increased demand for waged carers, jobs held primarily by women.
Christopherson comments, 'In all cases, women's changing employment
patterns within the broader labour market are at the heart of the incentives and capacities re-shaping caring services' (1997: 12). The need for
flexible workers has to be matched by flexible childcare.

The demand for childcare is mostly determined by the numbers of
women in the labour force; but the availability and types of provision are
determined by the nature of public policy: by the strength of voluntarist
traditions in caring work; the wage differentials between private and
public sectors; and so on. In the UK, childcare has not been seen as a
public service for children or for their mothers, but as an issue of labour
market supply. Unlike France, Italy or Scandinavia, where providing for
young children whose mothers work is both a children's issue and a labour
market issue, in the UK those who work in childcare typically work in
small private workplaces, or in private homes, and/or are self-employed,
or else work on a semi-voluntary or part-time basis. It has been difficult
therefore to get any kind of overview of the childcare workforce. The variety of qualifications and training routes, the modular nature of most

training and the fragmented pattern of childcare, have meant that it has been impossible to calculate the numbers who enter vocational training, or the destinations and subsequent career patterns of those who complete training. Therefore it is hard to estimate the success or efficiency, or even the usefulness, of training for childcare work in the UK. There is very little follow-up or feedback.

The research described here was carried out for the DfEE and is a small-scale qualitative study to investigate uptake on childcare training courses. It was carried out at two inner London Colleges of Further Education in 1996/97. A sample of 125 students, a group from each year of each of the childcare courses was interviewed. (These courses included BTec, Diploma and Certificate Nursery Nurse Qualifications, NVQs levels 2 and 3, and various miscellaneous or preparatory courses.) The average age of the students was 30, ranging from 16 to 52; and two thirds of the sample were from ethnic minority groups. Twelve of the students were men. Tutors and placement supervisors were also interviewed, and course documents scrutinized.

Childcare students and their attitudes to training

Students who apply for childcare courses have probably already gone through some kind of informal selection. Teachers and careers officers strongly encourage students to undertake courses that they perceive are most suited to students' ability and gender. Girl school-leavers who express an interest in working with children are likely to be advised to go in for teaching if their predicted or actual academic attainments are satisfactory, and directed towards childcare courses if they are not. Unqualified women who have spent time at home with their children and want to re-enter the workforce are perceived as lacking in confidence and are frequently encouraged to undertake childcare training, because it is regarded as building on something they can already do; look after children.

At the colleges we investigated, the students were perceived as low achievers; rare exceptions to this pattern were usually counselled out or advised to do another course. Although there was some variation between courses, the most able students being entered for the BTec and the least able being entered for certificate courses, all tutors considered almost all students ill-prepared for the courses educationally, and often emotionally.

They do not understand the academic level required or the depth or complexity of the professional task. They lack study skills.

They can't think. Some have never read a book, have never researched anything.

The amount of work is quite a shock. They don't hear however much you tell them . . . there is a general view that its work with children and so it is not hard work.

They have tremendous emotional needs within themselves in terms of their own background that have to be satisfied.

A huge number of our students are looking for self-esteem, love even, through working with children – it's a problem we have particularly with our client group of students because some of them have been so emotionally damaged or traumatized through horrendous childhoods and adolescences. Some are so hung up on the work that they think that if they love the child and hug it that is enough to make the child respond, that if they want to do it, it will happen.

Given the perceptions of a majority of the students as ill-educated and struggling, the courses are perceived by tutors to have an implicit (although not explicit in terms of course content) remedial function. The tutors' job is not merely to teach course content but to identify the nature of underachievement and try to rectify it; to bring out the coping skills of the student and help them to apply these in work situations, on the assumption that their life experiences and getting through them makes them more empathetic practitioners.

They come out at the end of the course having grown and developed. They have this amazing ability to cope with what life throws at them – it is a strength in looking after children and certainly in coping with parents in a district like this.

If they can resolve the needs of the child within them then they will be satisfied and may become good workers. If they are just doing their own journey they will be dissatisfied and drop out. If they get to the end they will have a degree of empathy and some skills.

I feel strongly about FE [further education]. FE offers people another opportunity. Our education system has not got it right for everyone and probably never will. There has to be an organization that picks people up and gives them another chance to make good. We select the people who we think can make good childcare workers. We make one or two mistakes; we are taking a risk.

[The training] is to build confidence, they have little confidence to start with. We get them to realize their skills, particularly in putting pen to paper and get what they have written to make sense. Also giving them a thorough understanding of child development, which is fundamental, but also to be responsible people and help them to be successful, which includes boring things like punctuality, reliability and honesty.

Capable people wouldn't fit in well. For instance there was a woman with several years experience . . . the standard of her work was nothing below a Merit, so I counselled her off. The courses have a remedial function – even BTec.

While the tutors viewed some students as being in need of guidance, to the point of remedial attention, students in turn regarded learning tasks as painful. Academic failure was an ever-present concern.

I grew up around here and I was told by teachers that I would amount to nothing, so my basic instinct is to show them. In five weeks I get letters after my name – NNEB [National Nursery Examination Board]. For someone who was told that they couldn't do anything, it's a BIG achievement. The primary school hit me like a sledgehammer and only when I was 16 I started reading books.

There is streaming at school. At junior school I was put into the wrong group. It is humiliating at school; for a year I sat on my own and cried, but there is no support or sympathy.

Even more capable students expressed reservations about their school experience. This student, aged 38, had only returned to studying after long avoidance of anything to do with school.

school was . . . I went to an all girls grammar school. It was very academic . . . girls were pushed into going higher but a lot of them got pregnant because they couldn't face it . . . you were put down.

There were comments about the authoritarian nature of teaching as an occupation and school as a forcing house.

School is more tense, there is more shouting, children can't do the work.

Teachers aren't allowed to show they care, because there is pressure to do so much more.

They can teach, but they don't know much about children, they don't like them.

When you get into the education system . . . it's about reduction, control, manipulation, think about what they are here to learn, not their full potential.

You need to help them to find themselves, discover themselves, not push it down their throats like at school.

These attitudes to schooling and academic learning meant that students found it less threatening to stress their practical experience over and above any theoretical knowledge. Students, especially women, felt that they all brought intrinsic talent to the job of childcare, and this talent was at least as important, if not more important than any knowledge they acquired in the course of training.

The caring bit attracted me. I feel comfortable around children and they feel comfortable around me. But now I understand more about children.

It's intrinsic to being a woman.

You can use your own experience as a mum, you feel comfortable.

All the courses in the world will never give you that feeling of knowing and working with children. That feeling comes from within, it's a good good feeling.

At home it's the women's role, that's why women do it, they are used to it.

Mothering is natural, it's an instinct, it comes naturally to most mothers.

You need to be a little bit mumsy to work with babies, it comes from within.

Whether trained or not, if you are not a natural, you can't hack it, you've got to get down to their level.

Almost all of our respondents, therefore, considered that aptitude was more important or as least as important as training. The most frequently mentioned qualities that were seen as important in caring for children – patience, kindness, understanding, tolerance, flexibility, consistency, reliability – were seen as qualities that students brought with them rather than qualities they had acquired through training.

Tied in with this view of themselves as already caring and competent women, was a view of young children as a more vulnerable group, uniquely susceptible to their influence.

They are vulnerable, I want to protect them, they depend on you. When they are older they don't.

I enjoy helping them, the first five or seven years are important to their life; it's important to help them on their way. By 9 or 10 they have learnt it all. The older children answer you back; they are harder to control.

They are more open to learning; older children are more stubborn.

We can control them more. You say don't do it and they understand. You say it to an older child and they get back at you.

Small children, they are still thinking your way, they don't know how to contradict. Older children are contrary, but small children are fruitful. They will tell you everything, they will tell you the truth.

They are easier to teach; they don't argue with you; they do whatever you say. You have some power over them. You can tell them.

It's less stressful than working with older children or adults.

At that age they are very tender and need more help to settle down.

It's very satisfying to see their achievements; forming the letter 'a'; getting out of nappies; just simple things. Not that they wouldn't have done it anyway, but with a bit of encouragement they can feel confident with you.

It's rewarding. You see their face light up. You've taught this child something.

But as well as being docile, young children are often good company.

They think differently from us the way they express themselves, the things that they do and how they say it. They confide, relate.

They perk you up, they are so lively and cheerful, they bring out the kid in you.

If personal attributes and experience matter so much, then what is the point of coming on a course? Knowledge was regarded as prescriptive and theoretical, a certain amount of facts that had to be swallowed in order to get the qualification. For many of the women with their own children, the child development that was taught was regarded as superfluous; and the theory was unrelated to practice.

It's given us lots of knowledge, health issues, diseases; without it we wouldn't know what half the words meant . . .

I learnt about safety aspects, child–adult ratios; now I understand.

I've learnt nothing new about children; no, no, no – children don't change, they're the same all over the world . . .

No, I haven't learnt anything, even the child development was repeating what you know because of your own children – like a vicious circle.

This bit of paper is not going to make me any better. I've been in childcare 22 years but I don't feel I'm learning anything new.

Essay writing is hard, those who have a lot to offer might get left out, it's the bit that isn't learnt that is important.

Studying and reading books is not going to help you understand children. If a child is upset and wants to be cuddled, or something is troubling them, you are not going to get it from reading books.

For a minority of students, mostly older women, the course had opened their eyes to the pleasure of learning:

It's good, you can never stop learning. Surely you want to extend your thinking. This course is an opportunity to go further if you want to.

There has to be a challenge, but if it was easy there would be no point – how can I gather the evidence, how can I prove what you have to do? It seemed like a mountain but I enjoyed tackling it.

Theory opens up wider knowledge: Freud, Bowlby, child development, how people perceive child development. Theory work comes in useful because it has opened up wider knowledge.

But that's the nature of childcare – new ideas, new policies and practices, the course updates and refreshes you; you can get stale, it opens you up. I've gained more knowledge, a wider perspective of childcare out there and how it functions.

We can use our brains and function and think.

I've learnt a hell of a lot on this course and I will continue to learn now.

The world of employment

All the childcare courses required placements, that is a period of time spent in a workplace during which performance is assessed. These placements were often difficult to organize, but ideally someone at the workplace would have responsibility for mentoring students. Different providers viewed the students differently. The most negative views of the students came from private and voluntary workplace settings where the students were supposed to get on with things by themselves with less back-up and support. In the schools the teachers saw the students as classroom assistants and therefore expected much less of them in the way of autonomy.

They seem to have no incentive and have not got a sense of where they are going; you have to push them – it's not to do with the course. They seem to come because it's a way of getting off the dole and they say I'll try childcare. It's a bit naïve.

(Coordinator, community nursery)

Sometimes I see them go and it's quite frightening that they could be in a job within a few months. I can only imagine they wouldn't get that far because nobody would want to employ them. About one quarter to be fair, probably about three quarters of the students we have are good.

(Nursery Nurse, private nursery)

I am disappointed with some students, they are not being assertive . . . 40 per cent would not make it. Some people do take a bit longer than others to get into it.

(Coordinator, community nursery)

Teachers made more positive comments.

It's very rare that we don't have a perfect student

(Headteacher)

I expect the percentage is really small, say 1 per cent that won't make it. Some of them do have problems with the coursework; keeping up with the academic side. Sometimes the placement may be going really well – a lot of the time we get what are called difficult students . . . but they are really marvellous here, they have got hands on.

(Teacher, special school)

Over seven or eight years of having them I have only had three who had absolutely no future.

(Teacher)

We asked students to rank the status of nursery nursing and other child-care jobs against a range of other jobs such as teaching, nursing, hair-dressing, shopwork, clerical, social work and domestic work. We asked How do you feel people think about the status of childcare as a profession?

For all the groups, local authority jobs in schools and local authority day nurseries ranked highest, and were seen to offer more status and respectability. The job that received the highest rating from most of the groups was that of a nursery nurse in a school, where, by proxy, she was seen as a teacher. Private day nursery staff were mostly ranked lower. Playgroup workers, childminders and nannies were consistently seen as having very low status on a par with domestic workers and cooks. The comments revealed that however much nursery nurses wished to convince themselves of their status, and thought that their work should be valued, in reality they understood that it was seen as a low status job by most people outside the profession.

You've got to go out in the world for very little.

A lot of people think that as a nursery nurse you are just there to wash their faces or take them to the toilet.

Anyone can get a job on a building site basically and it is the same with childcare, you're only getting the toys out and wipe bums. Its so depressing.

Parents sometimes look at you as if you were dirt.

A factory worker, something low down the scale.

Students were asked what they saw themselves doing when they finished the course. The options were: working for a local authority in a school or day nursery; working in home based care such as a nanny or childminder; working in a private-sector day nursery; going on to further education; or dropping out. Many of the respondents wanted a job in a school because the timetable fitted in with their own childcare arrangements, and because the job was perceived as more secure and responsible.

> I want to work in a nursery or a reception class. It's about the setting and the money although the money is way down the list. It's the organization really in the state sector and the people you meet.

But as noted above, there was a great deal of ambivalence about the job of nursery nurse in relation to that of teacher, and sharply perceived demarcations between them. Many considered that although they were doing a similar job to or even a better job than that of a teacher, their competence was unrecognized, for reasons of vocabulary, or because teachers themselves were ignorant of what went on.

> [What teacher's have is] access into the middle-class terminology that teachers use; it's learning the jargon to get involved in a conversation.

> We don't have to think about it, we just do it. It's the jargon. I comfort a child because he is sad, not because he is having an 'emotional crisis'

> We have heaps of experience and we want to be recognized for what we are doing. I know of people who look great on paper and then when they get to nursery they are frightened of children. One student teacher said to me, 'I suppose children having problems is like a virus in the computer'.

> Our practice is too sophisticated, a teacher with a degree can't believe what we do.

> You work hard but no result, you just see the teacher sitting back whilst you do all the work.

> There is not much real difference in the work, you get treated as an equal but you accept a lower pay.

> Teachers are not experienced, they are not mature, they can't take control.

> Parents feel more comfortable talking to nursery nurses. Teachers are a bit up there.

> In school nursery nurses are *nearly* on the level of the teacher but not quite. We do similar work. Parents treat [us] as nearly the same. If they didn't know who the teacher is and walked in they wouldn't know [the difference].

Generally, childminding and nannying were seen as unattractive options, and no one mentioned working in a playgroup as a possible career option. Nannying probably offers more job opportunities than any other aspect of childcare. But for most students, at least in inner London, nannying was not seen as a viable option, although one younger student did regard it as a possibility.

> A nanny is a good job these days; I can save a bit of money if I worked in an agency. I might do it for a bit, but not to live in. You have to live out. A single parent couldn't do it.

But this view was exceptional. Those respondents who expressed a view were negative about nannying.

> Nanny, that's even lower (than a childminder). It's like a hairdresser or apprentice hairdresser; a Saturday job, cook.

> Rich children choose a nanny because it sounds right and then they get you to do the housework.

> A nanny can do what she wants, it's a more relaxing job, not really stressful; you can sit down.

> I'd rather use a childminder than a nanny because I wouldn't want someone in the house.

> What, go on a course and become a childminder!

All students had done a placement in a private day nursery, and many were critical of what they had seen, both in terms of the practices with children, and in terms of the conditions of work.

> I went to one private day nursery . . . It was really disgusting the way they treated the children and the parents. The woman who ran it was just in it for the money. It was in an old church, they had taken the pews out and the room was divided by these big wooden screens. The day the children became 3 they went from one side to the other and did worksheets at the desks . . . they never moved from the desks except when they were taken out for antisocial behaviour or when they switched the TV on. In the other room the staff just sat and when I set something out for the children they said, 'Oh no, we don't do that here, we just watch them'.

> Private nurseries are not as good as the local authority nurseries, they do what they feel like doing.

> Government nurseries have in-service training once a term but private nurseries don't do it.

> There is bad practice in placements, mostly in private placements.

> You see very bad practice.

> Private nurseries, people seem to be totally unqualified and do the same work that a qualified person would be expected to do.

You get taken for advantage, skivvy, make the tea, do everything.

In a private day nursery you do what you are told, what she [the manager] lays down. In a local authority there are [regulations], it's laid down [properly].

Despite the low status of private day nursery work, and the criticisms of it, a sizeable group of respondents, many of whom were West African women, believed their future prospects lay in opening their own day nurseries. A minority of students, mainly those on BTEC courses saw themselves going on to further education, as teachers, social workers, psychologists or nurses, or in one case law. However the scanty evidence from college returns suggests that few do so.

For those who only managed to complete a certificate course, and were not accepted even for a nursery nurse course, because they were too young, or immature or lacked basic skills, working for an agency as a nanny or au pair or in a play centre were the only options.

the NNEB, if I didn't get on to it then maybe apply for a nanny agency, or work in a play centre

In answer to questions about long-term ambitions, many of the respondents were vague and said they did not know and could not imagine far ahead. For others, gaining a qualification and finding a job, any job, was the limit of their ambition.

just working

working full-time, well established as a nursery nurse . . .

working in a nursery

I've achieved what I set out to do; get a qualification.

Some of the women saw their future in domestic terms – predictably, given their view of themselves as natural mothers.

my own family, part-time work

married with another child. I'd like to be a kept woman. Years ago it was respectable, over the years that has changed, now that sort of role is rare, it's totally turned about.

to be a good mother and give a good education to my child

with children of my own

my own place, my own home

have a job, I hope it won't be that long, have a settled life, be married.

a lady of leisure but with children. I would love not to work. As women we've all got full-time jobs at home as well.

A handful of students had a long-term view of their careers, and saw themselves succeeding either having obtained another qualification, or in terms of management.

> I want to be more than a nursery nurse, I'm not content to sit on the bottom rung.

> I might change fields, for example police child protection, but you have to work in the police for five years in order to get into the unit.

> I'll be in management in a child-related career.

Despite being critical of placements in private nurseries, the most popular long-term career move was seen as starting up in business and opening a nursery. A majority of those from ethnic minority backgrounds, and almost all of those from West Africa, wanted to open a private nursery. Sometimes their bad experiences of placements were seen as an incentive to do better.

> I want to open my own nursery in Canada or America.

> own nursery in own country [Ghana]

> own nursery, but I'll need a management course before then.

> my own nursery in Ireland.

> a franchised nursery chain in the Cayman islands.

> my own nursery in Jamaica.

> an entrepreneur with my own nursery.

> I don't care where I am but in my own nursery

> own nursery, with my teaching experience [as a certificated teacher in Nigeria]

> a private nursery, they have a negative outlook, I'd like to make it more positive.

> I'm at a private day nursery. I am not really happy where I am. I'd like to open a day nursery and run it properly.

> I would like to have my own place. There are so many private nurseries and I know I could do so much better. All I need is the collateral to be able to go and get on with it.

Without any kind of follow-up, it is impossible to tell if these ambitions were realistic or fantasy. In this country collateral for buildings is hard to obtain, and the informant quoted above had tried very hard to obtain it. Certainly there is a rapidly expanding, and relatively unregulated, childcare market in many majority world countries (Penn 1997b).

We also asked the providers whether they themselves would recommend childcare as a job to a young person just starting out. Most of our respondents were not encouraging about the prospects of childcare workers and considered that nursery nurses if possible should aim to become teachers.

> I do say to the young students, especially if they are good, 'Why don't you go on and do teaching?' But they are fed up with having no money; they want to break out on their own. They say, 'I want to work and get money', so I say, 'Well do it for a couple of years and then think again.'
>
> (Nursery Nurse, school)

> No [to nursery nursing]. Maybe as a stepping stone to something else but it doesn't tend to be that without further training. People tend to stay here, they have been here a long time, especially the support staff. There are no career prospects or no promotion prospects within it.
>
> (Teacher)

> I don't know about a young girl, I would say maybe they would like to go into nursery teaching. The job I do is more suitable for a mum. If I would have gone into this career when I didn't have children I would have gone into teaching. I am lucky because I have had a partner to support me. If I didn't have a partner maybe I would have gone further.
>
> (Playgroup Supervisor)

Others considered that childcare was a viable career, providing the young person was ambitious.

> Yes, if you want it to be. You can move right through the hierarchy within the nursery and beyond if that is what you want.
>
> (Coordinator, workplace nursery)

> Yes if you are doing different things. I don't think anyone can stay in the same place for years and years. You need to set a goal and move on. There are opportunities. I will be a manager after three years experience.
>
> (Deputy Manager, private day nursery)

> Yes, there is a career ladder here. I've been [on] it for some years now. The role of the nursery officers has changed so much.
>
> (Deputy Manager, local authority day nursery)

> This is a good company to work for. They are keen to promote internally. They prefer to appoint from inside, somebody they know. I was promoted to third in charge within a year.
>
> (Nursery Nurse, private day nursery)

Despite the fact that they said there were good career opportunities, all of the providers quoted above said they themselves did not want to stay in

childcare work. The younger ones saw their future as essentially domestic.

> lady of leisure – no joking. I should be so lucky. I'm just trying to think
> about how to get to the end of the week. It's hard enough trying to
> think about getting married in two years time. Hopefully not going
> down or back into being a nursery nurse. It can be very stressful out
> there on the floor.
>
> > (Nursery Nurse, private day nursery)
>
> I'd like to have a family. I wouldn't especially want to have a family
> in London. Not bothered about working or carrying on working, I'd
> like to be at home with the children. I think it's something I can
> always go back to.
>
> > (Nursery Nurse, private day nursery)

Summary

Despite a plethora of new vocational qualifications, and a variety of work
and study routes to become qualified (Beaumont 1995), and all kinds of
competency based assessments in the workplace, childcare in the UK,
more often than not, tends to be a short-term and unsatisfactory career, in
which there is a considerable mismatch between hopes and aspirations,
and the reality of the workplace. A year after this study was completed, we
tried to trace those students who were due to qualify, to see whether or not
they had finished their course and obtained the work they wanted. Out of
the forty students we contacted, only two, both men, had full-time per-
manent posts. Of the rest, those who were working were mainly doing
temporary work in private nurseries. Another follow-up study has also
produced similar results (Foster 1996).

The research suggests that childcare work is seen as intrinsically a
woman's job – despite the trickle of male students – and draws on the
attributes and skills that women already see themselves as possessing,
rather than requiring the acquisition of new skills and professional com-
petences. This limited and feminized view of their work by childcarers
both reflects and is likely to contribute to poor conditions of employment
and limited career mobility. This view is also borne out by recent studies
in Australia (Burton and Petrie 1998) and New Zealand (Wylie *et al.* 1997)
which in this respect have similar labour market traditions to the UK.

Does this impoverished status matter either for the childcare workers or
for the children they care for? For many childcarers, caring for children
may carry intrinsic rewards, but rarely does it have any kind of long-term
future. Many, if not most, childcare workers are likely to have been
recruited from low achieving and often disadvantaged backgrounds, and
neither the level and content of the training, nor the work itself, much of
it home based or in small private-sector workplaces, is likely to change

their status very much. They do what poorer women have always done; that is service those who are wealthier and more successful. In that sense it is an exploitative arrangement. In terms of the workforce profiles needed for the new century, that is as flexible workers with continually upgraded skills and qualifications that enhance transferability across different kinds of jobs, childcare workers remain disadvantaged.

These findings suggest that within the UK, without further intervention in social policy, conceptions of work in this sector will remain narrow and gendered, that women carers' pay and conditions of work and career mobility will continue to be limited, and their lack of voice will continue to be conspicuous by its absence. If professionalization is a goal for those working with young children – and there are publicly expressed doubts about whether it should be (McKnight 1995) – common sense would suggest that the more lively and enquiring the workforce, the better the support they receive, and the more training they have, the better the outcomes for the children for whom they care. The new 'climbing frame' of qualifications linking diverse training courses together through transferable credits and work based competency assessments is a possible way forward (Abbott and Pugh 1998) although, as this section suggests, any approach to training is also dependent on a more coherent view of early childhood services.

Acknowledgements

This research was carried out with the assistance of Susan McQuail, who also provided valuable help and comments.

References

Abbott, L. and Pugh, G. (1998) *Training to Work in the Early Years: Developing the Climbing Frame.* Buckingham: Open University Press.
Beaumont, G. (1995) *Review of 100 NVQs/SVQs.* London: DfEE.
Beck, U. and Beck-Gernsheim, E. (1995) *The Normal Chaos of Love.* Cambridge: Polity.
Betcherman, G. (1997) Organizational change and its implications for employment and human resource development: an overview paper. Paper presented at the OECD/Ministry for Employment and Solidarity, Paris, December 1997.
Burton, J. and Petrie, A. (1998) Calculating the costs of care: Exploring issues of gender and work in the Australian Childcare Industry, unpublished paper.
Christopherson, S. (1997) *Childcare and Elderly Care: What Occupational Opportunities for Women?*, occasional papers no. 27. Paris: OECD; Labour Market and Social Policy.
Foster, M. (1996) Changing employment patterns for qualified nursery nurses: a potential difficulty for quality in children's learning. Unpublished paper given at the Learning for Life Triennial Conference, Warwick University, 1996.

McKnight, J. (1995) *The Careless Society: Community and its Counterfeits*. New York. Basic Books.

Penn, H. (1997a) *Childcare as a Gendered Occupation*. London. DfEE Research Report no. RR 23.

Penn, H. (1997b) *Review of Early Childhood Services in Developing and Transitional Countries*. Report prepared for Department of International Development. (Copies available from the author.)

Wylie, C., Podmore, V., Murrow, K. and Meagher-Lundberg, T. (1997) *Childcare/Early Childhood Education in a Labour Market Context in Australia, Sweden and the United Kingdom*, occasional paper 1997/2. Wellington: Labour Market Policy Group, Department of Labour, New Zealand.

Part five
Children as participants

Recent work in sociology has stressed the importance of regarding children as social actors; participants in, rather than recipients of, the social world around them (Qvortrup *et al.* 1994; James *et al.* 1998). From this perspective children, even very young children, are an important constituent and self-referent group in society, but are oppressed by other more powerful groups who have organized the social world to suit themselves. The concept of 'children's rights' is an attempt to redress the powerless position in which children find themselves, and the United Nations Convention on the Rights of the Child, although in some ways problematic, has been an important rallying point for those who consider children's interests to be neglected.

Part of this sociological approach to childhood is to try to consider events from the point of view of the child. This is now a significant area for research. For instance the Economic and Social Research Council (ESRC) in the UK has sponsored a major programme of research, 'Children from 5–16, which attempts to research childhood as a lived experience – what do children say about the situations in which they find themselves, and what opportunities do they have to influence such situations? This UK initiative is paralleled by others, for example in Finland, Germany and France.

This sociological perspective sits uncomfortably with a psychological approach. Psychologists for the most part look at children from an adult perspective; devising theories about how and why they function in the way that they do, how they are developing, and whether they are developing and learning in predicted and predictable ways. Much of the preschool literature is devoted to explaining these 'ages and stages'; observing children to place them on some notional continuum of learning, and planning and manipulating their environment in order to extend their learning so that they pass smoothly on to the next anticipated stage of their development. As Rose (1990) has pointed out, psychology has had a powerful normalizing function. The sociology of childhood school tries to avoid making assumptions about children's developmental progress. Instead, they argue that children themselves necessarily provide new and insightful comments on their own condition.

The next three chapters are all by sociologists whose work lies within this sociology of childhood tradition and who are critical of conventional approaches to working with young children.

Chris Holligan offers a challenging perspective on adult activities in a nursery. He uses the ideas of Foucault, who was Professor of History and Systems of Thought at the College de France, and whose powerful theorizing has influenced sociologists, philosophers and historians, although he has often been underrated in the UK. Foucault is one of a group of mainly French postmodern thinkers. He was a profound and meticulous scholar, and his analysis of Greek and Latin texts, especially the concepts of the body and the self, as the foundation for contemporary ethical thinking is widely praised for its contribution to intellectual history. His insistence on the importance of scrutiny and 'deconstruction' of the ideas and assumptions that govern everyday events, and in particular institutional life, are more controversial, but his stature is such that they deserve serious consideration. The group of researchers he assembled around him in Paris in the 1970s included a group examining everyday life in crèches, subsequently written up by Mozère under the title *Le Printemps des Crèches* (Mozère 1992). The French system of crèches is medically run and under the jurisdiction of the Ministry of Health, and the focus on bodily well-being is greater than one would find in many other countries; nevertheless the insight that bodily self-care and control of the body is an important face of institutional life for children is a valuable one. In one sense it is very obvious that adults exercise powerful control over children's movements, governing when and how they are allowed to use their bodies, what clothes they wear, how clean they must be, when they can go to the toilet, when and where and what they can eat, when they must sit still, when they are allowed to go outside, what they can do when they are outside, and generally how they comport themselves. Children may be able to exercise some choices in self-care, but the framework in which they exercise choice is essentially limited. The question is whether and how these limits are significant.

Holligan uses this kind of Foucaultian deconstruction as a basis for investigating nursery education. Based on his research in a number of nursery schools in Scotland, he shows how the underlying discourse of nursery staff emphasizes the surveillance and control of children's movements and their bodily functions, as an insidious means of shaping their behaviour. From this perspective, the 'observation' techniques that have been regarded by early years practitioners as a means of interpreting the behaviour and learning strategies of individual children could be perceived by the children themselves as their being 'watched', a further notch of bodily control, much as a prison guard might watch prisoners! Such an analysis is likely to be very unfamiliar to, and even resented by, those working in early childhood, but Holligan argues that, like other important sociological or philosophical insights, these ideas may offer us a worthwhile tool for examining nursery practice, particularly in the increasingly important context of children's rights.

Harriet Strandell tried to understand the concept of play from a children's perspective. She carried out ethnographic research in nurseries in Finland, and concluded, as Woodhead does from a rather different perspective, that the conventional notion of 'play' has a belittling quality; it is tolerated as a special childish activity in which children indulge. She suggests that 'play' is often a form of subversiveness; a way in which children can reassert their own control over a situation in which adults are exerting their power. This implies a solidarity between children against grown-ups, a perspective also emphasized by Corsaro (1985), and indeed by many children's writers as diverse as Robert Louis Stevenson, E. Nesbit and Roald Dahl.

Strandell also suggests that adults continually try to interpret and inject meaning into children's actions, whereas children may be much more casual than adults suppose and cruise between events and activities. Adults find such apparently arbitrary behaviour uncomfortable; in adult terms, a child who concentrates and is absorbed in an activity is learning, and one who flits between activities is failing to learn. But Strandell's point is that, as outsiders, nursery staff do not *know* what is going on between children or what they are thinking, yet they feel obliged to provide explanations.

Finally in this section, Priscilla Alderson, whose expertise is in the field of ethics and medical and social interventions, uses the United Nations Convention on the Rights of the Child as a framework for considering how adults interact with young children. She argues that even very young and inarticulate children have a point of view and feelings that should be respected, irrespective of the situations in which they find themselves. She offers a critique of conventional beliefs about the helplessness of babies and very young children, and argues that any decision making on their behalf has to take their rights fully into account.

References

Corsaro, W. (1985) *Friendship and Peer Culture in the Early Years*. Norwood, NJ: Ablex.

James, A., Jenks, C. and Prout, A. (1998) *Theorizing Childhood*. Cambridge: Polity Press.

Mozère, L. (1992) *Le Printemps des Crèches*. Paris: Harmattan.

Qvortrup, J., Bardy, M., Sgritta, G. and Wintersberger, H. (eds) (1994) *Childhood Matters: Social Theory, Practice and Politics*. Aldershot: Avebury Press.

Rose, N. (1990) *Governing the Soul; The Shaping of the Private Self*. London: Routledge.

8

Discipline and normalization in the nursery: the Foucaultian gaze

Chris Holligan

Introduction

The purpose of this chapter is to indicate how concepts of child-centred nursery education look when subjected to the critical gaze of Michel Foucault. The basis for this analysis consists of three case studies of teaching staffs' perceptions of children learning values. Sociologically orientated critiques of the nursery do however exist. For example Hartley (1993) utilizes Weber's ideas, coming to the conclusion that professional practice 'equips' children for life in post-industrial bureaucratic organizations.

Foucault (1977) argues that power can be seen positively as something that is productive of realities, domains of objects and rituals of truth. Persons and the knowledge that may be gained about them belong to this production. According to Merquior, for Foucault, 'every knowledge, even science, is a tool of the will to power . . . particular branches of knowledge obey strategies of domination, in fact 'invent' their objects so that man and earth can be better controlled' (1991: 146). In her critique of the discourse of child-centred education, Walkerdine argues that, 'the whole pedagogy itself is designed to permit the possibility of certain things considered "natural" and "normal" to children. The practices are set up to produce certain responses, based on a theoretical edifice which defines them as natural. Their presence, therefore becomes normal, their absence pathological' (1986: 67).

In analysing any structure of domination Foucault treats power, knowledge and the body as interrelated concepts. Human bodies are produced to become 'docile bodies' as a result of corrective regimes of discipline. Modern power aims to control individuals by exerting influence over 'the soul'. Its pervasive character directs attitudes, discourses, learning processes and everyday living. The modern, post-Enlightenment forms of control succeed through their 'gentleness'; normalization is achieved by processes of activity that are subjected to surveillance.

A technology of power is embedded within hierarchical social relationships that demand domination and subordination. To achieve its goal, power demands an intimate knowledge of its objects, which it can then set about 'producing'. The human sciences, for Foucault, are not neutral bodies of knowledge; instead they support the process of subjugation. Discipline is 'an art of the body' to render it obedient. Human sciences such as developmental psychology focus on details, movements and gestures and through such an atomistic approach try to alter 'the soul'. Timetables, daily routines and teaching–learning strategies establish such 'docile bodies'. Such disciplinary methods conspire to 'normalize' the individual whose behaviour is then subjected to surveillance to ensure normalization. As a post-structuralist, Foucault (1977) describes how the 'humanity' of modern kinds of governance reposition citizens into tighter forms of self-regulation through their discursive practices.

Power and knowledge

Modernity is constituted by the liberal–humanistic paradigm; knowledge, for example, is positioned as distinct from power and described as the disinterested search for truth. Power is conceived as abstract, a 'thing-like' entity monopolized by some institutions who then exercise it (oppressively) over others. Such a view leads to the conclusion that power distorts knowledge. Thus 'truth' and 'knowledge' are only possible under conditions where power is absent or not being exercised (Lyotard 1984). Foucault refers to such powerful discourses as 'regimes of truth', for example medicine, psychiatry and other kinds of disciplinary knowledge including educational psychology; professional discourses contain hidden politics. Foucault argues that truth, through its relationship with knowledge, is itself a discourse with powerful effects: 'Modern humanism is therefore mistaken in drawing this line between knowledge and power. Knowledge and power are integrated with one another and there is no point in dreaming of a time when knowledge will cease to depend on power, this is just a way of reviving humanism in a utopian guise' (Foucault 1980: 52).

For Foucault truth is produced by complex processes. What *counts* as true is what matters for Foucault. He sees it as being produced under the control of large institutions such as universities, schools and the media, who also organize its diffusion and consumption. Power is diffuse, but nevertheless real and is manifested in a network of social relationships. 'Discipline' is seen as a specific technology of power whereby individuals are both an 'object of power' and 'an instrument through which power is exercised'.

Discourses and power–knowledge

The focus of power–knowledge formations lies in discourse and the discursive practices through which 'regimes of truth' are constructed, thus:

> Discourses are . . . about what can be said, and thought, but also about who can speak, when, where and with what authority. Discourses embody meaning and social relationships, they constitute both subjectivity and power relations . . . Thus, discourses construct certain possibilities for thought. They order and combine words in particular ways and exclude or displace other combinations.
>
> (Ball 1990: 17)

For example, the discourse of educational psychology contributes to the constitution of the category of 'special educational need' and the discourse of psychometrics legitimates the labelling of persons as being of 'low' or 'high' intelligence; discourses constitute the objects about which they refer. Normally one is unaware of a discourse as such, instead it is a 'given' and not questioned. It helps produce particular lines of reasoning that are socially conventional and defines what issues are legitimate or what questions are meaningful. So a discourse can be said to 'speak' but we don't hear it as discourse. Such an absent presence is particularly powerful, as it gives an impersonal authority to those who speak about things; power acts through the discourse that they use to speak. Educational discourses of knowledge and morals seek to marginalize the body as merely a site of physical exercise and punishment. For Foucault however modernity involves the regulation of life through the body. Modern discipline asserts power over and through the body with the aim of producing 'docile bodies' and 'obedient souls'.

In disciplining the body persons as subjects become governable; bodies are measured, categorized and normalized. Macdonell argues that:

> the techniques of discipline do not torture or brand the body to make it signify. Instead, they distribute bodies to various places and activities. They prescribe the bodies movements, impose norms on its activity, watch out for any deviation, and exclude the non-conforming. In these ways the body is connected with processes of meaning: it is tied to an identity, a level of ability, the specification of a job.
>
> (1991: 109)

Persons are, in the Foucaultian scheme of things, constructed through knowledgeable discourses related to the exercise of power. Subjective experience is an important aspect of our psychological identity and is argued to be socially constituted by factors that individuals internalize unconsciously. For Foucault confession does not emancipate; it is rather a discourse whose power constrains one uniquely.

Observation, normalization and examination

For Foucault the exercise of modern disciplinary power is captured in the panopticon, the nineteenth-century Benthamite design for a prison. Here individual cells encircle a central observation tower. Each individual is isolated from the others and constantly observed, but they don't see who observes them or know if they are being observed. So they learn an awareness that they might be observed and begin to alter their behaviour to what they think is expected. Disciplinary power functions through the technologies of observation and surveillance. Disciplinary power separates, analyses and differentiates; its categorizations are embodied in records and results. Examination or assessment results place individuals in a field of surveillance – they become objects for a branch of knowledge and therefore a site for the exercise of power. Normalization facilitates the production of evaluative discursive practices that define individuals; a person is 'good at' and is 'poor at' or has 'developmental needs'. Foucault talks about this 'normalizing gaze' as a system of surveillance imposed on individuals as they are encouraged to show and express their 'needs' to others. The power of normalization, it is argued, resides in its apparent neutrality and therefore its objectivity. This normalization operates at a younger and younger age, not only for children with 'special needs', but for all children through baseline assessment regimes. They have to be kept under close surveillance to see how normal they are becoming.

The research study: values in the nursery

Research background

The research enquiry was conducted during the 1990s in a Scottish town and involved three case studies of nursery schools. One was located in an affluent middle-class suburb and the others were both based in areas of multiple social deprivation. Each of the two latter communities has received substantial funding for many years from the European Social Fund aimed at achieving community regeneration. Teaching staff in these nurseries took part in semi-structured interviews on an individual basis. We attempted to follow Burgess (1993) and adopt a 'conversational mode' for the interviews. These data were analysed qualitatively (Bulmer 1984; Bryman and Burgess 1994).

Since the project was set up to investigate staff's perceptions of 'values in the nursery', the in-depth interviews addressed this theme: in what forms can Foucault be 'found' in the nursery?

Training the body

Poor area nurseries

The structure of producing normalized individuals into the social body is particularly transparent in professional practice. For example, in the nurseries in poor communities accounts taken as representative by staff of their approach include:

> During their time at nursery I hope to make them more aware of themselves socially and physically in particular through toilet training and eating habits.

Normalizing deviance (discipline as 'corrective' not punitive) constitutes an intrinsic part of practice and one also finds evidence of a 'discourse of derision' against some parents, thus:

> They lack a lot of stimulus in other areas of development and their play is below the norm in most cases because of poor parenting. So right from the beginning we have to start and train in various aspects like sand and water, building materials . . . we are aware that the kind of opportunity does not exist in the home in the majority of cases.

> A particular child came in with no values of how a book should be treated, it was something to be tossed around and played with.

Aggressive bodies must also be regulated:

> Many are noncooperative, very selfish and when it comes to values if you can't get what you want you just punch somebody or bite them or kick them until you get it or just grab if off somebody.

Both the linguistic and domestic behaviours are subject very closely to regulative norms:

> A great many children have speech problems and attend therapy on a regular basis and have great language deprivation.

The power–knowledge expertise of the speech therapist assists in the process of legitimatizing the exercise of professional power over those who might otherwise become modern day lepers. As Foucault might argue, to ensure the continued effectiveness of its panopticon system of surveillance the state has to gain access into the private lives of its citizens; domestic practices are evaluated as revealing a private deviance:

> Not one child was able to say that this was a cup and that a saucer. It was a mug and a plate. And on investigation with the parents they said they never used cups or saucers, just mugs.

Once homes have been monitored through the child's behaviours as a 'window' then disciplinary power may extend to re-educating parents:

> We have brought parents in and discussed how to go about acquiring the skills the children are going to need in school and discuss

with them in the home. Often when I've asked them to carry out a certain programme or taken a book home to encourage speech development they have done it and come back with it every day. And that's been quite good and helpful because they didn't know how to do that.

Enhancing professional power–knowledge in relation to parents may entail locating practices in the sphere of their private leisure interests, thus:

One way of really getting in with parents is when we go swimming, that is a good opportunity because parents have to be with their children swimming so they see what we do with the children in the water.

Producing 'docile bodies' beyond the normal boundaries of the classroom is reinforced through the transference of techniques of disciplinary observation to the primary caretakers.

Rich area nursery
Foucault argues that the production of docile bodies can occur in different ways depending upon normative rules that structure institutional contexts. An interesting example, in the rich area nursery, concerns the physical appearance of a Chinese child whom the others perceived as 'looking different':

The wee Chinese girl that you saw this morning well they asked, 'Who's she?', because she stuck out as being a bit different. They wanted to know who she was, she looked different, I think that's as far as it went.

Regimes that regulate and reinforce the physical interactions of children were often referred to by staff, thus

Taking a turn with making the chocolate crispies that's encouraged, [we say] you can make one, but if it's not your turn you can wait.

Also, as self-regulation is central to the successful achievement of a 'microphysics of power' staff try to avoid 'interventions' in children's play, thus

It's quite seldom that we have to intervene. At the beginning these rules are established that there are only five people allowed in the house or five allowed in the bricks corner.

The peer group assist staff in the creation of corrective discipline in the case of non-docile bodies, thus,

He was quite a difficult child, the same as the one we have this year, he's boisterous, wild. Our kids tend to pick up on anything that goes wrong. The more isolated cases stand out. They know they are not socially normal and if it involves that child they will tell you, but they wouldn't have told you if it had been anybody else.

Group pressures of this kind were not reported on by staff in the poor area nurseries, but they did report on high levels of physical strategies used by children to exert pressure. Creating docile bodies would seem to follow non-identical routes amongst different social classes. Staff make assumptions about social class:

> Basically we assume that the values that we are driving home are also being driven home at home. Daddy is not in prison for six months as he might be in another area; we don't have that here.

Foucault's term 'docile bodies' includes within it a psychological meaning with power acting through and upon 'the body' to engineer the modern self. Many examples from staff reveal their wish to have the children integrate 'as bodies' with other children socially, thus:

> One wee boy is very, very quiet, very observant really, taking in all the rest of the goings on in the nursery, but up until now he's not really tried to integrate at all, but recently he's began to accept himself ever so slightly and I gave a bit of encouragement

Children perceived as being 'shy children' are brought into the body of the peer group to 'assist their development'. Unlike the children in the poor area nurseries these children seem to have more thoroughly incorporated social rules:

> We don't really have that problem of having to sort out dropping litter. In fact that was one thing that came up on the trip – the woman in the café said, 'What well behaved children!' And Elia said, 'Is it noticeable?', and she replied, 'Yes, other groups come in here and we've got litter up to there.' The same with the garden; we seldom have to shout, 'Do not stand all over that'; if a ball goes into the plants most will come and say, 'The ball's in the bushes', and not trample their way into it.

As in the other nurseries the processes of baking and making things requires learning of routine physical details:

> When they are baking they must wash their hands and not lick the spoon every time they stir the mixture. If they are doing jelly or crispies there's a guide book for them to follow so they know to wash their hands. When they go to the toilet they know to wash their hands so that they don't pick up germs.

Rules about tools must be obeyed:

> With scissors and simple tools we don't want them to hurt themselves. We try to teach them the correct way to use the tools provided other than as weapons.

Bodies can pose a threat to order and must sometimes be physically partitioned off from the community, thus:

Sometimes you get a child who will not say he's sorry and that is a problem. What I say is, 'Well you'll just have to sit on a chair until you're going to say you're sorry.

Confession, recording and discipline

Poor area nurseries
Confession of subjective experience is a key part of the hidden discourse of professional practice, which for Foucault aids self-regulation as well as adding to the effectiveness of education's 'emancipatory' practices:

> Even when they are upset we don't always know why they are upset because they haven't got the vocabulary to tell us. By the time they leave us after a year that is greatly improved.

A process of 'checking' and observational assessment constitutes a major element of the work of teaching staff. For Foucault, recording and assessment is an integral part of the structures of domination. For example, 'checking' in nursery differentiates amongst a range of behaviours and attitudes; such as suspected cases of child abuse through to documenting progress in curricular areas:

> We may find a child is being difficult in the nursery or is unusually weepy. There may be underlying reasons for it and we have to check carefully.

At times knowledge and power would appear to be shared with parents, particularly when official agencies are involved.

> I feel records must be shared with parents. If I have to write to the Reporter of the Children's Panel I feel parents have the right to know what I'm saying about their child.

Interestingly however the code of medical practitioners was said to prohibit the sharing of child assessments with teachers, and sometimes with parents. The teacher felt that 'issues of confidentiality' may interfere with 'planning for the child'.

Walkerdine (1986) draws attention to the discourse of child development as involving the imputation of universal biologically inescapable needs to the child. Children's putative needs are at the heart the recording and observational processes. Typical rationales in the nurseries include:

> The curriculum is adjusted to a child's particular needs. You are aware he's an individual with special emotional and physical needs especially at a crisis time.

> Sharing incidents in the family helps us to meet the needs of the child, if we understand the background and the reasons for certain behaviours then we can do something about it.

Needs are sometimes conflated with values. In using the local authority's official 'Children Profile' form (it has sections for recording progress in social, emotional and cognitive domains) a teacher explained how:

> We assess where the child is at, what kinds of attitudes, what kinds of sharing of experiences, of feelings is he ready for or not. Can he express himself, negotiate with peers and adults? These are all hidden values and they have to be assessed whether the child is capable of doing that or not.

If explicit 'confession' is inadequate as a means of getting to know the child then activities can be arranged to ensure the teacher can gaze into 'the soul' of the learner:

> A very therapeutic activity is clay. How they play with it is an indicator that maybe something is troubling them and if that comes out it is an indicator that maybe we should be asking some questions here . . . some conflicts in their heads about what is happening at home.

Rich area nursery

Confession is sometimes sought from children by staff about their social attitudes and values; attempts to secure confessions can fail:

> When we initially got that doll a lot of children would not play with it and we asked them why. I don't think they said because it was black. They just said we don't like it, we just don't like it. We asked them why and we really didn't get anywhere.

Staff may seek confessions as a way of understanding children's relationships and in the following case reinforce the value of 'public confession'. In this situation a third child tried to be part of a group of two children playing together:

> They were reluctant to include her and one of them started whispering to the other one and I wasn't sure whether it was a whisper that had anything to do with her so I spoke to Gemma and said, 'What was it that you were whispering to Ann?' And she told me what she had said and I felt it was reasonable to say, 'It's not really nice for the person who's not hearing what you're saying because they think you are saying something about them. You shouldn't really be doing that . . . you should share things that you want to say to people.'

Surveillance as assessment

Poor area nurseries

Assessment as an integral part of preschool education is included in the recent Scottish Office curriculum framework for 'children in their Preschool year' (Scottish Office 1997). Interestingly, the visibility of the learning experience to the professional gaze is highlighted in that document through the choice of colour photographs to record and present examples of 'good practice' in the nursery. One particular photograph reinforces Foucault's position. A member of staff is sitting down looking intensely while writing observational assessments about a child playing on a ladder. Within the nurseries staff posit assessment as central to their professional task as educators.

> Constantly the nursery staff are observing. It is the most crucial part of the nursery work and when to observe, how to observe and how long to observe takes time . . . Observations are very much part of the training of nursery nurses and teachers at college.

In line with Foucault's claim that the power of discursive practices help to constitute learners as both subjects and objects of knowledge, staff do not perceive themselves as 'imposing things' on children. In each child's 'little file' staff put their assessment entries:

> If there is a particularly good piece of play going on it would be noted in the file so at the Parents' Consultation Day I can say, 'On such and such a day your child did a very nice piece of work' . . . So most of our day is spent observing, we only interact with the child when the child's needs demand it. We don't impose things on the child.

Observational assessment helps regulate the direction that docile bodies in the making are encouraged to follow, in time–space zones created by staff (see King 1978; Hartley 1993):

> We've got to know whether in fact a child uses all areas of the nursery and if a child isn't using them we ask why . . . we then work out some kind of strategy to see that he completes all areas of the nursery. We would encourage the child to be somehow directed into these areas to make sure he's experiencing the whole curriculum.

The regional (governmental) observational profiles establish a uniformity of approach from staff and prescribe a focus:

> The Profile heightening your awareness of what you are looking for. It's easy to get working away and stop thinking. I feel the Profile helps you to keep questioning your approach to the children. It gives you a compact all round picture of the child's development, covering everything you want to be looking for in the child.

The science of developmental psychology as a powerful discursive practice is, as postmodernists argue, clearly involved in the creation of the 'normal child', who becomes 'good at' what are legitimated as being in keeping with required ideals of the self.

Rich area nursery
According to Foucault, the panopticon as an apparatus for surveillance is to be understood as:

A diagram of power reduced to its ideal form . . . it is a figure of political technology that may and must be detached from any specific use
. . . It is prevalent in its applications . . . Whenever one is dealing with
a multiplicity of individuals on whom a task or a particular form of
behaviour must be imposed, the panoptic schema may be used.

(1977: 205)

What form does the panopticon gaze take in the rich area? Promoting
social participation was claimed to be important:

I noticed he was lacking self-confidence so I encouraged him to join
in. I would say that is one of the main things we do.

Evaluative observations may sometimes involve sociological inference:

In the main the parents give the children the best of whatever they
can materially, or giving time in the home in things that will encourage [learning].

As far as trips are concerned we did start taking children along to Safe-
ways to shop. But we gave it up as in the back of my mind it wasn't
an experience they were deprived of . . . That also applied to the
library. There are a lot of things that we don't do because the parents
do it.

Some observations entail direct disciplinary interventions, thus

Sometimes you've got to nip that in the bud so that it doesn't blos-
som into something else.

You take them aside and just speak to them and say, 'Would you like
that done to you?' Say it was when someone had been hit hard and
they answer, 'No'. So then you ask, 'Well why did you do that?'

Formalized assessment procedures can be called upon to help staff cope
with those children who appear to differ considerably from the norm.

We use outside advice when we have a child who's handicapped in
some way with learning difficulties, like an autistic child . . . Then an
educational psychologist comes and assesses that child mainly to see
what school is best for them.

Discussion

An article in the *Independent* (2 April 1998) entitled 'Electronic CVs for
every citizen' outlined that the Labour Party was considering CVs that
would give everyone a number 'from the cradle to the grave'. Information
technology is clearly facilitating further the state's knowledge of our life-
span if details of our 'cultural fingerprints' become mandatory. Clearly it
is foreseeable that current methods of recording and reporting in the

nursery might be adapted for inclusion into a nationwide format, enabling vastly greater control and docility. Walzer argues, in line with teachers' values, that, 'The function of discipline is to create useful subjects, men and women who conform to a standard, who are certifiably sane or healthy or docile or competent, not free agents who invent their own standards (1991: 59).

Foucault is described by Walzer as being focused 'on what he thinks of as the "micro-fascism" of everyday life' (Walzer 1991: 72). Throughout our examination of the empirical data, staffs' concern with normality was striking. Taylor claims that the notion of normality is central to the focus of modern technologies of control. He argues that Foucault's thesis is that:

> What is wielded through the modern technologies of control is something quite different, in that it is not concerned with law, but with normalisation . . . it is above all concerned with bringing about a certain result, defined as health or good function . . . The new kind of power is productive. It brings about a new kind of subject and new kinds of desire and behaviour [*sic*] which belong to him. It is concerned to form us as modern individuals.
>
> (1991: 75–6)

Clearly the practical strategies for producing 'child development' reported upon in this chapter are consistent with his claims.

Taylor interprets Foucault further to mean that:

> The objectifying and domination of inner nature comes about in fact not just through a change of attitude, but through training in an interiorization of certain disciplines. The disciplines of organised bodily movements, of the employment of time, of ordered dispositions of living/working space – the disciplines which build this new way of being are social.
>
> (1991: 76–7)

Viewed in the light of Foucault's theoretical framework, the desirable outcomes for children's learning and baseline assessments can be conceived of as officially mandating those educational conditions for the production of 'modern children'. Foucault is clearly 'in' the nursery.

Clearly, his perspective offers a radically different and subversive conception concerning the nature of children's experience of nursery education and its purposes. His claims ought to heighten our awareness of the possibility that under the guise of observational and assessment processes is an extensive system of surveillance. Such an argument encourages us to consider how oppressive it might feel as a child being watched continually, even if as adults we do it with the best intentions and with the support of the teaching profession. Surely a good way to resist the potential 'micro-fascisms' of teaching is to realize that there are different ways of interpreting 'best practice'. Alternative critiques of the received wisdom about child-centred education alert us to the importance of trying really hard to think about life in the nursery from a child's perspective.

Acknowledgement

I am grateful to my colleagues in Educational Studies and to John Robertson, Head of Curricular Studies for facilitating the production of this chapter.

References

Ball, S. (1990) *Politics and Policy-Making in Education: Explorations in Policy Sociology*. London: Routledge.

Bryman, A. and Burgess, R.G. (eds) (1994) *Analysing Qualitative Data*. London: Routledge.

Bulmer, M. (ed.) (1984) *Sociological Research Methods*. London: Macmillan.

Burgess, R.G. (1993) *In the Field: An Introduction to Field Research*. London: Routledge.

Foucault, M. (1977) *Discipline and Punish: The Birth of the Prison*. London: Penguin Books.

Foucault, M. (1980) *Power/Knowledge: Selected Interviews and Other Writings, 1972–77*. Brighton: Harvester Press.

Hartley, D. (1993) *Understanding the Nursery School*. London: Cassell.

King, R. (1978) *All Things Bright and Beautiful? A Sociological Study of Infant Classrooms*. Chichester: Wiley.

Lyotard, J.F. (1984) *The Postmodern Condition: A Report on Knowledge*. Manchester: Manchester University Press.

Macdonell, D. (1991) *Theories of Discourse: An Introduction*. Oxford: Basil Blackwell.

Merquior, J.G. (1991) *Foucault*. London: Fontana.

Scottish Office (1997) *A Curriculum Framework for Children in their Preschool Year*. Edinburgh: SOEID.

Taylor, C. (1991) Foucault on freedom and truth, in P. Hoy (ed.) (1991) *Foucault: A Critical Reader*. Oxford: Basil Blackwell.

Walkerdine, V. (1986) Post-structuralist theory and everyday social practices: the family and the school, in S. Wilkinson (ed.) *Feminist Social Psychology: Developing Theory and Practice*. Milton Keynes: Open University Press.

Walzer, M. (1991) The politics of Michel Foucault, in P. Hoy (ed.) *Foucault: A Critical Reader*. Oxford: Basil Blackwell.

9

What is the use of children's play: preparation or social participation?

Harriet Strandell

Free play in the big room

Participants: Risto (4), Tero (4) and Olli (6), boys

> *Risto:* You be my big brother and I'll be your little brother.
> *Tero:* No you be grandpa.
> *Risto:* We don't need a grandpa, 'cos these are soldiers.
> *Tero:* Yeh.
> *Risto:* They're big boys.
> *Tero:* And these are toy weapons, OK?

Doing things on a fantasy or symbolic level accounts for a considerable part of children's communication with each other. In modern times, children's pretend play has become a kind of archetype child activity. It is regarded as something children have the right to do, as a warrant for a healthy childhood, protecting them from insecurity and worries; an expression of children's real nature. Play is an important element in the protection model of childhood.

On the other hand, in modern Western society play has become marginalized and locked into itself in a world of its own. It has grown into a highly differentiated and separate activity – an activity that separates children from the real, adult world. It has become one of the expressions for the banishment of children to the margins of society. Play has become the expression of a kind of activity that has no place in real society; something easy that children engage in while waiting for entrance into society. Play has become trivialized. As a metaphor, the word 'play', when coupled with 'child' connotes 'triviality' (Thorne 1993: 5). The modern play discourse thus contains the marginalization and exclusion of children from society, and thus from influence in real life. Exclusion and protection are two sides of the same coin, implying each other (Engelbert 1994).

In the most widespread modern version, the pedagogical, play is made an instrument for *learning* adult competencies; 'real world things'. In developmental psychology and pedagogics, symbolic play is considered instrumental for basic developmental functions in childhood. In a form of preschool pedagogy that has been called 'invisible pedagogy' (Bernstein 1975: 116–18), play is the basic concept, becoming a kind of a diagnostic tool: from children's external behaviour and doings in arranged play contexts conclusions are drawn about the children's inner state, their developmental stage (Bernstein 1975). Children's play has become a working tool for professionals engaged in the upbringing of children. The pedagogical discourse also operates with standards for what is good play: the standards of the operation of daycare centres can, for example, be evaluated by monitoring children's play (Helenius 1993: 89).

In these kinds of pedagogical discourses play is treated as a supervised and curricularized activity, far from anthropology's view on play as an activity in its own right, as a situated activity, where the main motive for children to come together is 'to be where the action is' (Sutton-Smith 1982: 69).

Play: from preparation to participation

Instrumental interests in children's play tend to shut children up into a play world, and *separate the play world from real life*, that is from the social reality that surrounds the play situation. The problem of the relationship between play and reality is solved by removing play from the real-life context. In play, children are seen as practising or *simulating* real actions and relationships between people. Play is regarded as coping with reality – but reality in a very distanced and abstract way; a reality that exists in another time and in another place. The reality is located in a future where the children have progressed to another stage of childhood or left childhood altogether. Play is cut off from the immediate social reality of which it is part, at the same time and in the same place. Since play is regarded as a preparation for a future reality, there is a lack of interest in the relation of play to the immediate reality surrounding it. The question of how play relates to real life is far from clear: 'Children's doll play is a favourite context for developmentalists and clinicians . . . The question of how and when we should use children's play narratives to examine their understanding of other people and events remains an open one, and one that is important to explore' (Dunn 1988: 8–9).

But what if the play world is not a world of its own? What if it is not apart from the real world, but instead one of the means of making it and operating in it? Not by preparing for it, but by using play as a (communicative) *resource for participation in everyday life?* A communicative perspective on play has been discussed by Gregory Bateson (1973). In Bateson's view, playfulness can be used by children as a framing device; a metacommunicative signal indicating a shift from a serious to a non-serious position. Playfulness can be used in any kind of activity, and not only in play situations. Play can be used as a resource in the process of attributing meaning to action, in line with other resources for engaging in joint action with other persons.

I wish to consider play not as a competence or a means of reaching adult competence by practising it in play, but as a resource used in everyday life activities. In this chapter I will take a *constructivist* view on reality, combining interactionist and ethnomethodological approaches to that construction process. In a constructionist view, there is no 'real world' that pre-exists human symbolic language. Versions of reality are made in social interaction, by attaching meaning to actions; social life is an interpretive process (Bruner 1986: 93–105, 1990: 24–5; Denzin 1989: 12). Doing reality, then, is a kind of *negotiation on meaning*, conducted in terms of language (Bruner 1986: 57–9). The meaning of an action lies in its *effect*, that is in the responses to it. In the response, the responder imputes intentions to the action and acts according to his or her own interpretation of what has been done (Bruner 1981: 43–4).

The questions of social order that have to be addressed in the everyday life of the daycare centre, in order to participate in it, are basically of the same kind as those of any other institution in society where people engage in joint actions with other people (regardless of whether they are populated by children or adults). As social actors children are not essentially different from adults (Bruner and Haste 1987).

The method

The everyday life context of children that will be explored in this article stems from a study conducted in three municipal daycare centres in the Helsinki region (Strandell 1994). Finnish daycare centres play a central role in the life of many children under school age (7 years). Most of the children in the study attended their centre for seven to nine hours a day, which in no way differs from the average attendance in daycare centres. The time spent in the centre thus fills a considerable part of the child's waking hours. The children do not come to the daycare centre just to play and be together with other children for a while. They are there from early morning to late in the afternoon, while their parents are working or studying. The children take part in all kinds of everyday life activities, like having breakfast and lunch (a hot meal) and snacks, and resting or sleeping. There is a reason, then, for treating daycare life as an everyday life context.

The empirical data consists of ethnographical observation of the social interaction between the children in three groups, consisting of 18–20 children each. The age of the children ranged from 3 to 6 years. Each group was followed for about eight weeks. All kinds of activities and situations occurring during the day were studied, including situations where the children seemed to be doing nothing at all. Both verbal and non-verbal interaction were recorded, using only pen and paper (Strandell 1997).

Organizing relationships and activities narratively

Narration is a central means of negotiating meaning. Interpretation requires the telling of a story. Storytelling is a way of creating possible worlds, and possible courses of action. The power of narration lies in that it is about human intentions and human actions; there is a human push to organize experience narratively (Bruner 1990: 78–9). A story always operates in the borderlands between fantasy and reality, and there is no sharp dividing line between them. Because stories are about what could have happened or how things could be, they are excellent tools in constructing reality (Bruner 1986: 11–19, 1990: 67–9).

Narrative interpretation is a human way of functioning that is in no way child specific. Children do, however, get involved in it extensively, because the structure of symbolic play is narrative. Symbolic play is based on developing a plot; telling a story.

The narrator's voice – telling the story – is a powerful resource in defining the situation and its meaning (Auwärter 1986). And this is valid not only in the internal play world, but in real life, in participating in everyday events and reproducing social relationships. Acting on the narrative speech level gives power to influence the course of action: children can define what the activity and the situations are about. Maybe that is why children usually seem to be more attracted by acting on the narrative speech level than acting in already created and fixed roles?

Free play in the hall

Participants: Eero (3) and Jussi (4), boys

Eero and Jussi are playing in the sandpit in the hall.

> *Eero:* I once saw a sort of tractor with a trailer, it was almost a lorry. Ville's got a trailer.
> *Jussi:* So's Kalle.
> *Eero:* This is a Ville-lorry like . . . [?]
> *Jussi:* Look, it can do . . . [?]
> *Eero:* You could be with it every day.
> *Jussi:* No I couldn't, we've got the day off tomorrow.
> *Eero:* Oh, a day off.

Woven into the fictive story in this episode is another story, of how Eero could get Jussi to be with him. The hint that Eero wants Jussi to play with him is revealed when he says 'You could be with it every day' and is confirmed when Jussi points out a reality of daycare centre life: 'No I couldn't, we've got the day off tomorrow.' Here the narrative intrigue carries negotiations on who will be with whom. At the end Jussi and Eero shift from a fictive to a reality context. In the rest of the episode Eero and Jussi mostly negotiate on a reality basis:

Eero: Will you be with me?
Jussi: No.
Eero: Who're you going to be with?
Jussi: Mika, when he gets here.

Clearly, the instruments of narrative construction are here used in order to organize everyday life; to negotiate on 'who should be together with whom' and how this being together should be planned. It's interesting to look at the situation in which the negotiation takes place. The two boys have been discussing and doing different things together for a long while before the above episode begins. Against this background, they do not seem to be in need of getting involved, because they are already involved. Is Eero maybe involved in 'meta-negotiating', in learning 'situated rules of social life', trying out different ways of handling social relationships? Social integration is one of the most important channels to participation in the everyday life of the daycare centre. Becoming socially involved is a constantly recurrent theme during the day at the centre (see Corsaro 1985: 126, 150).

In the next episode we can follow a somewhat more sophisticated way of elaborating social relationships, using in a very elegant way the instruments of narrative play to weave negotiations on social relationships into a fictive story. Developing a story is here made the frame for coping with the actual social situation the children are in.

Free play in the singing room

Participants: Liisa (5), Anu (5) and Rita (5), girls

Anu and Rita are crawling behind a giant cloth dog in the corner of the singing room. They open two umbrellas above them as a roof. They can hardly be seen from outside. Liisa enters the room. She stands looking at the dog corner, listening to Anu and Rita, who are talking to one another. Liisa attempts to get involved by saying 'Hi'. Anu says to her, 'We're building a house'. A little later, however, Anu says, 'It's raining outside', and, 'Liisa, you're not to come in', whereby Liisa answers, 'I can watch you from here'.

Liisa climbs up on to the dog, then back on top of the cupboard. Rita and Anu are conversing all the time, 'furnishing' their house.

Liisa: It's stopped raining.
Rita: No it hasn't! It's raining here.
Anu: Yes, and it should be dark.

Anu switches the light off. (The switch is right above her.)

Liisa: This door must be kept closed.

Liisa goes to close the sliding door. Then she returns to the corner.

Liisa: Is it dark enough?
Anu: Shall we let Liisa come and play with us now?
Rita: No!

After the answer 'No'! Liisa is presented with additional conditions for participation, 'Go and shut the other door', and the negotiations continue. At the end of the episode, the fact that Liisa belongs to another unit is used as an argument for excluding her: 'Luckily you're a Ladybird! Luckily it's our turn!'

The above excerpt from an episode is a negotiation on social participation using the narrative dimensions inherent in pretend play. It is a negotiation on whether Liisa can enter the activity and on what conditions. The frame of the negotiations is a pretend play, inside which the negotiations waver between being conducted in real life and woven into the storytelling. By saying, 'It's stopped raining', Liisa inserts herself in the story and gets a hold on developing the plot. For a while, the negotiations are conducted on a symbolic level. Anu's utterance, 'Shall we let Liisa come and play with us now?' makes it quite clear that the children involved really define the situation as a negotiation on the conditions for Liisa's participation.

By referring to a rule of the daycare centre saying that the different units have the right to use the big room at different hours, Anu puts the three children in different positions with different negotiating powers. Liisa does not have the right to be in the big room (a fact that the teacher also confirms a little later). This rule of the daycare centre makes Liisa's participation 'from the margin' understandable.

Was Liisa integrated in the course of events or not? The episode can be interpreted in several ways. If we look at the episode as a play context, maybe Liisa can be said to be part of the developing of the story; at least the narrative structure of the negotiations gives her a chance to participate in the storytelling. If, however, we consider the episode as a negotiation on social relationships, using narrative means, the case is more dubious. Anu's and Rita's responses to Liisa's openings shift between total rejection and giving her signals indicating that maybe the case can still be discussed: 'Go and shut the other door'. All in all, the episode shows that social participation is no one-dimensional phenomenon, but operates on several interconnected levels.

Participation or not, the point is how different kinds of social and spatial divisions, rules, categorizations according to age, time-schedules, daily routines and other structures of everyday life condition the children's discussions and their ways of organizing their activities during the day. This organizing can be 'camouflaged', wholly or partially, as fantasy and done on a fantasy level.

Bad quality of play or a problematic play concept?

To overcome the separateness built into the play concept, and to conceptualize children's actions and the ways in which children create meaning in their actions in relation to the social order and the social structure of the institutional contexts of which they are part is a sociological challenge. The concept of 'children's culture' has – like the play concept – been criticized for separating children's actions from questions of social order and structure. James, Jenks and Prout (1998) pay attention to the intersection between ordering properties and subjective experience, and want to see the concept of children's culture as 'a form of social action contextualized by the many ways in which children choose to engage with the social institutions and structures that shape the form and process of their everyday lives' (James *et al.* 1998: 88).

The next episode can be used for discussing the intersection between ordering properties and children's actions; how actions are conditioned by the institutional setting. The episode does not have the narratively ordered structure of the previous episodes. It seems to be more fragmented and evolves in several directions. The episode can also be used for discussion about how a course of action can be differently interpreted, depending on what kind of interpretive frame/childhood discourse is used or what kind it is put into.

Free play in the big room

Participants: Marko (6), Jussi (4), boys; Mari (3), girl

Marko and Jussi remain in the big room when Tomi and Jouni go out. The boys are romping on a mattress.

> *Jussi:* Let's start . . . [?]
> *Marko:* No, not that.

Jussi runs here and there about the room. Then he steams into the dining room. Marko runs after him, shouting:

> *Marko:* I know what we can play, Jussi.

The boys return a moment later and continue romping on the mattress.
  Marko pushes a soft toy up his sweater, jumps again, does a somersault, stands up and says:

> *Marko:* I'm going to show Hanna.

Marko goes off to the dining room with Jussi following. Jussi is giggling all the time. Marko goes and shows Hanna his big tummy. The boys then return to the big room. Jussi leaps off a bench on to the mattress. Marko gets up on the swing and swings backwards and forwards.
  After jumping and swinging for a moment Jussi says:

> *Jussi:* I don't want to play with you anymore. I'm going to be with Aki.

Jussi goes out into the entrance hall.

> *Marko:* No, stay with me, you can . . . [?]

Jussi has gone out into the entrance hall, Marko running after him. A moment later the boys return to the big room.

> *Marko:* Let's shut the door.

Jussi goes and closes the door to the hall. Marko shuts the sliding door to the dining room. The boys resume their jumping and swinging.
A buzzing sound can be heard in the entrance hall.

> *Jussi:* I'm going to see . . .

Jussi runs into the hall, then comes back. After a while Mari enters the room. Jussi says, 'Don't come in here' to her. She collects a piece of cloth and leaves the room. Marko suggests to Jussi that they should clean up; they discuss what either one should do. They put things into proper places and leave the room.

To daycare teachers this mostly sounds like bad quality of play. When play is used as a working method and a normative concept, the episode looks like play that is continuously disturbed and never has a real chance to develop. It seems just to confirm that children cannot concentrate on what they are doing. Symbolic play – which 3–6-year-old children are supposed to engage in – is loaded with presumed criteria that the activity should satisfy in order to pass as (good) play, such as a focus inwards, duration and 'screening off' what is going on around, development of role characters and actions of role characters.

From my research point of view, however, the problem is not the activity, but the (pedagogical) play concept largely in use in early childhood education, which does not take into account the institutional context of the activity. In the episode above, the social turbulence surrounding the boys has the effect of pulling their attention in many directions simultaneously. The episode is full of impulses from the outer world, which split the activity up into sequences with no necessary inner connections. In 'free' activities children are on the *move*, both in a physical and in a social sense. Children typically do not limit their concentration only to the activity they are engaged in at that moment; simultaneously they look around, 'absorbing' what is going on around them. Sometimes this orientation 'outwards' results in leaving the activity and joining in something else. One of the main results of the study lies in the contextualization of children's actions, in constructing the context of children's actions as being *wider* than consisting of just one separable activity. The context includes the whole social 'scene' (or parts of it), the whole group of children and adults, and all ongoing activities (or parts of them). Children are *participants in a social system.* They curiously investigate what's going on around them, focusing towards other people, other activities and other places. Acting like the children in this episode can also be seen as a way of acting plainly as social beings with no purpose in addition to that: getting informed and chatting can be regarded as part of upholding social relationships and participation in everyday life.

Originally William Corsaro's study of children's interaction in a daycare centre (Corsaro 1985) drew my attention to the flexibility and mobility in children's activities. He noted that activity episodes were usually short and were easily interrupted or terminated, resulting in much leaving and entering, and that much of the interaction consisted in negotiations on how to get access to activities and on protecting interactive space.

In my own research, I chose to characterize children's doings as a never ceasing *flow of activity* (see Strandell 1997: 450–1, 455–7), having no clear beginnings or endings, and going through more or less constant changes in defining the activity, in social structure, in content and often also in spatial location. Activities slip into new activities, and are abandoned temporarily or definitely. One activity splits into several, or activities fuse to become one. Usually there are several activities going on at the same time, with the children commuting between them.

Do children's activities have to be defined?

The episode can also be used for a discussion on different *knowledge interests*. When childhood ethnography is conducted in *educational settings*, as in this case, children are surrounded by adults doing professional work on and together with them. Groups of professionals apparently have knowledge interests that are more pragmatic and normative than those of the researcher, because knowledge is put into practice. The process of discussing my findings with people who work professionally with children set me thinking about different ways of 'knowing children', leading to different ways of seeing and interpreting what's going on between the children.

Whenever I have presented my findings and interpretations of what children do in the social milieu of the daycare centre and how they attach meaning to actions, I have been astonished to hear how ready my listeners have been to put phenomena and children into fixed categories of meaning: to know what a child is and what he or she needs; to know what is good and what is bad; and to offer explanations for why things are as they are. I had a feeling that there was some sort of recontextualization or 'translation' process going on: findings were in a way absorbed by the childhood discourses influential at the time.

In the translation process, findings were put into different kinds of social discourses: quite often the *childhood as a social problem* discourse, but sometimes also in the *children as competent social actors* discourse. I connect the need to 'translate' findings to the process in which professionals *create the child as the object* of their 'child-work' (Oldman 1994) and in which the child has to be clearly defined, in order to become a 'good' object of child-work. In the process of creating the child as the object of child-work, *the child becomes defined*. From this point of view, the above episode is problematic, because it is not so clear what the children are doing, and the 'usefulness' of their activities is dubious. The activity cannot be coded and put into fixed categories with labels on. If an activity cannot be conceptually controlled, it can hardly become pedagogically instrumentalized, or used for controlling purposes.

Actually, one of the resources children use in dealing with the control directed towards their activities is playfulness. Nonsense rhymes, ritual framing, playful language use, performances, commuting between serious and non-serious positions, laughter, exaggerations and exuberance are powerful means of defining what is going on in situations, and at the same time ways by which children posit themselves out of reach of adult control of their activities.

In an early stage of the fieldwork I noticed that some of the most playful situations, where children amused themselves greatly, were not at all aimed for play, in the teachers' structuring of the day. They were meal times, singing sessions or gymnastics. On looking more closely at how these situations are socially organized, they turn out to be *controlled* activities, where the children's influence is circumscribed, compared to 'free play' activities. Things have to be done in a certain way and in a certain order. The teachers also usually intervene frequently; correcting, helping and prohibiting the children.

Maybe one of the lessons from my research is not whether children are dependents or competent actors, autonomous subjects or social problems. It is more about *not* placing them in fixed categories that can be labelled. Maybe we could – in childhood research and in professional child-work – learn from one of the findings of the study: that children often seem to be more attracted by acting on a narrative level than acting in already created and fixed roles. The story never becomes fixed; it changes and stays open-ended as long as it is told. Maybe we should do more work on 'unfixing' the concept of play, withdraw from the self-evident and normative position it has whenever children's activities are discussed, and pay more attention to how play and playfulness are used in social organization.

References

Auwärter, M. (1986) Development of communicative skills: the construction of fictional reality in children's play, in J. Cook-Gumperz, W. Corsaro and J. Streeck (eds) *Children's Worlds and Children's Language*. Berlin: Mouton de Gruyter.
Bateson, G. (1973) *Steps to an Ecology of Mind. Collected Essays on Anthropology, Psychiatry, Evolution and Epistemology*. St Albans: Paladin.

Bernstein, B. (1975) *Class, Codes and Control, volume 3: Towards a Theory of Educational Transmissions*. London: Routledge and Kegan Paul.

Bruner, J. (1981) The pragmatics of acquisition, in W. Deutsch (ed.) *The Child's Construction of Language*. London: Academic Press.

Bruner, J. (1986) *Actual Minds, Possible Worlds*. Cambridge, MA: Harvard University Press.

Bruner, J. (1990) *Acts of Meaning*. Cambridge, MA: Harvard University Press.

Bruner, J. and H. Haste (eds) (1987) *Making Sense. The Child's Construction of the World*. London: Methuen.

Corsaro, W. (1985) *Friendship and Peer Culture in the Early Years*. Norwood, NJ: Ablex.

Denzin, N. (1989) *Interpretive Interactionism*. London: Sage.

Dunn, J. (1988) *The Beginnings of Social Understanding*. Cambridge, MA: Harvard University Press.

Engelbert, A. (1994) Worlds of childhood: differentiated but different, in J. Qvortrup, M. Bardy, G. Sgritta and H. Wintersberger (eds) *Childhood Matters: Social Theory, Practice and Politics*. Aldershot: Avebury.

Helenius, A. (1993) *Leikin kehitys varhaislapsuudessa*. Helsinki: Kirjayhtymä.

James, A., Jenks, C. and Prout, A. (1998) *Theorizing Childhood*. Cambridge: Polity Press.

Oldman, D. (1994) Adult–child relations as class relations, in J. Qvortrup, M. Bardy, G. Sgritta and H. Wintersberger (eds) *Childhood Matters: Social Theory, Practice and Politics*. Aldershot: Avebury.

Strandell, H. (1994) *Sociala mötesplatser för barn: Aktivitetsprofiler och förhandlingskulturer på daghem*. Helsinki: Gaudeamus.

Strandell, H. (1997) Doing reality with play: play as a children's resource in organizing everyday life in day care centres, *Childhood*, 4(4): 445–64.

Sutton-Smith, B. (1982) A Performance Theory of Peer Relations, in K. Borman (ed.) *The Social Life of Children in a Changing Society*. Hillsdale, NJ: Lawrence Erlbaum.

Thorne, B. (1993) *Gender Play: Girls and Boys in School*. New Brunswick, NJ: Rutgers University Press.

The rights of young children

Priscilla Alderson

Implicit and explicit ideas about children's development and social status, and about adult–child relationships, affect attitudes towards children's rights. This chapter considers the relevance of the 54 articles of the 1989 UN Convention on the Rights of the Child to young children, especially babies. Do babies have any rights? And, if so, what would these rights be? What are rights, and what are their strengths and limitations? The practical value, particularly of participation rights, which involve informing, respecting and consulting with young children, will be described.

Three kinds of rights

The Convention begins, 'in recognition of the inherent dignity and of the equal and inalienable rights of all members of the human family [as] the foundation of freedom, justice and peace in the world'. Children's rights are divided into three main, and partly overlapping, kinds: provision, protection and participation rights. Participation includes taking part in society and in making personal decisions that affect the child.

Probably everyone supports children's provision rights, for example, to food and clean water, necessary warmth and the best available healthcare. Similarly, most people agree that children should be protected from neglect and abuse. There is less agreement on the third kind of rights, participation or autonomy rights, and listening to the voice of the child. 'Isn't that something to do with children being able to decide whether to go to school?' is a frequent criticism. 'And anyway, that has nothing to do with babies. They don't have voices or views.' However, babies do have a range of participation rights.

Strengths and limitations of children's rights

The strengths of the Convention rights are that they are *formal, internationally agreed standards* for the *legal protection* of all children. Every country in the world except the USA and Somalia has ratified the Convention, and undertaken to change national law to accord with it, and to inform 'adults and children alike' about the Convention. Governments also undertake to report to the UN every five years on progress they have made in implementing the Convention's rights. Rights are linked to legal entitlements, which are standards that can be claimed and defended, if necessary in the courts.

This strength is also a limitation of all rights. So, for example, we cannot talk about a baby's right to a loving family. Love cannot be willed or enforced; parents cannot be prosecuted for not being loving enough. The Convention preamble acknowledges the importance for every child to grow up 'in an atmosphere of happiness, love and understanding'. But these cannot be rights. Instead, the Convention sets all possible standards that can be enforced to assist families in providing loving care.

Rights are limited in other ways. Some rights are *aspirational*, not yet fully realizable, but only 'to the maximum extent of [each nation's] available resources' (4).[1] Rights are not *absolute* but *conditional*, affected by the 'evolving capacities of the child', the 'responsibilities, rights and duties of parents'(5) and the national law. 'The best interests of the child must be the primary consideration' (1, 21). Rights cannot be exercised in ways that would harm the child or other people. They must 'respect the rights and reputations of others', as well as 'national security and public order, health and morals' (13).

Rights are sometimes seen as *selfish* claims, however they are really about solidarity, justice and fair distribution. In claiming a right, you acknowledge everyone else's equal claim to it, and therefore reaffirm the worth and dignity of every person. Children's rights are part of promoting 'social progress and better standards of life in larger freedom'.

The next sections go through some of the rights in the Convention that relate to babies, under the headings provision, protection and participation. Some rights could go under more than one of the three main headings. The child is defined as anyone under the age of 18. The British government chose to apply the Convention 'only following a live birth'.

Providing for babies

Standards of care

All services for children 'shall conform with the standards established by competent authorities, particularly in the areas of safety, health, in the number and suitability of their staff as well as competent supervision' (3). This can involve setting agreed standards for all health, care and education services, with registration and inspection to see that the standards are kept. There are great difficulties in agreeing on standards that can be clearly defined and assessed in early years services (Ensing 1996). So far there has been little attempt to involve young children in selecting the criteria or in thinking of ways to assess their satisfaction or unhappiness with a service (Elfer and Selleck 1999).

Healthcare

The child has the right to 'the enjoyment of the highest attainable standard of health and to facilities for treatment of illness and rehabilitation of health', especially 'to diminish infant and child mortality' (24). State parties shall develop primary healthcare, and provide 'adequate nutritious foods and clean drinking water . . . appropriate pre- and post-natal health care for mothers . . . health education [including] basic knowledge of child health and nutrition, the advantages of breast feeding, hygiene, and environmental sanitation and the prevention of accidents . . . and family planning services' (24).

From their first weeks children share in their own healthcare. The baby is the most active partner in breast or bottle feeding. With breast feeding, the baby creates the demand that builds up the supply. Babies can be wiser than 'experts', who advise, say, four-hourly feeding, which inhibits the milk supply. Very soon, babies start to share in dressing, by holding their arms flexibly to help to put on sleeves, instead of being like limp or rigid dolls. Soon their participation becomes so sophisticated that, for example, a child aged 15 months can put away the groceries shopping in the correct places.

Martin Woodhead (1997) criticizes experts who dress up their own opinions as children's universal 'needs', such as children's need to be responsible. Yet babies seem to be so keen to struggle towards independence, to feed themselves, initiate games and interactions, and to cooperate and help. Parents and other carers and staff in early years centres play key roles in helping babies to become responsible for their self-care, and in being adventurous yet cautious enough to avoid injuries. One example is when adults wait for children to test and decide whether to take a risk, such as climbing on a low wall, to see how careful they can be and how they gradually increase their strength and skilful mobility. Another example is how, when given the choice, 1-year-olds soon learn when they feel cold enough to need a coat. When adults trust their views appropriately, they encourage babies to develop reciprocal trust with their caring adults. Yet adult controls are often framed as healthcare ('You'll get a cold. You'll be too tired. Eat that up it's good for you.') when they have more to do with adults' convenience. Unrealistic ideas about how much a child should eat or sleep or wear or run about can lead to unnecessarily labelling children as having sleep or feeding problems or being hyperactive, and to battles, which greater confidence in babies' self-care could prevent (Leidloff 1976).

Review when looked after

Any child cared for by authorities has the right to 'periodic review of the treatment provided to the child and all other circumstances relevant to his or her placement' (25). From as early as possible, the young child's feelings should be considered. There could be a reversed routine, in which adults attend to the child's wishes, unless they can show that this is unnecessary or inadvisable, instead of having to justify respecting young children's views (Alderson and Montgomery 1996).

Financial support

Every child has the right to social security and insurance, in accordance with the national law, and to help with achieving the 'full realisation of this right' (26). While poorer countries are unable to honour this right, richer ones are increasingly moving away from it and expecting parents to pay for all their child's needs up to the age of 18, 21 or older. O'Neill (1994) reviews the negative effects of the way liberal societies are privatizing parenting and abandoning collective responsibilities for children.

Standard of living

Every child has the right 'to a standard of living adequate for the child's physical, mental, spiritual, moral and social development . . . State parties, in accordance with national conditions and within their means, shall take appropriate measures to assist parents and others responsible for the child [when in need] to implement this right', such as with nutrition, clothing and housing (27).

Children across the world are moving in larger numbers into the poorest sectors of their society (Qvortrup *et al.* 1994). There is evidence that the most damaging kind of poverty, measured by health, accident, education and crime factors, is comparative poverty, through wide and increasing differences between the richest and poorest sectors of society. The steepest differences have developed in the UK in recent years (Wilkinson 1994). Babies in social class V are twice as likely to die as those in social class I/II. Much higher accident rates occur among poorer families (Roberts *et al.* 1995).

Education

Primary education shall be 'compulsory and free to all' (28). Fulfilling this article will mean that babies are born to educated parents, thus raising their chances of survival. Education includes 'the preparation of the child for responsible life in a free society, in the spirit of understanding, peace, tolerance, equality of sexes, and friendship among all peoples' (29). Educational opportunities for teenage mothers are increased at schools and colleges that provide facilities for their babies.

Cultural life

The child has the right 'to rest and leisure, to engage in play . . . and to participate freely in cultural life and the arts' (31). Many details of daily life, such as in babies' food, clothes, housing and transport, express their culture and their social status. Early years centres can be public places where children meet as citizens to enjoy their shared cultural life (Dahlberg *et al.*, 1999).

Publicizing the Convention

State parties undertake 'to make the principles of the Convention widely known, by appropriate and active means, to adults and children alike' (42). The British government has done comparatively little to publicize the Convention. Ideas from the beautiful South African photograph posters illustrating the Convention could be copied in this country and displayed in health and early years settings as well as other public places to increase public awareness of babies' rights.

Protecting babies

These rights concern protection from neglect and abuse of body or mind, and from discrimination.

Privacy and good reputation

'No child shall be subjected to arbitrary or unlawful interference with his or her privacy, family, home or correspondence, nor to unlawful attacks on his or her honour and reputation' (16). This article can affect babies whose parents have HIV, or are in prison or mental hospital, or if the mother has been raped, or is in some other great stigmatizing difficulty for which the baby is in no way responsible. In UK health law, babies have as much right to privacy as adults (Montgomery 1997). They can be severely harmed by 'attacks on their reputation' because they are unable to answer or challenge attacks that may arouse damaging prejudices against them among their relatives or neighbours or professionals caring for them, which could have lifelong effects. Professionals should avoid making inaccurate or potentially damaging records of babies in their care. Research on babies can risk unlawful interference and high ethical standards are especially important (Royal College of Paediatrics and Child Health 1992).

Violence

States shall 'protect the child from all forms of physical or mental violence, injury or abuse, neglect or negligent treatment, maltreatment or exploitation' (19). This is another right that especially applies to babies as the most defenceless and vulnerable people. Most British babies are smacked and are more likely to be smacked than older children. One study of over 400 mothers found that more than three quarters of the mothers admitted to 'tapping' their baby during the first year, and over a third had done so more than once during the previous week (Smith 1995). In the UK, children are the only people who can, in law, be hit, which implies a belief that children are not fully human beings who feel shame and pain and can be reasoned with like adults (Newell 1989). The UK's record on physical punishment was especially criticized by the UN Committee on the Rights of the Child.

Special protection

Children temporarily deprived of their family environment 'shall be entitled to special protection and assistance provided by the State' (20). In cases of adoption and other alternative care, 'due regard shall be paid to the desirability of continuity in a child's upbringing and to the child's ethnic, religious, cultural and linguistic background' (20). This right is also important in all settings where children are cared for part-time, partly to ensure reasonable continuity between home and daycare. Anti-racist measures are also important in centres attended only by white indigenous children, who otherwise quickly learn racist attitudes (Brown 1989; CRE 1990; Siraj-Blatchford 1996). Regard for ethnic, religious and cultural background begins from birth in the way the baby and mother are cared for.

Mass media

State parties shall 'encourage the mass media to disseminate information and material of social and cultural benefit to the child and in accordance with the spirit of the [Convention]' (17). Babies are often used in films, magazines and advertising, obviously without their consent. This raises questions about whether stricter standards for the media, to protect babies individually and generally from ridicule or exploitation, are desirable. Alternatively, many images of babies in the media may be welcomed as one kind of social inclusion.

However, countless media references to babies show how much they are socially excluded. So many accounts are dismissive or hostile, or oddly ignore babies. For example, in June 1998 a news headline during the court case of a childminder after the death of a baby said 'How can we protect parents?'. The free baby books given to mothers in UK antenatal clinics discuss postnatal depression, but not postnatal elation. Much of the stress of having a new baby is likely to be due to negative attitudes and the way mothers and babies are excluded from so many aspects of society.

Exploitation, sale of children, cruel treatment, imprisonment and war

The child shall be 'protected from economic exploitation and from performing any work that is likely to be hazardous' (32), from the illicit use of drugs (33), and from sexual and pornographic exploitation (34). State parties shall prevent 'the abduction of, the sale of or traffic in children' (35), and shall 'protect the child against all other forms of exploitation prejudicial to any aspects of the child's welfare' (36). 'No child shall be subjected to torture or other cruel, inhuman or degrading treatment, or be deprived of his or her liberty unlawfully. Every child deprived of liberty shall be treated with humanity and respect for the inherent dignity of the human person' (37). States parties shall 'take all appropriate measures to promote physical and psychological recovery and social reintegration of a child victim' after neglect or abuse, cruel treatment or armed conflict (39).

Babies are affected by hazardous work when they live near polluting workplaces, and when work conditions harm their parents' health before, during and after the pregnancy. Many babies live in families involved in illegal drug taking and selling, and in crime to support addiction. Their parents may be imprisoned; the baby may be removed from the mother at birth and suffer agonizing withdrawal symptoms and long-term disrupted relationships. Breastfeeding provides a natural way to wean babies gradually off addictive drugs.

Adult-centred systems of penal justice ignore the children concerned, who may be the main casualties, growing up fearful, stigmatized, depressed and in poverty – not conditions that prevent future crime. The number of women prisoners in the UK is rising rapidly for reasons such as debt or petty theft, which are associated with the great increase in poverty among young and single parent families. Although babies can stay in prison, they have to leave at an age when close contact with their mother is still crucial, and they are not helped in their 'social reintegration'. International policing is beginning to develop ways of protecting children from sexual tourism, traffic in children and pornography involving them.

Young children are often the first to suffer in war, which is now often conducted in civilian areas. The billions of dollars spent each year on arms are directed away from health and education services and from water and agriculture programmes. And these are further damaged by warfare, while casualties fill the hospitals. Debts linked to arms sales further drain national economies. Demands for repayment, with the policies of the World Bank encouraging cash crops and the economizing on all services for people, prevent the repair of the social fabric on which babies' lives and well-being depend. Children are also especially affected, in that most people in many of these war-torn countries are children and young parents, unlike the aging Western societies.

Babies and participation

Provision and protection rights enjoy wide support, but participation rights are seen as more controversial. This review of babies' rights, however, has emphasized participation aspects of provisions and protection, and in turn they weave into participation rights.

Right to life

'Every child has the inherent right to life'. State parties 'shall ensure to the maximum extent possible the survival and development of the child' (6). This article mainly refers to unnecessary death through poverty and preventable, treatable malnutrition, injury and disease. Yet 'life' means more than survival and involves a reasonable quality of life. Babies also have a right to release from a life filled with suffering, and from zealous but useless over-treatment, raising agonizing dilemmas between the right to die, and the right to live (Royal College of Paediatrics and Child Health 1997).

Name, identity and family

'The child shall be registered immediately after birth and shall have the right to a name, the right to acquire a nationality and, as far as possible, the right to know and be cared for by his or her parents' (7). The child has the right 'to preserve his or her identity, including nationality, name and family relations' (8). And if the child is illegally deprived of these, there should be help 'with a view to speedily re-establishing his or her identity' (8). States should 'ensure recognition of the principles that both parents have common responsibilities for the upbringing and development of the child' (18). The child and parents should not be separated 'unless this is in the best interests of the child' (9). States 'shall take measures to combat the illicit transfer and non-return of children abroad' (11).

Participation rights begin when babies are welcomed into their family and community, and by 'taking due account of the importance of the traditions and cultural values of each people for the protection and harmonious development of the child' (preamble).

Knowing the harm that can arise in family relationships after early separation, such as in special-care baby units (Klaus and Kennel 1976), professionals have a duty to question all such separations and avoid them when possible. In the UK, as in many countries, young parents are among the poorest members of society and those in paid employment often work the longest hours. Some have to live and work far away from their children, when economic pressures disregard children's rights to family life.

Inclusive communities

'A mentally or physically disabled child should enjoy a full and decent life, in conditions that ensure dignity, promote self-reliance, and facilitate the child's active participation in the community'. The eventual aim for all services for disabled children should 'be conducive to the child's achieving the fullest possible social integration and individual development' (23). International understanding, skills and capabilities in the care of these children should be improved, according to the Convention. When disabled and non-disabled children play and learn together, many of the children play together in integrated groups and sensitively help one another (Alderson and Goodey 1998; Cleves School 1999).

Freedom of expression

'State parties shall assure to the child who is capable of forming his or her own views the right to express those views freely in all matters affecting the child, the views of the child being given due weight in accordance with the age and maturity of the child' (12). The child shall have the right: 'to freedom of expression [including] freedom to seek, receive and impart information of all kinds . . . through any medium of the child's choice' (13).

The key participation right is the right to express a view. At first this is making contented or unhappy noises. Babies do appear to have strong and sensible views (leaving aside esoteric debates about how much these are inborn or learned), and they respond to adults who interact with them (Stern 1977) and listen to and learn from babies. For example, babies' protests against being separated from their parents when in hospital eventually led to hospital staff learning from their distress, and it is now routine in UK hospitals for parents to be with their child, a standard partly learned from the majority world, which is spreading around Europe (European Association for Children in Hospitals 1993). When parents share with health professionals in giving care, they can both make more informed decisions for the child (Alderson 1990). Babies' objections to being left in a strange place with strangers are a cue for adults to spend time on handing over care, and exchanging information about the baby's habits and preferences, how these are subtly expressed, and how the staff can respond so that they can give more appropriate and mutually rewarding care.

Very soon babies express themselves through play and can be seen to make and express choices, showing intense concentration and enjoyment (Goldschmeid and Jackson 1994). Babies' skills develop into the autonomous imaginative play encouraged in some nurseries (Penn 1997).

Freedom of expression, and the right to be heard and responded to, can begin to be honoured or withheld from birth.

Freedom of information

The ability to make informed decisions, such as to cooperate with the caring adult, depends on being informed. Babies develop trust (or mistrust) in their carers and willingness to cooperate with them (or not) through their experiences. These include reassuring explanations long before babies understand words. Children learn to talk by being spoken to for months, as if they can already talk. 'Information' can include physical contact and other body language, games, pointing and holding objects and pictures, and many other means of supplementing or replacing words, the constant examples of how other people interact, which babies soon imitate, and activities such as sharing in feeding and playing.

From the second year, telling a story can help children to understand and cooperate with stressful experiences like hospital treatment and surgery, as if the story about the beginning, middle and end of the treatment helps children to make sense of the ordeal (Alderson 1993). Some children need extra information. For example, blind babies lie very still in order to hear intently when someone enters the room. If they are suddenly picked up, they are distressed and their parents become upset by this reaction. If parents talk while they enter the room, the baby can enjoy their arrival and want to be picked up. In a sense, information is power, helping the child to have security through some feeling of control, instead of feeling suspended in helpless uncertainty. Children are then better able to see how to cooperate instead of making fearful protests.

Freedom of thought and association

The child has the right to 'freedom of thought, conscience and religion' (14) and to 'association and peaceful assembly' (15). Babies have thoughts, at least in the sense of desires for food, nurture, companionship, rest and distinct feelings about the different individuals around them. In the words of the UK Children Act 1989, they have ascertainable wishes and feelings. Many adults judge babies as good, obedient, lazy, greedy or naughty, long before babies are morally aware and have conscience enough to be able to be good or naughty. From about 12 months they begin to be aware of moral choices about whether to comply or not with their parents' wishes and warnings. Hitting children on the grounds that they are not yet morally reasonable still assumes that they can reason out why they are being hit, and what the adult disapproves of, and what different kind of behaviour is wanted.

Frequent premature judgements about a 'naughty' baby can easily become self-fulfilling, and lead to early rejections and punishments, which restrict 'freedom of thought'. They make babies feel anxious, uncertain and 'bad' (Miller 1983) so that they can become harder to care for. Another approach is to see newborn babies as amoral, but as having more or less energy and determination. Some adults value this energy; others feel threatened and exhausted by it. Quiet babies tend to be seen as 'good' whereas energetic noisy babies can easily become 'very good' – exuberant, happy, outgoing and actively helpful – or else 'bad'. Respecting babies' freedom of thought means reserving judgement and trying to understand their behaviours from their point of view, besides encouraging their loving respect for other people's thoughts and feelings, helping them to listen to their growing conscience, and to live in harmony and mutual respect with others.

Freedom of religion, association and peaceful assembly are important rights for families to enjoy so that babies can live as members of free communities. Minority societies increasingly confine children into institutions and enclosed spaces: home, car, nursery. They often exclude babies from many public spaces and gatherings, including parties, religious meetings, weddings and funerals, although as symbols of hope and renewal babies can bring profound meaning to these ceremonies.

Participation rights helpfully alert adults to new ways of seeing how they can live more fully in partnership with babies, seeing them as active contributors to their family and community. To treat babies with respect from the start affirms their own humanity and that of the carers, and helps to set the foundations of their self-respect and respect for others.

This chapter has considered beliefs about babies and rights, rather than discussing in detail the policy and practice implications that flow from these beliefs. The chapter's main purpose is to encourage new approaches to the attitudes that underlie early years policies.

Note

1 Figures in brackets refer to the relevant article of the UN Convention on the Rights of the Child.

References

Alderson, P. (1990) *Choosing for Children: Parents' Consent to Surgery.* Oxford: Oxford University Press.

Alderson, P. (1993) *Children's Consent to Surgery.* Buckingham: Open University Press.

Alderson, P. and Montgomery, J. (1996) *Health Care Choices: Making Decisions with Children.* London: Institute for Public Policy Research.

Alderson, P. and Goodey, C. (1998) *Enabling Education: Experiences in Special and Ordinary Schools.* London: Tufnell Press.

Brown, B. (1989) Anti-racist practice is good practice, in V. Williams (ed.) *Babies in Daycare.* London: The Day Care Trust.

Cleves School (1999) *Learning and Inclusion: the Cleves School Experience*, P. Alderson (ed.). London: David Fulton Publishers.

CRE (Commission for Racial Equality) (1989) *From Cradle to School: A Practical Guidance to Race Equality and Childcare*. London: Commission for Racial Equality.

Dahlberg, G., Moss, P. and Pence, P. (1999) *Beyond Quality in Early Childhood Services*. London: Falmer Press.

Elfer, P. and Sellick, D. (1999) The Best of Both Worlds: Enhancing the Experience of Young Children in the Nursery. Unpublished paper, London. National Children's Bureau.

Ensing, J. (1996) Inspection of early years in schools, in C. Nutbrown (ed.) *Respectful Educators – Capable Learners: Children's Rights in Early Education*. London: Paul Chapman.

European Association for Children in Hospital (1993) Charter for children in hospital, *Bulletin of Medical Ethics*, 92: 13–15.

Goldschmeid, E. and Jackson, S. (1994) *People Under Three: Young Children in Day Care*. London: Routledge.

Klaus, M. and Kennel, J. (1976) *Maternal Infant Bonding*. St Louis, MO: C. Mosby.

Leidloff, J. (1976) *The Continuum Concept*. London: Futura.

Miller, A. (1983) *Thou Shalt not be Aware: Society's Betrayal of the Child*. London: Pluto.

Montgomery, J. (1997) *Health Care Law*. Oxford: Oxford University Press.

Newell, P. (1989) *Children are People Too: the Case against Physical Punishment*. London: Bedford Square Press.

O'Neill, J. (1994) *The Missing Child in Liberal Theory*. Toronto: University of Toronto Press.

Penn, H. (1997) *Comparing Nurseries: The Experiences of Children and Staff in Day Nurseries in Spain, Italy and the UK*. London: Paul Chapman.

Qvortrup, J., Bardy, M., Sgritta, G. and Winterberger, H. (eds) (1994) *Childhood Matters: Social Theory, Practice and Politics*. Aldershot: Avebury.

Roberts, H., Smith, S. and Bryce, C. (1995) *Children at Risk? Safety as a Social Value*. Buckingham: Open University Press.

Royal College of Paediatrics and Child Health (formerly British Paediatric Association) (1992) *Ethical Guidelines on Medical Research with Children*. London: RCPCH.

Royal College of Paediatrics and Child Health (1997) *Withholding or Withdrawing Life Saving Treatment in Children*. London: RCPCH.

Siraj-Blatchford, I. (1996) Language, culture and difference: challenging inequalities and promoting respect, in C. Nutbrown (ed.) *Respectful Educators – Capable Learners: Children's Rights in Early Education*. London: Paul Chapman.

Smith, M. (1995) A community study of physical violence to children and accompanying social variables. Conference abstract, International Society for the Prevention of Child Abuse and Neglect, Fifth European Conference, Oslo.

Stern, D. (1977) *The First Relationship: Infant and Mother*. Edinburgh: Fontana.

United Nations Committee on the Rights of the Child (1995) Commentary on the UK Submission. Geneva: UN.

Wilkinson, R. (1994) *Unfair Shares: The Effects of Widening Income Differences on the Welfare of the Young*. Barkingside: Barnardo's.

Woodhead, M. (1997) Psychology and the cultural construction of children's needs, in A. James and A. Prout (eds) *Constructing and Reconstructing Childhood*. Cambridge: Polity.

Part six
Research and practice

In this book, there have been a number of persistent themes. What kinds of assumptions about children and childhood underpin daily practice? How powerful is the wider sociocultural and historical context in shaping early childhood services and daily practices with young children? What kind of theoretical bases do we draw on in discussing and developing daily practice? How does practice develop and change? In this last section we look at the role played by research.

The conventional model of research is of a specialized, expert and 'neutral' research team coming in to a site to carry out a specific and predetermined inquiry into certain aspects of practice. Often there is a nod to practitioners in the form of steering committees or an advisory group or some other attempt to enable practitioners to inform the research process. The results are then 'written up' by the research team, and disseminated to select audiences, sometimes including the practitioners themselves. This is not necessarily a negative process for practitioners and is sometimes a very useful one, depending on the nature of the involvement and the way in which the feedback is handled. Oakley and Roberts (1996) distinguish three different kinds of research evaluations: formative, process and outcome measures.

> Formative evaluations involve small-scale efforts to identify issues and relevant strategies prior to (and independently of) designing and implementing programmes of intervention. Process evaluations study the ways in which services or interventions are delivered; they are designed to describe what goes on, rather than to establish whether it works or not. Only a third type of evaluation, outcome evaluations, are designed in such a way that they can generate answers to questions about the effectiveness of particular interventions in changing specified outcomes.
>
> (Oakley and Roberts 1996: 6)

The most robust research enquiry, the 'gold standard' is the randomized controlled trial (RCT). This is a procedure evolved for the clinical testing of medical interventions such as drugs, in which half the sample are randomly allocated to take the drug, and their progress is compared with the other half of the sample, who do not receive the treatment. Oakley argues that RCTs can be used to good effect in evaluating nurseries – and other social interventions – and showing in what way children who have used the nurseries differ from those who have not. She also argues that RCTs are not necessarily unethical or alienating: they can closely involve practitioners; they can take account of process; and where resources are scarce, some decision has in any case to be made about how resources are allocated; and they have the overwhelming advantage of providing 'hard' evidence about how well the children do, using whatever criteria the practitioners or parents think important, compared with children who have not been through the same route.

But this kind of outcome based research is a very different approach to knowledge and to evidence from that explored in the previous two chapters. Anne Edwards and Gunilla Dahlberg ask in what ways can researchers contribute to the development of practice in early years settings, and conversely are there ways in which practitioners can draw on research to develop their practice? Although they write from differing perspectives, they would both agree with the following ideas about knowledge and learning in practice:

1 Knowledge always undergoes construction and transformation in use.
2 Learning is an integral aspect of activity in and with the world at all times. That learning occurs is not problematic.
3 What is learned is always complexly problematic.
4 Acquisition of knowledge is not a simple matter of taking in knowledge; rather, things assumed to be natural categories . . . require reconceptualization as cultural, social products.

(Lave 1996: 8)

Gunilla Dahlberg draws on the work being undertaken in Reggio Emilia to argue that a broad philosophical understanding is necessary in working with young children, since practice is predicated on many kinds of assumptions about the nature of children and the nature of knowledge. Reggio Emilia is a commune or small city in northern Italy, which, under the leadership of the psychologist Loris Malaguzzi, has developed a nursery system that has had world-wide renown. A touring exhibition of the work of the children from the nurseries is available, and has been shown, for example, at the Bethnal Green Toy Museum in London. There is a wide consensus that the work of the children is remarkable in its range and depth (Gura 1997). Dahlberg argues that this is due to the way in which Malaguzzi understood and applied wider philosophical debates about the nature of knowledge to the nurseries; he was very well informed about and continually drew on a postmodern perspective that emphasized the tentative and relative nature of knowledge, and the processes by which it is continually being created and revised. Dahlberg calls this a 'co-constructionist' approach.

Because existing knowledge about children and the curriculum was 'deconstructed' and its philosophical and historical roots explored, it was possible to involve an early years community of staff, parents, politicians and children, in working together to define, implement and document and 'reconstruct' or 'co-construct' their own ideas, a process which proved much richer than anyone had anticipated – what Malaguzzi ironically called the 'hundred languages of children'. This approach does not distinguish between 'research' on the one hand, and practice on the other, but sees them as inextricably fused.

Dahlberg provides a very illuminating and enthusiastic account, but the intensity and level of abstraction of this philosophical debate is sometimes hard to appreciate in such a pragmatic context as the UK. Anne Edwards adopts a rather different kind of sociocultural approach towards research and practice. She draws on the psychological notions of 'situated learning' and 'community of practice' (discussed in Part one), to describe her work with practitioners in the north of England. Like Dahlberg, she accepts that what early years workers know and do is rooted in their own past histories and in the contexts in which they practice, but is less concerned to engage in the wider philosophical debate. Her focus is initially much narrower. She describes how she and her colleagues held sustained discussions with a small group of practitioners from diverse backgrounds on the topic of young children's learning, which then led on to the practitioners introducing new activities and reflecting on how well they had worked. The intention, as with Reggio Emilia, has been the deconstruction and reconstruction of practice; destabilizing existing interpretations and the supported construction of new ways of being and seeing.

In her chapter, Edwards, like Dahlberg, argues that research does not need to be outside of practice but can be a fruitful part of it. The researcher need not, as so often happens, come in from the outside, do an esoteric piece of work and then disappear, leaving others to make what they can, if anything, of the findings. Using the 'community of practice' concept, she also argues that there are overlapping communities of practice, and the agendas, priorities and procedures of researchers, politicians, managers and others concerned with early years are part of the 'problem space', the areas of overlap that must be negotiated. Such overlaps, however problematic, are also enriching – they offer a valuable opportunity for 'the conversational development of informed practical knowledge' (Chapter 12, page 198).

References

Gura, P. (ed.) (1997) *Reflections on Early Education and Care Inspired by Visits to Reggio Emilia*. London: British Association for Early Childhood Education.

Lave, J. (1996) *The Practice of Learning*, in S. Chaiklin and J. Lave (eds) *Understanding Practice: Perspectives on Activity and Context*. Cambridge: Cambridge University Press.

Oakley, A. and Roberts, H. (eds) (1996) *Evaluating Social Interventions*. London: Social Science Research Unit/Barnados.

Everything is a beginning and everything is dangerous: some reflections on the Reggio Emilia experience

Gunilla Dahlberg

In the Nordic countries, there is a lot of exciting work currently underway drawing its inspiration from Reggio Emilia. At the Stockholm Institute of Education we are in the process of implementing a large-scale project entitled 'Early Childhood Pedagogy in a Changing World'. With funding from the Swedish government, an entire community comprising 28 preschools is working with inspiration from Emilia, while building on and reconstructing its own tradition in the field of early childhood pedagogy. The project involves not only children, teachers and parents from the respective preschools, but politicians and administrators from the local community. We are furthermore cooperating with the Reggio Emilia Institute in Stockholm.

In connection with this project I'm often asked, 'Why Reggio? Aren't the Scandinavian preschools and daycare centres also world renowned?' And they are; but for me the Reggio experience represents a challenge to the prevailing tradition of what early childhood pedagogy is, should and can be. It also symbolizes 'part of a dream come true' – to quote our friends in Reggio; the hope of promoting children's rights and status, at a time when management theories and simple quality indicators are on the agenda!

In a chapter such as this it is difficult to do justice to the Reggio Emilia experience. This is largely because of the web of discourses that constitute this experience. Some of these discourses are familiar to me; others remain to be discovered and explored. But before problematizing the Reggio experience, I would like to say that my perspective – which is also that of Reggio Emilia – presupposes that we are continuously constructing our world. This means that my interpretations, conceptualizations and meaning making are productive and, as such, become part of their construction. Accordingly, constructions are neither neutral nor innocent; quite the contrary. They display both power and control.

Reggio Emilia – against a nostalgic vision of the child

Today there are differing opinions as to how we might understand our times. However, there appears to be a shared sentiment that we are living through more than the chronological end of an era and are facing profound transformations. Seyla Benhabib has articulated this quite aptly:

> As the twentieth century draws to a close, there is little question that we are living through more than the chronological end of an epoch. To invoke a distinction familiar to the Greeks, it is not only kronos which is holding sway over our lives; but our kairos as well, our lived time . . . time is imbued with symbolic meaning, is caught in the throes of forces of which we only have a dim understanding at the present. The many 'postisms' like posthumanism, post-structuralism, postmodernism, post-Fordism, post-Keynesianism and *post-histoire* circulating in our intellectual and cultural lives, are at one level only expressions of a deeply shared sense that certain aspects of our social, symbolic and political universe have been profoundly and most likely irretrievably transformed.
>
> (1992: 1)

It is not at all surprising that a feeling of distress and erosion of trust prevails when times change. However, in my view, Malaguzzi and the Reggio Emilia experience have not drawn sustenance from a nostalgic yearning for the good old times. Their view of our times and the child neither builds on narratives of 'futurity and progress', nor of 'decline and nostalgia' (Jenks 1994). Instead they have engaged in a dialogue with the present, exploring their everyday pedagogical practice in relation to different scientific and philosophical perspectives. To quote Loris Malaguzzi (personal communication), 'Pedagogy is not created by itself; it is only created within the context of a loving relationship or by confronting the present'.

Malaguzzi also pointed out that what he embraced was not a naïve optimism, but rather a sceptical attitude toward the presumed certainties of the past, the present and the future.

A pluralist perspective

The discussions surrounding children in Reggio Emilia are the product of the war experience and of twenty long years of fascism/fascist repression. After the war, and the immeasurable loss associated therewith, many people dreamed of nothing other than building a decent society in which to live. As in many countries, it was believed that society had to give precedence to the lives of children. According to Bengt Borjesson:[1]

> World War II was the unsurpassable social landslide in the history of the twentieth century; of the countless metaphorical themes which

emerge in connection with this course of events, it is the test of strength/tug-of-war between the authoritarian and fascist administrations/regimes, on one hand, and the democratic societies, on the other, which has engraved itself on the consciousness of every thinking human being during this epoch.

(1995: 133)

This tug-of-war, between the authoritarian and the democratic, was very apparent in Reggio Emilia's struggle of the 1960s and 1970s. In an interview that my colleagues and I conducted with Bonacci, the Mayor of Reggio Emilia during that period, it became obvious how important it was for many people in Reggio to break with authoritarian tradition and build a society based on democratic values. In our interview, we asked Bonacci what prompted the people of Reggio Emilia to design an early childhood education system founded on the perspective of the child. He replied that the fascist experience had taught them that people who conformed and obeyed were dangerous, and that in building a new society it was imperative to safeguard and communicate that lesson, and nurture and maintain a vision of children who can think and act for themselves. The mission was to teach children not to obey!

While enacting a broad social vision, it is quite obvious that this vision has not been framed within modernist concerns for progress and universal explanations. Like postmodernist and poststructuralist thinkers, the pedagogues of Reggio Emilia have not adhered to modernist claims of truth, but instead attempted to move away from the legacy of modernity with its universalism and binary oppositions between order and disorder, nature and culture, the rational and the irrational, thinking and feeling, and so on. To build a base for democratic politics, Malaguzzi, apart from his Gramscian heritage, was surely supported by his pragmatic outlook and his inspiration from Dewey. In fact, from my perspective, his pragmatism was very much that of Rorty: 'Pragmatism is to me, as I have said, a philosophy of solidarity rather than of despair' (1991: 33).

Malaguzzi also held the conviction that a pragmatic approach could not be accomplished without a pluralistic orientation and the commitment of children, parents, teachers, administrators and politicians.

By entering into a dialogue with both their own local practice and with different scientific and philosophical perspectives, the children, the pedagogues, the parents and others in Reggio Emilia have managed to construct their own local narrative. Malaguzzi was embroiled in continuous discussions about objectivity, truth and relativism, and their relationship to human beings' sense of self-reliance.

An important factor that helps to explain the success of the Reggio experience is the region's long history of active citizenship. Putnam (1993), who has studied the level of economic development and civic performance in Italy, has found that, in addition to this particular historic legacy, the Emilia Romagna region also boasts strong, effective and responsive political institutions supported by local organizations. This 'social capital' has created the necessary precondition for social relationships characterized by trust and cooperation, in Putnam's phrase, 'making democracy work'. According to Putnam, this 'social capital' has also been a precondition for the strong economic growth of the region.

The intellectual mission of Loris Malaguzzi and his colleagues

What is so terribly impressive and exceptional about the Reggio experience and the work of Loris Malaguzzi is the way in which they have challenged the dominating discourses of our time, specifically in the field of early childhood pedagogy – a most unique undertaking for a pedagogical practice! This was achieved by deconstructing the way in which the field has been socially constituted within a scientific, political and ethical context and then reconstructing and redefining children's and teachers' subjectivities. That is, Loris Malaguzzi and those associated with him have tried to understand what kinds of thoughts, conceptions, ideas, societal structures and behavioural patterns have dominated the field and how these discourses have shaped our conceptions and images of the child and childhood, the way we interact with children and the kind of environment we create for them. I would like to add that their practice has revolutionized pedagogics by virtually transforming the entire web of relationships within the field.

As I see it, all of this was possible because Malaguzzi was extremely familiar with the field and its traditions, but he also had the courage and originality to choreograph his own thinking. By placing himself and the Reggio practice in continuous dialogue with different scientific and philosophical perspectives, not to mention the worlds of poetry, architecture, art and so on, he, together with the pedagogues, succeeded in exposing our cultural heritage and opening up new possibilities, a new space, outside the ahistorical laws and imperatives of contemporary science and philosophy. This is not unlike what Bourdieu and Foucault, among others, accomplished. Hultqvist writes about Foucault:

> For him knowledge production in favour of society rather implies the ability or the method to see something other than the given; to think in a way other than the customary and to see in a way other than what one is used to. This implies shaking off the straitjacket of hegemonic discourses, calling into question and reformulating the established truth.
>
> (1995: 18)

Another important factor that has contributed to the success of the Reggio project is the fact that self-interest and private interests appear not to have superseded higher ideals and objectives. This has required a certain degree of sacrifice on the part of those involved and a genuine belief in the good of the cause to ensure a professional relationship with pedagogical practice.

A social constructionist view and an anti-representational approach

In Reggio they share a social constructionist view based on such concepts as construction, co-construction and reconstruction. In the scientific world there is a marked tendency to conceptualize the world as something we describe and represent in our heads, but according to the social constructionist view we are all active observers and participants, continuously constituting and constructing the world we live in. Heinz von Foerster to whom Malaguzzi often referred, argued that: 'Objectivity is a subject's false view that observing can take place without him' (quoted in Israel 1992: 109).

For Malaguzzi, the notion that we cannot describe our world without taking notice and being aware of the fact that we are describing it, was nurtured by the inspiration he drew from a variety of disciplines. In this connection, he was known to cite scientists and philosophers representing, for example, the new quantum mechanics associated with chaos theory and the new cybernetics, as well as the science of mathematics.

Coupled with Malaguzzi's social constructionist perspective is his awareness of the power of the process representation. As a result, the pedagogues in Reggio have been very much against a textbook approach to their practice with prescribed rules, goals and methods. This explains why they do not have a 'programme or a curriculum' that can be readily transferred and applied to another cultural context. I recall Malaguzzi inquiring once, very seriously, if the Swedish pedagogues visiting Reggio were working with 'The Dove', 'The Dove' being one of the most well known thematic works in Reggio. 'Do you have doves in your squares, like in Reggio?' he continued. I had to answer, 'No!'

Gregory Bateson's (1988) contextual and relational epistemology, together with his critique of ingrained conceptions of consciousness, the world and our civilization, have been very important in this regard. Bateson has argued that we should understand our world as patterns that are related and interconnected, rather than fixed and separate. He wanted to view these patterns more like a synergetic dance of cooperating parts. Bateson also claimed that we live with the illusion that the map is the territory, the landscape, and the name is the same as the named.

In relation to this he argued that if we could only acknowledge the illusion and break the pattern and see that 'the name of the name is not the name and the name of the relation is not the relation' (Bateson 1988: 3), we could then change this relationship and create a new space for pedagogy.

Reggio shares this anti foundationalist and anti-representationalist perspective with the neo-pragmatists. Cherryholmes, with respect to pragmatic thinking, has pointed out that:

> In place of talk about programs and projects, we prefer to talk about conjectures and images and contradictions and ambiguities that accompany ideas that we value, when we choose our way of life and society. We believe that we will never fully understand and nail down these ideas because their meanings will continue to shift and drift. These are not reasons for despair. It is just the way things are, as we understand them, when we cope with education, society and living.
>
> (1994: 205)

Time and again Malaguzzi cited the mathematician Lewis Carroll, author of *Alice in Wonderland*. I do not know whether he read Carroll's *Sylvie and Bruno Concluded*, but I suspect that he might have been inspired by the following passage. The storyteller meets a character called Mein Herr, and the following conversation takes place:

> Mein Herr looked so thoroughly bewildered that I thought it best to change the subject. 'What a useful thing a pocket-map is!' I remarked.
>
> 'That's another thing we've learned from *your* Nation', said Mein Herr, 'map-making. But we've carried it much further than *you*. What do you consider the *largest* map that would be really useful?'
>
> 'About 6 inches to the mile.'
>
> 'Only *six inches!*' exclaimed Mein Herr. 'We very soon got to six *yards* to the mile. Then we tried a *hundred* yards to the mile. And then came the grandest idea of all! We actually made a map of the country on the scale of *a mile to the mile!*' 'Have you used it much?' I enquired.
>
> 'It has never been spread out, yet,' Mein Herr said: 'the farmers objected: They said it would cover the whole country, and shut out the sunlight! So we now use the country itself, as its own map, and I assure you it does nearly as well.'
>
> (Carroll [1893] 1973: 556–7)

A pedagogy that speaks in a child's voice

Deconstruction has made it possible for Reggio Emilia to recognize that children, teachers and parents can be differently constructed. By calling into question theories, where identities are perceived as stable and unified wholes, they have been able to conceptualize identity, not as something given, but as socially constructed and co-constructed. Accordingly, they see identities not as essentials, but as historically formed in everyday practices and in relation to power. Through this endeavour they have been able to construct another child, the *rich child,* with lots of potential, instead of the poor child – the deficit or the child at risk, with limited capacities and in need of protection; so common in educational settings. The *rich child* is seen as a co-constructer of his or her own world. The image of the *rich child* also constructs the *rich pedagogue*, who is perfectly comfortable with the idea of having the potential to be co-constructors of their own identity. The representation of the *rich child* also constructs *rich parents*.

From my perspective, developmental psychology can be a real hindrance when it comes to creating a pedagogy that speaks in the voice of the child. The field of developmental psychology does not have very much of a critical orientation. It is largely confined to changes in orientation that are methodological in nature, such as interactionism, contextualism, ethnography and so on. The search for definite structures and stages – like Piaget's operational structures – surely represses contradictions and ambiguity and promotes normalization. But as Docker (1994) maintains, structures can also be conceived of as without a centre: open to interpretation without an end; unconfined; unreduced; unfinalized; untotalized; not continuous; non-linear; and where truth is never arrived at – a view that seems more in keeping with the Reggio Emilia perspective.

Reggio also stands outside the pedagogical canon, where the child is seen as active and resourceful, but where the teacher still owns the questions and the answers. Even if many of us working with children try to approach our work from a child's perspective and work thematically, it seems that we have not been able to detach ourselves from our cultural heritage, wherein the teacher monopolizes most of the classroom time, and where the teachers ask the questions; questions that are not real questions since the teacher already knows the answers.

Since the Reggio discourse has been able to stand in dialogue with, but also in confrontation with a very hegemonic child developmental discourse by adopting a social constructionist perspective, it has, to a great extent, been able to disrupt processes of normalization, standardization and neutralization and make way for and celebrate diversity, difference and pluralism.

A playful textuality

As demonstrated thus far, I think that Reggio Emilia has anticipated poststructuralist perspectives and various motifs of postmodernism by creating a space for and by inviting contradiction and by welcoming challenges, Reggio has been able to choreograph 'a playful textuality'. The *atelierista* (artist in residence) has been important in breaking this new ground. By employing different media and a complexity of meaning, the *atelierista* has played a vital role in making new and exciting connections.

This makes the Reggio practice rich in paradox and irony. Malaguzzi often said, 'For upbringing to be successful you need a jester in your pocket'. In this context, with echoes of the work of Bronfenbrenner, he also said, 'For upbringing to be really successful, there needs to be at least one crazy uncle around who astonishes'.

This, I assume, has been possible because Reggio Emilia has turned away from the modernist idea of organic unity and encouraged multiple languages, confrontation and ambivalence and ambiguity. Therefore, people favouring a strong modernist idea of organic unity often find the practice at Reggio Emilia too noisy and containing too much 'dirt and pollution'.

The Reggio Emilia pedagogy is like a Rabelaisian approach, an intercontextuality that combines carnival and public square games, feasts, masks, theatre, philosophies and cosmologies (Bachtin 1986). Reggio Emilia and its preschools also join in 'carnivalesque activities'. During a visit to Reggio, I took part in an ecological marathon where children, teachers and parents – in fact the whole community – were participating, together with marathon runners, fire-eaters, masked people walking on stilts, and so on. And when you hear the names of some of the project work produced by the children in the preschools you get a similar impression: an amusement park for birds, the mob, the dinosaurs and so on. The whole milieu speaks of a collective adventure.

Reggio – contributing to a narrative of self-reflection

But what is perhaps even more important, uncommon and unique, both for pedagogues and scientists, is that they always see their own social constructions as a beginning and as having the potential of being dangerous. This is related to their epistemological idea that constructions and representations are productive and, therefore, neither neutral nor innocent. With that knowledge they are always keeping their own practice open for criticism through self-reflection and documentation. This documentation can be seen as narratives of children's and teacher's lives and, as such, they are, in Rorty's words, a way of 'telling the story of one's contribution to a community' (1991: 21). It is also a contribution to a narrative of a reflexive project of the self, since documentation serves as a means of identifying the techniques by which we constructed ourselves and our relationship with the world and how we make ourselves into subjects. The more aware we are of these practices of the self, the greater the space for altering these practices (Foucault 1991; Gore 1993).

But as Carlina Rinaldi, one of the pedagogue in Reggio Emilia, has pointed out, when the dialogue is made into an object of inquiry the dangers and responsibilities will increase as practices become visible. And there is no guarantee that these practices will be consistent with our expectations. This means that practices must always be open for rethinking and reformulation and we must learn to live with uncertainty.

To end, I would like to say that Reggio Emilia, in my opinion, has been able to institute a new horizon, a new freedom or perhaps a new regime of truth. One could even suggest that Reggio has created *a new university!*

Note

1 All translations in the text have been made by the author.

References

Bachtin, M. (1986) *Rabelais och Skratlets Historia*. Stockholm: Grebo.

Bateson, G. (1988) *Ande och Natur. En Nodvandig Enhet*. Stockholm: Symposium.

Benhabib, S. (1992) *Situating the Self*. Cambridge: Polity Press.

Borjesson, B. (1995) Det ideologiskt omstridda barnet, in L. Dahlgren and K. Hultqvist (eds) *Seendet och Seendets Villkor. En Bok om Barns och Ungas, Valfard*. Stockholm: HLS Forlag.

Carroll, L. ([1893]1973) *Sylvie and Bruno Concluded: Lewis Carroll, the Complete Works*. London. The Nonesuch Press (first published 1893).

Cherryholmes, C.H. (1994) Dialogue: pragmatism, poststructuralism and socially useful theorizing, *Curriculum Inquiry*, 24(2): 194–213.

Docker, J. (1994) *Postmodernism and Popular Culture: A Cultural History*. Cambridge: Cambridge University Press.

Foucault, M. (1991) Governmentality, in G. Burcell, C. Gordon and P. Miller (eds) *The Foucault Effect: Studies in Governmentality*. Chicago, IL: University of Chicago Press.

Gore, J. (1993) *The Struggle for Pedagogies: Critical and Feminist Discourses as Regimes of Truth*. New York: Routledge.

Hultqvist, K. (1995) En nutidshistoris om barns valfard i Sverige, in L. Dahlgren and K. Hultqvist *Seendet och Seendets Villkor. En Bok om Barns och Ungas Valfard*. Stockholm: HLS Forlag.

Jenks, C. (1994) Child abuse in the postmodern context: an issue of social identity, *Childhood*, 2(3): 3.

Putnam, R.O. (1993) *Making Democracy Work: Civic Traditions in Modern Italy*. Princeton, NJ: Princeton University Press.

Rorty, R. (1991) *Objectivity, Relativism, and Truth*. Philosophical Papers, vol 1. Cambridge: Cambridge University Press.

12 | Research and practice: is there a dialogue?

Anne Edwards

Some preliminary questions

What is research?

First of all is research a process or a product? Is it primarily a way of operating systematically as we gather information in complex social settings? Or is it simply what researchers find out and package enticingly for application in other settings? If it is a process, what are its purposes? Should we expect it to illuminate aspects of practice? Or should it solve problems of practice? If illumination is an aim, are research products found primarily in the enlightenment of the practitioners who choose to interpret their settings with these new insights in mind? If problem solving is the purpose, are research products seen only as commodities to be taken into new settings and used? These questions, in turn, raise others about practice and knowledge.

What is practice?

Does practice in early childhood services consist largely of routines and rituals that have their roots in the professional histories of each element of the service? Is practice mainly the carrying out of carefully constructed action plans? Or is it primarily the exercise of informed professional judgements in complex settings? Who are the practitioners? Are we operating with a form of debilitating inverse snobbery when we designate only those who work directly with children or parents to be practitioners and then protect them from the sharp edges of informed professional debate about their roles and functions? Are policy makers, local strategists, managers and researchers also practitioners with children's well-being at the centre of their concerns?

What is knowledge?

Is knowledge a commodity that can be used or applied universally? Is it a set of propositions to be tested? Is it the cultural capital of a particular professional group? Does it lie at the source of our dispositions to interpret and act in particular ways? To what extent is it simply constructed in the settings in which it is used? How can knowledge communities, wherever they are situated, be refreshed? How can research based knowledge inform practice?

The research–practice link is not a simple one. Indeed in the education field it has a long and troubled history with disappointments on both sides. Mary Kennedy has explored four lines of argument that are often used to explain the apparent failure of research to influence educational practice over six decades in the USA (Kennedy 1997). These arguments are familiar ones: the research itself is insufficiently authoritative or persuasive; the research is irrelevant to practice; research ideas are inaccessible to practitioners; the educational system is itself either unable to cope with the changes that research suggests or conversely the system is too unstable and unable to engage with systemic change. Her conclusion is that researchers and school based practitioners should recognize that both research and practice are influenced by, and are even 'victims of' the same shifting social and political context. Our disappointment, she explains, doubtless stems from false expectations about the relationship between research and practice. Instead we should acknowledge the 'ambivalent and ambiguous character of education' and in doing so actually enhance its relevance and accessibility.

Kennedy's arguments point to an exploration of relationships between research and practice in early childhood services in the sociocultural settings in which each have developed and are currently being constructed. Any exploration will need to answer some of the preliminary questions. I shall attempt this examination of the relationship between research and practice by starting with a view of practice as informed action carried out by professionals who demonstrate dispositions to interpret their settings in particular ways and select responses to their interpretations. Practitioners, according to this view, are using the practical knowledge of their professions to anticipate events and maintain control of them. If research based knowledge is to influence practice it consequently has to become part of the constant cycle of interpretation and response that is at the core of informed professional action in complex settings.

Clearly, therefore, research is not simply a product that can be applied universally to solve the problems of practice. If it is to enhance practice, research has to be able to inform both the interpretations and responses of practitioners. It needs to become embedded in the practical knowledge of the community of practitioners and inform practitioners' ways of seeing and being as they work with clients. At the same time it needs to so sensitive to the existing values and expertise, that is cultural capital, that practitioners already bring to bear on their professional decision making.

This view of research–practice links makes considerable demands on social science researchers and is based firmly on an idea of research as illuminative and clarificatory. In addition it expects research to have the potential to become part of the practices themselves. The possibility that social science research processes might have some impact on their fields of study is, of course, recognized in codes of ethical research practice and in acknowledgement of the powers and responsibilities of social researchers as they 'spiral in and out' of research participants' lives (Giddens 1990). Seth Chaiklin has taken the interactivity and illuminatory qualities of social science research and practice further, in his celebration of what he terms 'theory/practice' (Chaiklin 1993). Chaiklin's theory/practice as a form of social science aims at developing a 'theoretical account of societally significant practices' and producing analytical descriptions that are potentially useful to practitioners in enhancing their understanding of practice.

Chaiklin is operating within a sociocultural framework that emphasizes: the power of history in shaping the possibilities for action available in any setting; and the centrality of practitioners' knowledge and beliefs to how they interact with those possibilities. A sociocultural perspective suggests that in order to develop practice, practitioners need to be able to distinguish between cultural capital, which can usefully be used, and cultural baggage, which inhibits the development of practice. Furthermore, they need to see how their practices are positioned in other complex sets of relationships between other practitioners, policies and clients. Accordingly, early childhood professionals should, in Kennedy's terms, be alert to the 'ambivalent and ambiguous character' of these services and the implications of this for their practices.

Kennedy's warning about the instability of policy driven social settings is also aimed at researchers. They too are positioned vulnerably in sets of governmental research priorities. In addition, Chaiklin's direct attention to how research and practice inform each other requires researchers to examine how the lenses that they place over practice and the contexts of practice can usefully produce the illumination and clarification of practices for practitioners. Researchers also come to the practice of research with their own mixtures of capital and baggage. And so complex are the settings of practice that it is unlikely that one set of research lenses, whether shaped by, for example, psychology or sociology, can do justice to what expert practitioners have to take into account as they make informed judgements in practice. For research to illuminate and clarify practice, it needs to be able to accommodate the complexities of practice and its contexts. For this reason we shall now look more closely at what sociocultural psychology can offer those interested in links between research and practice.

A sociocultural perspective on informed practice

Sociocultural psychology emphasizes relationships between individuals, actions, meanings, contexts, communities and cultural histories (see, for example, Resnick *et al.* 1991; Chaiklin and Lave 1993; Wertsch *et al.* 1995a). Wertsch *et al.* describe a sociocultural approach to the study of human action as follows: 'The goal of a sociocultural approach is to explicate the relations between human action, on the one hand, and the cultural, institutional, and historical situations in which this action occurs on the other' (Wertsch *et al.* 1995b: 11).

It would seem, therefore, that a sociocultural framing of practice and its development would have some mileage for research in and on early childhood services, where cultural, institutional and historical constraints and possibilities have so much impact on practice and its meanings. The value of a sociocultural framework lies both in enhancing researchers' understandings of the complexities of practice and in alerting us to ways in which practice might be developed. Let us therefore look at some of the key tenets of sociocultural psychology and in so doing clarify still further some possible responses to the preliminary questions. A prime concern evident in these tenets is how knowledge is used and developed in the communities in which practice occurs.

A *community of practice* is a place where knowledge is used in action and developed into forms that are acceptable within each community (Lave and Wenger 1991). Communities of practice have shared histories and values and as a result ascribe common meanings to objects and events. It is quite easy to see, for example, primary education as a community of practice with its shared history, values and meanings. It is less easy to see preschool provision as a coherent community of practice. Diverse histories have resulted in different priorities and therefore different ways of interpreting children, children's needs and the resources available to meet those needs.

Knowledge, within a sociocultural framework, is owned and developed in the communities in which it is used. Its origins lie in the sociocultural history of specific knowledge communities. One becomes a member of a community of practice through increasing engagement with the knowledge in use in that community. The knowledge of the community is mediated by more expert members through the ways that the tools and artifacts of the community are used and most particularly through the meanings ascribed to the tools. Here the tools of early years provision include both language and material resources such as jigsaws or dressing-up clothes. Tool use in nursery settings can be seen in, for example, how an adult highlights an aspect of role play or shares a nursery rhyme. Crudely, an educationally trained professional might use a rhyme to enhance a child's familiarity with language, whereas a care orientated practitioner may be more concerned with how the rhyme might distract a child from an altercation with another. Neither use would be inappropriate, but different training and associated cultures would lead to different interpretations of, and responses to, similar events, and different meanings being ascribed to the tools available.

Action is consequently central to this notion of *knowledge in use* in a community of practice. As practitioners become more expert in the practice of a community they move from being peripheral participants in the action and knowledge use and draw ever-increasingly on the body of knowledge that informs the community. In so doing they interpret the demands of practice and respond in more skilful ways and, in turn, contribute to the knowledge construction process of the professional community.

Identity, as intentional action in a context that one interprets and acts upon, is therefore an important concept. Identity, that is, a sense of what one can do, leads one's actions. In terms of professional identity, the more that practitioners understand their practice and the possibilities for responses available in the places in which they practice, and the more they use this practical knowledge while engaged in practice, the more developed their practice becomes. Professional identities are therefore heavily rooted in the actions, expectations, meanings and possibilities employed by previous generations. These expectations, meanings and possibilities for action are powerfully evident in the ways that tools and artifacts (for example, language, resources, sites of practice and so on) are used to construct knowledge. Michael Cole explains the situation more generally when he describes how humans develop in cultures that pre-exist their entry: '. . . the common starting point of all socio–cultural–historical viewpoints . . . is [humans'] need to inhabit an environment transformed by the activity of prior members of their species' (1995: 190). His explanation reminds us of just how great the challenge is for those who wish to develop new configurations of existing communities of practices with new priorities for knowledgeable practice.

This brief outline of the tenets of sociocultural approaches to knowledge and practice therefore raises a number of issues. These include the dangers of closed communities of practice that are forever recycling old and tired knowledge and the challenges presented when communities are required to change rapidly in order to accommodate new external demands.

Adapting professional practice to cope with new external demands is a major concern for early childhood practitioners in England and Wales, who are having to work with the educational demands of *Desirable Outcomes* (SCAA 1996). It was this challenge that was presented to Angela Anning and myself at the School of Education at the University of Leeds when we were asked to collaborate with three local authorities in the professional development of key practitioners through the construction of an educationally orientated curriculum for children from birth to 5 (Anning and Edwards in press). The collaboration provides a useful case study of the power of sociocultural approaches to understanding and enabling dialogues between research and informed practice.

A case study of a research–practice collaboration

The collaboration involved our working with 25 early years workers from diverse backgrounds and with a wide range of different responsibilities as they attempted to meet the educational demands of *Desirable Outcomes* (SCAA 1996) in order to ensure that children achieved the educational entitlement outlined by the document.

Probably more than any other UK initiative, *Desirable Outcomes* seems likely to promote increased cohesion in early years provision. But cohesion can come in many guises. The fragmentary nature of UK early years provision, drawing on healthcare, nursery nursing, social work, voluntary work and education, has ensured that the various sources of practice have been able to retain important features of their own sociocultural histories and have sustained quite distinct practitioner identities through considerable variations in knowledge and practice. Each professional grouping therefore has its own strengths, which are validated and refined in its daily practice.

One of the challenges facing providers when the project started, was to ensure that early years professionals were enabled to provide children's educational entitlement in ways that allowed them to work confidently with children while they were building new identities as educators as well as carers. The aim was therefore cohesion without colonization.

In planning the project we worked with three principles, which we hoped would address some of the issues outlined.

- We were aiming at the creation of a new community of practice, which drew together professionals from diverse backgrounds, with a common focus on supporting the learning of very young children.
- We wanted the study to support practitioners as they acquired new understandings and dealt with the demands made on them.
- We wanted the study to change practice and to leave practitioners well placed to sustain the changed practices, and to share them once the project had finished.

Key words therefore were community of practice, action and knowledge, taking us to a central concern with supporting the development of increasingly informed professional identities in action in early years settings.

Importantly our project aimed at creating a new form of professional practice; one that allowed early years workers to attend more directly to young children as learners and to develop their roles as active supporters of that learning within a broad curriculum framework. The meanings ascribed to existing tools and artifacts in the preschool settings were likely therefore to change, the sites of practice were not necessarily likely to contain experts in the new forms of practice and the settings themselves were unlikely to license the use of such expertise, even if it did exist. We were aiming at an all-embracing change in practice, practitioners and the sites of practice.

We therefore decided to focus on:

- informing the professional identities of practitioners by enabling them to become users of research and encouraging them to use research based knowledge in practice;
- setting up situations in which practitioners would work with familiar tools and artifacts in ways that allowed them to ascribe new (educational) meanings to them, by drawing on their research based knowledge in their evaluations of their actions;
- creating opportunities for informed discussion across settings of practice and the sharing of meanings being ascribed to aspects of practice by colleagues in their settings.

These focuses led us to case study enquiries followed by action research, and particularly the notion of action research embedded within sets of learning networks that enabled collaboration across settings and between practitioners, providers and higher education.

Figure 12.1 provides an outline of the 18-month project. Step One lasted for four months and during that period we met monthly for workshops led by Angela Anning or me on, for example, young children and literacy, action research, working with parents and supporting children as learners. Step Two also lasted for four months. Here colleagues worked in their own settings, undertaking case study work in the areas of children's learning in numeracy or literacy and a short piece of action research based on their case studies. We met regularly, and Angela and I visited the settings to offer feedback and advice on both the research process and research based practice. During Steps One and Two colleagues were also sent research digests prepared by Angela or me on, for example, early literacy and early numeracy. Step Three lasted for ten months. Having dipped their toes into research based practice in Step Two, in Step Three participants undertook major research based curriculum development work in their own settings with their colleagues. Again we visited settings and regular workshops were held to discuss work in progress.

Consistent themes at workshop meetings throughout each step of the study were: working with evidence; observing children and their interactions with adults; and Vygotskian notions of how adults assist young children to become learners through, for example, engagement in 'joint involvement episodes' (JIEs). Schaffer's work on JIEs (Schaffer 1992) appeared to strike an important chord with the group. Its relevance is perhaps unsurprising. It emphasizes how adults can assist the language and cognitive development of young learners by paying joint attention to and jointly acting on a topic. With young children topics include objects or some feature of the environment, but as children develop the topics can be symbolic and become central features in conversations between children and others.

The idea inherent in JIEs is that children learn to distinguish, act upon and represent features of the world beyond their close relationships with

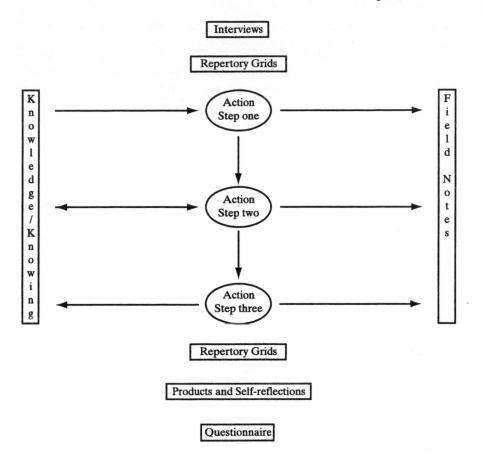

Figure 12.1 The design of the study

caregivers as part of that relationship. They learn to look outside the boundaries and private meanings of the relationship and take on for themselves the meanings ascribed to important cultural objects by their community. Helping children to understand objects and their meanings is, of course, central to the work of practitioners in well resourced nurseries. Therefore developing the capacity of nursery professionals to see the educational implications of actions on and around objects was central to the project.

Figure 12.1 shows that we are also gathering additional information through interviews, repertory grids and a questionnaire, but I shall not be referring to these here. Instead I shall concentrate on the professional learning that appeared to be contributing to the development of shared understandings of practice. The data are the self-reflections produced by participants at the end of Step Three, supplemented by field notes written at monthly meetings. Three of the individual studies give some flavour of the project and the processes it employed.

Melissa was a nursery teacher in a large nursery school. Alison was the head of an early years centre. Her background was nursery nursing followed by a social work training. Molly was head of a nursery and she trained as a nursery nurse. Melissa, Alison and Molly all focused on the construction areas of their settings; however they had different intentions.

Melissa's nursery had a well established High Scope system in place. As one part of Step Three she intended to use the construction area and the impetus provided by the project to enhance children's language use in their construction play and particularly to encourage the nursery assistants in her team to make the most of the language opportunities available in the construction area. The first focus was the use of positional language. Play people and farm animals were added to the wooden bricks in the construction area to enable children to make enclosures. The children did as anticipated and the staff encouraged positional language as they played with the children. Staff all made notes on their interactions and brought them to planning meetings. Melissa's evaluation of this element of her project includes the following statement.

> The adults discovered the ease of using existing resources to enable children to develop their language skills. Also they assessed the knowledge of the children through making notes about skills demonstrated in the construction area. They also saw the value of resources being added to the construction area in providing the opportunities for further learning and in being able to assess existing skills through their own involvement.

Alison's starting point was a feeling that by focusing on number and computation, while interacting with children, her team's approach to mathematics was limited. Her Step Two observations explored that hunch and led her to conclude that this was likely to be due to the staff's lack of confidence in that area of the curriculum. Her observations also revealed that opportunities to work with blocks and small construction materials were limited and that the construction area was under resourced. The focus of Alison's project in Step Three therefore became: establishing and resourcing a construction area; developing mathematical opportunities in the area; and raising staff awareness and improving mathematical knowledge and understanding.

Staff in Alison's early years centre carried out detailed and finely focused observations of children as they engaged with the materials available and they worked conversationally with the children in the construction area. These observations were discussed and used to focus later observations, and provided Alison with the opportunity to feed in her increasingly informed understanding of how children are supported as learners. As researchers, we found practitioners' observations of children annotated and cross-referenced and later reflections added (when, for example, David Wood's helpful observation that, while older children are recruited to curricula younger children are captured (Wood 1988), had been discussed in a workshop). This appeared as a consoling addition to the observation notes where a nursery worker had recorded her failed attempts to cajole a 3-year-old to work with shapes while bikes were available. Importantly, Wood's general observation about young children also prompted a written reflection in the additional notes, on the timing and pacing of interventions with young children.

Molly already had an established construction area in the nursery but was dissatisfied with the quality of the activities that occurred there. Her focus was the development of children's mark-making skills in the construction area. Having observed at Step Two that her staff seemed uneasy about extending children's activities and thinking in the construction area, she started by modelling the kinds of interaction she would like to see. She followed this by discussing the criteria with which she evaluated her own actions with the staff. She then involved the staff in observing the children and each other interacting with the children at Step Three.

In all three examples the emphasis was on enhancing the capacity of nursery staff to interact knowledgeably with the children and to support them as learners in the construction area by encouraging their more focused use of the materials (tools and artifacts) available, and through their own increasingly informed interactions with them.

In each setting, staff were asked to make detailed observations of the children at play in the areas, and to identify what they thought the children had learnt and what they too had learnt. Melissa, Alison and Molly developed their goals for their nurseries through familiarization with current research, discussion with colleagues from other settings and from their own case study research in their own environments at Step Two of the project. They then helped their colleagues to use the same information and skills in their work with children.

The focus in the project was therefore on knowledge construction and hence informed identity construction at two levels. Firstly, at Steps One and Two attention was paid to informing the professional identities of the 25 project participants. Their identities were validated, for example, in discussions of the case study evidence brought to our monthly meetings and by the insightful interpretations they were making when they looked in detail and in increasingly informed ways at their own settings. Their participation in the project appeared to be enhancing their ways of seeing and being as they worked in the complex settings that are nurseries.

For example, at a workshop during Step Two Molly reflected on the way she had been working with her staff and commented, 'You know, perhaps it's not a question of getting them or making them do things. It's more helping them to see what they can do and helping them to do it. Isn't it? At least now I think it is.'

At a workshop during Step Three Alison was discussing the increasing emphasis she and her colleagues were placing on knowledge of curriculum when staff were interacting with children: 'It's a question of getting the balance between the child and the planned curriculum. You need to keep the curriculum lead while observing and interacting with a child. So when you are assessing you catch what they can do rather than what we want done.'

The second level of identity construction came into play at Step Three, when the 25 participants worked more directly with their colleagues in their workplaces to support their developing understandings of the educational potential available in familiar features of nursery settings and consequently their increasingly informed identities. Step Three also witnessed a further development in the professional identities of the original 25 participants as they were able to use the networks established in the first two steps to support them in their new roles as supporters of the learning of workplace colleagues.

In attempting to assist the informing and forming of a community of practice, the project: focused on informing the professional identities of practitioners through engagement in evidence based practice; encouraged the development of new meanings around familiar tools and artifacts; and set up the opportunity for the development of a new discourse of informed educational practice to be used by preschool professionals. How successful were we?

Key outcomes of the project

In summary it did seem that, if not a community of practice, at least a community of understanding was developed. We perhaps need to wait to see what happens over the next few years in each of the settings before we can go so far as to suggest that a coherent community of practice has been created. The curriculum materials produced as a result of the project (Anning and Edwards 1999) may assist such a development but that will be another evaluation. Let us, therefore, look at the three focuses of our initiative and consider the extent to which our activities in each of these three areas assisted the development of a community of understanding.

Informed professional identities

Accessing identities, or ways of seeing and being, is notoriously difficult. However, recent work on discourse and cognition does help us. Derek Edwards, for example, suggests that who we are, and why we are who we are, are embedded in sets of social practices (D. Edwards 1997). Furthermore, one way of accessing who we are is to examine how we talk about those practices. John Shotter takes a similar line when he argues, 'we can both discover and display the nature of the resources people use, by studying how they 'shape' the everyday communicative activities in which they are involved in practice, that is people 'see' and 'act' through their use of words, just as much as through their use of eyes and limbs' (Shotter 1993: 15).

Shotter's use of the term 'resources' is very much in line with the stance on informed identity construction that we have been taking. We aimed at increasing the intellectual resources available to professionals as they made decisions about practice; that is, as they acted intentionally in their workplaces. The evaluations and workshop discussions of practice suggest that members of the group were drawing on the intellectual resources offered by research and discussed within the group, and were consequently seeing and operating in new and informed ways in their settings.

The ascription of meanings to tools and artifacts

This focus was central to our aim of changing practice in sustainable ways. If practitioners were able to use familiar materials in new and informed ways as they worked with children then we might have some confidence that we were *en route* to creating a community of practice that would be able to offer children their educational entitlement from birth to 5. Every self-evaluation at the end of Step Three provided evidence of this occurring. The collaborative action research process at Step Three and the focus of each project on adult interaction, whether over material artifacts or songs, appeared to provide the vehicle for enhancing practitioners' understandings of their roles in JIEs and indeed the importance of these for children.

Developing a new discourse of professional practice

Networking within the group between local authorities, between settings and between higher education and practitioners became a taken-for-granted element of the project. As a group of 25 key participants and higher education staff we exhibited the features of a community of practice discussed by Lave and Wenger (Lave and Wenger 1991). The group became a place where knowledge was used and produced and where we developed a shared history and sets of values and expectations. We understood each other.

The role of research in generating new professional understandings

How would we evaluate the role of research in these developments? We certainly put as much stress on the use of research as on engaging in the research process as part of our emphasis on informed identities engaging in intentional action. The case study work at Step Two allowed practitioners to explore the previously taken-for-granted, informed by the research literature and conversations with other practitioners. As a result, assumptions about immediate professional contexts were destabilized. Their subsequent action research at Step Three was carefully set within an already well established professional network, where it was understood that research could illuminate and inform interpretations of practice and provide a range of possible responses.

As action researchers the participants were not working in isolation, rationally testing research based knowledge in attempts to solve the problems of practice. Instead they were part of a wider network, developing what John Elliott, drawing on Giddens (1984), describes as 'discursive consciousness' (Elliott 1993). Elliott argues that changes in pedagogy depend upon teachers' capacity to take on the 'collaborative reconstruction' of professional cultures and that reconstruction, in turn, depends on practitioners' opportunities to structure new forms of practical consciousness by engaging with an augmented store of mutual knowledge. Elliott's notion of action research here, therefore, has a great deal in common with sociocultural notions of the development of practitioners as informed actors, who draw upon and contribute to the knowledge in use in their communities of practice. His analysis also points to particular roles for researchers in creating the conditions under which practitioners' self-awareness might develop, and in augmenting, where useful, the knowledge base of the community of practice.

We were helped in finding a rationale for creating the conditions for the development of discursive consciousness by the need to address the demands of *Desirable Outcomes*. Indeed, the research project became what Engestrom, within a sociocultural framework, describes as an object, or 'problem space', 'at which activity is directed' (Engestrom 1993). The research project allowed participants to operate across the boundaries of their own professional settings and to work with common research tools on activities, the meanings of which were mediated by common access to the research base on children's learning in mathematics and language. In their activities, participants not only appropriated current understandings of, for example, children's learning, but also in interaction over research and in their own actions, started to create new forms of practical knowledge.

How are research–practice dialogues achieved and sustained?

Research–practice dialogues in the project just outlined occurred in university workshops, in nursery settings and wherever practitioners read the research digests they were sent. Discussions were premised on issues that arose from practice and insights from research were used to extend currently held understandings of the potential for practitioners' actions in the events being described.

We found ourselves strongly in agreement with Hirst's emphasis on the development of practical reasoning through the mutual informing of research and practice during conversations about practice (Hirst 1996). Our role as researchers was to open up for scrutiny assumptions about practice and add our research based perspectives to the analyses of practice that occurred. In that way we not only refined our own understandings of cultures and contexts but also informed practitioners' interpretations of taken-for-granted events. The destabilizing of existing interpretations and the supported construction of new ways of being and seeing were the core purposes of our conversations about practice.

But our conversations were simply starting points for the construction of new professional identities in action, as insights from discussions were drawn upon in practice and brought back to later conversations. Three features of our project therefore seem to have been important.

- The case studies in Step Two and the action research that occurred in Step Three became the vehicles through which participants could use their researcher lenses when interpreting and responding to the immediate demands of daily practice, and so more firmly construct their understandings in action.
- Sites for conversations, for example workshops or visits, that are close to the concerns of practice needed to be set up with the expectation that issues derived from practice were likely to drive the direction of ensuing conversations.
- The 25 participants established their own group based learning culture, in which knowledge was constructed and refined both before and after it was drawn upon in practice. The questioning of assumptions and a growing understanding of the complexity of adults' educational roles became central to the discourse of that culture.

We had established a learning network into which research based knowledge was fed when evidence from discussions of practice provided the opportunity. But we had also, through case study and action research requirements, contrived the need for regular injections of research based insights. Our model was less complicated than that offered by Huberman, but is very much in sympathy with his notion of networks that alter teaching (Huberman 1995). Huberman too suggests the importance of: destabilizing current assumptions through the fresh insights that external expertise can bring; and providing opportunities for the supported construction of new understandings of practice. He particularly emphasizes the weaknesses of what he calls closed networks when compared with the opportunities for development that are available in open networks that are receptive to new interpretations of old practices.

Sociocultural perspectives on learning, knowledge and action appear to offer a useful way forward for the development of practices in early childhood services and for the development of research on, for example, how practitioners are supported as learners. An important premise, however, is attention to the position of researchers and settings based practitioners in any dialogues about practice. A preliminary question considered the wisdom of regarding only those who work directly with clients as practitioners. It is an important issue.

I've argued elsewhere (A. Edwards 1997) that researchers are also members of a community of practice and that communities are enriched by overlapping membership. In such overlaps participants retain core membership of the communities whose practices are central to their work, but become 'peripheral participants' (Lave and Wenger 1991) in the overlapping communities. Were we to acknowledge that research, management, strategic development and so on were also practices with their own communities in which knowledge is developed and used and in which practitioners make informed professional judgements, we could begin to see the value that might be gained from overt attempts at ensuring that, at times, these communities overlap, through working in Engestrom's 'problem space' (Engestrom 1993) on issues where aspects of the expertise of all contributing communities can be brought to bear on the conversational development of informed practical knowledge.

References

Anning, A. and Edwards, A. (in press) *Promoting Children's Learning from Birth to Five: Developing the New Early Years Professional.* Buckingham: Open University Press.

Anning, A. and Edwards, A. (1999) *A Curriculum for Literacy and Mathematical Thinking for Young Children Aged 0–4.* Leeds: University of Leeds, School of Education, unpublished paper.

Chaiklin, S. (1993) Understanding the social science practice of understanding practice, in S. Chaiklin and J. Lave (eds) *Understanding Practice.* Cambridge: Cambridge University Press.

Chaiklin, S. and Lave, J. (eds) (1993) *Understanding Practice.* Cambridge: Cambridge University Press.

Cole, M. (1995) Socio–cultural–historical psychology: some general remarks and a proposal for a new kind of cultural–genetic methodology, in J. Wertsch, P. Del Rio and A. Alvarez (eds) *Sociocultural Studies of Mind.* Cambridge: Cambridge University Press.

Edwards, A. (1997) Possible futures in initial teacher training in the primary phase, in A. Hudson and D. Lambert (eds) *Exploring Futures in Initial Teacher Education: Changing Key for Changing Times.* London: Bedford Way Papers.

Edwards, D. (1997) *Discourse and Cognition.* London: Sage.

Elliott, J. (1993) What have we learned from action research in school-based evaluation?, *Educational Action Research,* 1(1): 175–86.

Engestrom, Y. (1993) Developmental studies of work as a testbench of activity theory: the case of primary care medical practice, in S. Chaiklin and J. Lave (eds) *Understanding Practice.* Cambridge: Cambridge University Press.

Giddens, A. (1984) *The Constitution of Society.* Cambridge: Polity Press.

Giddens, A. (1990) *The Consequences of Modernity.* Cambridge: Polity Press.

Hirst, P. (1996) The demands of professional practice and preparation for teaching, in J. Furlong and R. Smith (eds) *The Role of Higher Education in Teacher Education*. London: Kogan Page.

Huberman, M. (1995) Networks that alter teaching, *Teachers and Teaching: Theory and Practice*, 1(2): 193–211.

Kennedy, M. (1997) The connection between research and practice, *Educational Researcher*, 26(7): 4–12.

Lave, J. and Wenger, E. (1991) *Situated Learning: Legitimate Peripheral Participation*. Cambridge: Cambridge University Press.

Resnick, L., Levine, J. and Teasley, S. (eds) (1991) *Perspectives on Socially Shared Cognition*. Washington: American Psychological Association.

SCAA (School Curriculum and Assessment Authority) (1996) *Desirable Outcomes for Children's Learning on Entering Compulsory Education*. London: Department for Education and Employment/SCAA.

Schaffer, R. (1992) Joint involvement episodes as contexts for cognitive development, in H. McGurk (ed.) *Childhood Social Development: Contemporary Perspectives*. Hove: Lawrence Erlbaum.

Shotter, J. (1993) *Cultural Politics of Everyday Life*. Buckingham: Open University Press.

Wertsch, J., Del Rio, P. and Alvarez, A. (eds) (1995a) *Sociocultural Studies of Mind*. Cambridge: Cambridge University Press.

Wertsch, J., Del Rio, P. and Alvarez, A. (1995b) Sociocultural studies: history, action and mediation, in J. Wertsch, P. Del Rio and A. Alvarez (eds) *Sociocultural Studies of Mind*. Cambridge: Cambridge University Press.

Wood, D. (1988) *How Children Think and Learn*. Oxford: Blackwell.

Index

TRAINING TO WORK IN THE EARLY YEARS
DEVELOPING THE CLIMBING FRAME

Lesley Abbott and Gillian Pugh

In the present context of change and development in the early years field the availability of appropriate training for all those working with young children is of paramount importance. Research shows that one of the most important factors determining the quality of early childhood care and education is the quality of the adults who work with them. The book builds on recommendations made by the Rumbold Committee, the RSA Start Right Report and the National Commission for Education in highlighting key issues, developments and opportunities. More importantly it signals ways in which government policy must change in order to meet the requirements which the authors recommend.

Written by key people in the early years field together with input from students at various stages in their training, the book will be a valuable resource for trainers, students and practitioners concerned to explore ways in which the need for appropriate initial and continuing professional development can be met.

The authors represent a broad spectrum of early childhood establishments, organizations and training institutions both nationally and internationally.

Contents
Early Years training in context – Changing minds: young children and society – Facing some difficulties – Early years educators: skills, knowledge and understanding – Teacher training for the early years – The development of quality services through competence-based qualifications – Praxis NVQ early years assessment centre – a case study: putting the candidate at the heart of the process – Early childhood studies degrees – The pathways to professionalism project – a case study: making an early childhood studies degree accessible – Painting the cabbages red . . .! Differentially trained adults working together in early years settings to promote children's learning – A European perspective on early years training – Training to work in the early years: the way ahead – Appendix – Bibliography – Index.

208pp   0 335 20030 3 (Paperback)   0 335 20031 1 (Hardback)

What is architecture for children?

Architects are far from unanimous in their concepts of the way architecture should be designed to accommodate the needs of children today. Christoph Mackler, for example, puts it concisely: 'There is no such thing as architecture for children'. Mackler designed his kindergarten as a small town with houses, bridge, street and square. He takes children seriously as small adults and provides them with a space in which they have a wide variety of opportunities to develop. The design also acknowledges the single-family houses opposite the kindergarten by reiterating the theme of the gable. At the same time, he sets the building apart from the monotonous external rendering of the surrounding housing estate by his use of warm-toned, dark-red clinker brick. A further contrast to the neighbouring buildings is achieved by cutting through the gabled structures with a white wall to render visible, from the outside, the corridor that links the group rooms.

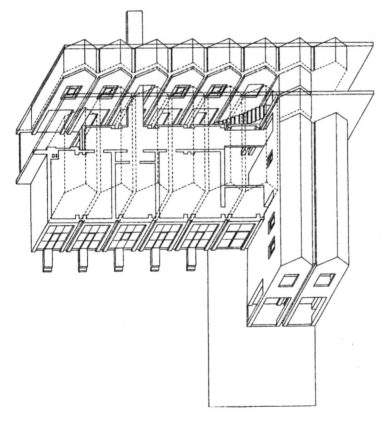

Figure 5.1 Christoph Mackler's kindergarten built as a series of terraced houses round a square

Andreas Keller in Rodelheim is similarly reluctant to use childlike forms. He has created a long, two-storey, bar-like structure. A hint of 1920s architecture is present in the references to the nearby estates built in that decade. With a completely glazed upper floor, the light opens out to the green space of the nearby park, thus achieving a fluid transition from architecture to nature. Keller has reduced any obvious pandering to children to a few details such as a low look-out window on the entrance floor. A distinctive feature of the building is the sunshade provided in the form of a cantilevered roof with aluminium sheathing reminiscent of the wings of a plane.

Fairytale castles and building bricks

Almost diametrically opposed to the concepts just mentioned are the kindergarten designs by the Austrian painter and ecologist, Friedensreich Hundertwasser. For him, creating architecture for children means making their wishes and dreams come true. In this sense the architect is merely an intermediary between the fantasies of children and the reality of the world. Hundertwasser has designed a kind of fairytale castle, whose onion domes and cosy corners make it seem very playful. He has pursued not only the aim of building for children, but also his concept of reconciliation between man and nature. The entire building is covered by a roof that is a meadow planted with trees. In this way the developed site (reclaimed industrial land) is returned to nature, the building having been gently 'slipped under its skin'.

Within the scope of this programme, a number of architects have interpreted 'architecture for children' as an architecture that takes up themes that hold a certain fascination for children: castles, towers, fire brigade, ship, cave, gallery and building blocks. Remembering their own former ideas and wishes, they have broken out of the restrictive mould of functionality to create an enormous diversity of spatial concepts. Of course, the reference to vivid childhood images neither constitutes architecture nor serves as a substitute.

In the same spirit, the firm of Worner and Partner designed their kindergarten as a 'building brick castle'. A sequence of building bricks is used to create an inner courtyard covered by a glass roof and forbiddingly closed to the outside world like a castle. The same motifs are repeated in the interior design. Another kindergarten designed by Uwe Laske defines itself as a large 'play object', with a round tower, oriels and gangway. This rich diversity is meant to encourage the children to act spontaneously, moving around and exploring. In spite of his attempts to accommodate the needs of children, the architect has not allowed himself to get bogged down in multiple design elements, preferring to give the long building a relatively clear form.

Michael Kleinert's concept for a kindergarten is similar to that of Uwe

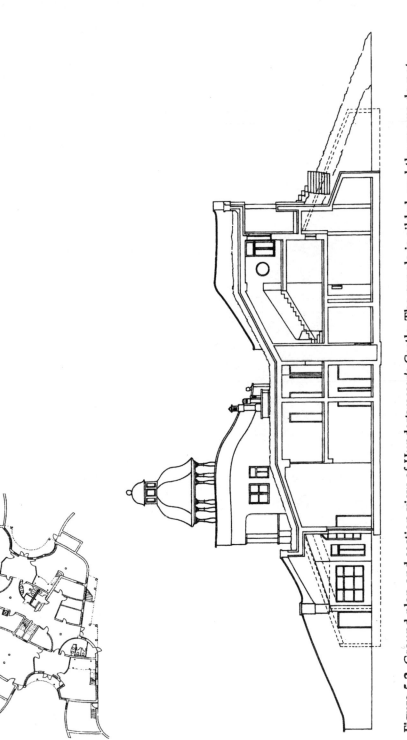

Figure 5.2 Ground plan and section view of Hundertwasser's Castle. The cupola is gilded, and the rooms do not have straight lines

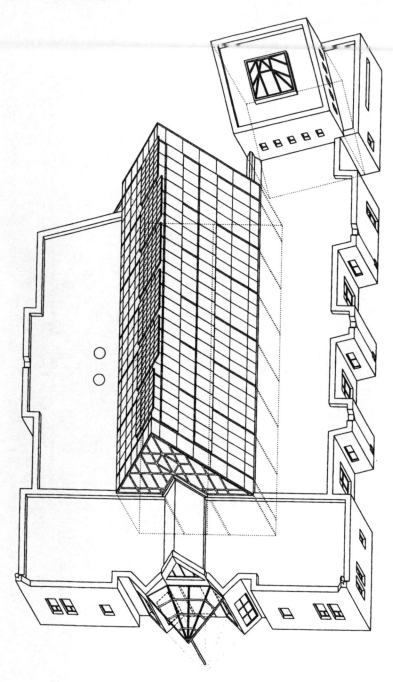

Figure 5.3 Solar heated kindergarten in a site at the back of a supermarket. The inside playspace is a tropical garden.